Wrestling With the Rabbis

~

Throughout the Hebrew Scriptures

Daniel Mann

Mann, Daniel, Author

**Wrestling With the Rabbis ~
Throughout the Hebrew Scriptures**

A Word of Gratitude

The publication of this book would not have been possible without the encouragement and support of my wife Anita.

However, I want to reserve the greatest gratitude to Our Savior ~ Jesus Christ who, through my many tears and struggles, has opened my eyes to the riches of His Word.

Table of Contents - Chapter Summaries

PART 1 - SCRIPTURE

Today's Orthodox Jews are Talmudic Jews in contrast to Biblical Jews. This means that they esteem the Talmud - a vast collection of ancient rabbinic writings compiled around 550 AD - above all other writings, even Scripture.`

Jesus had accused the scribes, lawyers and Pharisees of distorting the Hebrew Scriptures with esoteric interpretations only accessible to the leaned. The rabbis have distorted the meaning of the Bible in various ways to suit their own tastes.

According to the Rabbis, Paul misunderstood the Hebrew Scriptures and attempted to impugn Judaism by alleging that the Mosaic Law inevitably placed everyone under a curse (Galatians 3:10-12). However, this is the message of the entire Bible.

"Sola Scriptura" reflects the teachings of the Bible that God's words must prevail over all other words or statements of truth or moral imperatives. This preeminence of God's Word is consistently found in the NT and the teachings of Jesus but not among the rabbis.

How should we regard Genesis 1-3, which describes the creation and the Fall of humanity into sin and death? Is it historical or non-historical, as the theistic evolutionists (TEs) maintain?

PART 2 - SALVATION

CONCLUSION

INTRODUCTION

Let me warn you – this book is critical of Talmudic Judaism. Why? Because my people have turned away from the Words of God in favor of the words of men!

The first king of Israel, King Saul, was a fitting example of the Israelite leadership. God had directed him to utterly destroy the sinful Amalekites and even their animals. However, Saul was convinced that he knew better than God and did not follow His words. God sent the Prophet Samuel to Saul to reprimand him, but Saul defended his disobedience by claiming that he intended to sacrifice the choicest cattle to the Lord:

- …Samuel said, "Has the LORD as great delight in burnt offerings and sacrifices, as in obeying the voice of the LORD? Behold, to obey is better than sacrifice, and to listen than the fat of rams. For rebellion is as the sin of divination, and presumption is as iniquity and idolatry. Because you have rejected the word of the LORD, he has also rejected you from being king." (*1 Samuel 15:22-23 ESV*)

By rebelling against the Word of God, Saul had also rebelled against God. Samuel equated this rebellion with idolatry, a serious betrayal of the One who had appointed him king.

At first, it had seemed that Saul had been an excellent choice. He had been a very humble man, and humble men heed the Word of God. When Saul was chosen by Samuel to be king, according to the directions of God, Saul confessed his unworthiness:

- "Am I not a Benjaminite, from the least of the tribes of Israel? And is not my clan the humblest of all the clans of the tribe of Benjamin? Why then have you spoken to me in this way?" (*1 Samuel 9:21*)

However, after achieving success and acclaim, he soon found little need for humility and obedience to the Word of God. This has also been the story of Israel. Once their bellies were filled, they forgot their God.

I experienced a variation of this theme. I didn't feel good about myself. Having little success to speak of, I inflated myself with positive affirmations. One set of affirmations had to do with my Jewish identity. I convinced myself that because I belonged to such a successful race, I was superior to others. This became my drug of choice. However, as with any drug, we require increasingly higher doses to maintain the high. In time, we are hooked. The high is gone, but we still need the drug to get out of bed in the morning.

Through a life-threatening experience, I began to search and was found by Yeshuah the Messiah. However, over the next several years, I had to endure the most painful experience of withdrawal. During this time, my still very mysterious Lord was painfully revealing to me the nature of my addiction. He opened my eyes to the ugly lies I had been telling myself, and I was broken. I saw the deceit of my self-righteousness, but I also began to see the self-righteousness within others and even within my people, who I had once regarded as superior.

I also began to notice that even the Church was often held captive to this Gospel-rejecting malady. Paul had charged the Corinthian Church

- For it has been reported to me by Chloe's people that there is quarreling among you, my brothers. What I mean is that each one of you says, "I follow Paul," or "I follow Apollos," or "I follow Cephas," or "I follow Christ." (*1 Corinthians 1:11-12*)

11

They too had been boasting about their group affiliation. Belonging to the "right" group was psychologically uplifting but not according to the Lord. Paul, therefore, sarcastically reprimanded them:

- "[Don't]...go beyond what is written, that none of you may be puffed up in favor of one against another...What do you have that you did not receive? If then you received it, why do you boast as if you did not receive it? Already you have all you want! Already you have become rich! Without us you have become kings! And would that you did reign, so that we might share the rule with you!" (*1 Corinthians 4:6-8*)

I was beginning to see that *pride* is a destroyer, separating people from people and even from God. It is a disease that needs to be exposed for the good of the afflicted and for those who love them.

This is what Jesus did (*Matthew 23*). He exposed the corruption and was hated for it (*John 7:7*). I hope I am not hated for what I express in this book. However, we are told to expect persecution (*2 Timothy 3:12; John 15:18-20*).

Pride is also a deceiver. Consequently, in each chapter, I hope to expose the fallacies of the rabbinic interpretations of the Scriptures, both of the Old and of the New. This exposure is not only necessary for the spiritual health of the Jewish people but also for the spiritual health of the Church.

My Apology

My use of the Scriptures in this book is a hodge-podge of various translations. This is not because I was looking for the version that would justify my stance, but because I had written the chapters of this book at different periods in my life. In the earlier chapters, I tended to use the New King James Version (NKJV), and then I transitioned to the New International Version (NIV) and most recently to the English Standard Version (ESV). The few times that I did choose a translation because of its particular wording, I indicated the translation used.

SCRIPTURE

Chapter 1

TALMUDIC JUDAISM AND ITS DISREGARD OF THE SCRIPTURES

Today's Orthodox Jews are Talmudic Jews in contrast to Biblical Jews. This means that they esteem the Talmud - a vast collection of ancient rabbinic writings, compiled around 550 AD, above all other writings, even above the Hebrew Scriptures.

The Talmudic writings, including the Mischnah, represent a departure from the Hebrew Scriptures. According to its own statements, the Talmud has also superseded the Scriptures. For example:

- "Those who devote themselves to reading the Bible exercise a certain virtue, but not very much; those who study the Mishnah exercise virtue for which they will receive a reward; those, however, who take upon themselves to study the Gemarah exercise the highest virtue." (*Babha Metsia, fol. 33a*)

- "The Sacred Scriptures is like water, the Mischnah wine, and the Gemarah aromatic wine." (*Sopherim XV, 7, fol. 13b*)

- "He who transgresses the words of the scribes sins more gravely than the transgressors of the words of the law." (*Sanhedrin X, 3, f.88b*)

Not only does this constitute adding to the Law, something that God had forbidden (*Deuteronomy 4:2; 12:32*), it also involves replacing the Law with the commandments of men.

Isaiah had denounced Israel for teaching commandments of men, however holy they might appear, in place of those of God:

- And the Lord said: "Because this people draw near with their mouth and honor me with their lips, while their hearts are far from me, and their [faithfulness] fear of me is a commandment taught by men, therefore, behold, I will again do wonderful things with this people, with wonder upon wonder; and the wisdom of their wise men shall perish, and the discernment of their discerning men shall be hidden." (*Isaiah 29:13-14*)

Furthermore, God, through Moses, had repeatedly warned against receiving the words of men as if they were the Words of God:

- "But the prophet who presumes to speak a word in my name that I have not commanded him to speak, or who speaks in the name of other gods, that same prophet shall die." (*Deuteronomy 18:20*)

The rabbis have not only replaced the Bible with the Talmud, they even claim that the Talmud (also called the "Oral Law") represents the Word of God given to Moses on Mount Sinai, which he had orally passed on, according to the Mishnah:

- Moshe received the Torah from Sinai and transmitted it to Yehoshua [Joshua], and Yehoshua to the Elders, and the Elders to the Prophets, and the Prophets transmitted it to the Men of the Great Assembly. (*Pirke Avot 1:1*)

In the next chapter, I will argue that there is not a shred of evidence to support this claim made 1500 years after the giving of the Law on Mount Sinai. Nevertheless, the rabbis

15

argue that it must have been given by God because the Talmud is necessary:

- [Rabbi] Yosef Albo [*Sefer Halkkarim, 3:23*] offers the following philosophical proof for the existence of an oral law. R. Albo states that a perfect text must, by definition, be totally unambiguous and not require any additional information to be understood. Since the Torah is called perfect [*Psalms 19:8*], the Torah must not have any ambiguities. However, it does have ambiguities. For example, the verse [Deut. 6:4] "Hear O Israel! The L-rd is our G-d, the L-rd is one" is understood by Jews to imply absolute monotheism while it is understood by Christians to imply a trinity. How can a perfect Torah contain ambiguity? Only if the Torah includes an oral explanation that clarifies all ambiguities can it be called perfect [*cf. Maimonides, Moreh Nevuchim, 1:71*]. Therefore, R. Albo states, there must have been an oral tradition transmitted along with the written Torah. (www.aishdas.org/student/oral.htm)

The Talmud also teaches many things counter to what is found in the Scriptures. For example, it teaches the superiority of the Jews, something that Moses had repeatedly warned against:

- "Do not say in your heart, after the Lord your God has thrust them out before you, 'It is because of my righteousness that the Lord has brought me in to possess this land,' whereas it is because of the wickedness of these nations that the Lord is driving them out before you... Know, therefore, that the Lord your God is not giving you this good land to possess because of your righteousness, for you are a stubborn people." (*Deuteronomy 9:4, 6*)

Moses also warned our people to *not* take credit for their successes:

- "Beware lest you say in your heart, 'My power and the might of my hand have gotten me this wealth.' You shall remember the Lord your God, for it is he who gives you power to get wealth, that he may confirm his covenant that he swore to your fathers, as it is this day. And if you forget the Lord your God and go after other gods and serve them and worship them, I solemnly warn you today that you shall surely perish." (*Deuteronomy 8:17-19*)

Sadly, our people have gone after a very different god – a Talmudic invention. Accordingly, in *Why the Jews Rejected Jesus*, David Klinghoffer, concluded that Jewish rejection of Jesus is founded in "the mystic uniqueness of the Jewish essence or nature. There was something distinct about the Jewish soul...The Jewish soul feels the worlds, in a remarkably visceral way, as unredeemed."

He based his opinion upon Judah Loeb's famous interpretation of the Talmudic tractate, *Avodah Zarah*, which stated that God had offered the Torah to all the other nations first, "to see if they possessed a predisposition to the Torah, and did not find it in them," in contrast to what God found in the Jews.

This type of chauvinism – the aggrandizement of one's own people - is predictably found in all religions. For instance, the Koran reads:

- You are the best nation ever brought forth to men, bidding to honour, and forbidding dishonour, and believing in Allah. (*Surah 3:110-112*)

17

- The unbelievers of the People of the Book and the idolaters shall be in the Fire of Gehenna, therein dwelling forever; those are the worst of creatures. (*Surah 98:6*)

Why are the Hebrew Scriptures so different in this regard? Perhaps because they are not derived from man but from God!

Instead of being the light to the world, we have covered the light with the chauvinistic darkness of the Talmud. And the dreadful promised consequences have continually followed. Moses warned that we would be hated by the world. This prophecy has become a persistent fact of history, always accompanied by the disobedience of our people in turning from Scripture. This is not to exonerate the world for their malicious anti-Semitism. However, faithfulness to God requires us to expose and confess the sins of our people, as the Priest Ezra had prayed:

- "O my God, I am ashamed and blush to lift my face to you, my God, for our iniquities have risen higher than our heads, and our guilt has mounted up to the heavens. From the days of our fathers to this day we have been in great guilt. And for our iniquities we, our kings, and our priests have been given into the hand of the kings of the lands, to the sword, to captivity, to plundering, and to utter shame, as it is today. But now for a brief moment favor has been shown by the LORD our God, to leave us a remnant and to give us a secure hold within his holy place, that our God may brighten our eyes and grant us a little reviving in our slavery." (*Ezra 9:6-8*)

As it is today, God had granted "favor" to His people Israel "for a brief moment." However, Israel must once again hear the Words of their God. Jesus attempted to turn Israel back to

Him. However, He charged that they would not hear Him since they refused to even believe Moses. (*John 5:44-47*)

Meanwhile, the greatness and restoration of the Jewish nation has always accompanied a return to our God. (Adherence to the Talmud has brought despair and dispersion.) God built Israel into a great nation because of the faithfulness of King David. This greatness continued through much of Solomon's reign. It was restored, in great measure, under the faithful reigns of the great kings of Judah - Asa, Jehoshaphat, Hezekiah, and Josiah. All of these kings had revived Israel by returning them to the very Words of God rather than to the traditions of the elders or to their learned rabbis.

Even the modern rebirth of Israel had nothing to do with the Talmud. Instead, the Talmud has been a blight upon our people. Yet our G-d promises that He will open the eyes of disobedient Israel:

- "And I will pour out on the house of David and the inhabitants of Jerusalem a spirit of grace and pleas for mercy, so that, when they look on me [the speaker, God], on him whom they have pierced, they shall mourn for him [Jesus], as one mourns for an only child, and weep bitterly over him, as one weeps over a firstborn." (*Zechariah 12:10*)

What does our God require of us? Return:

- "Return, faithless Israel," declares the Lord. "I will not look on you in anger, for I am merciful, declares the Lord; I will not be angry forever. Only acknowledge your guilt, that you rebelled against the Lord your God." (*Jeremiah 3:12-13*)

How are we to return to God? By returning to His Word as the ancient Kings of Judah had done! For example, King Josiah was notified by Hilkiah the priest that he had found "the Book of the Law of the LORD given through Moses" (*2 Chronicles 34:14*). Evidently, it had been missing for so long that no one noticed its absence until it was found. The godly King Josiah immediately understood the importance of this Book and directed the priest:

- "Go, inquire of the LORD for me and for those who are left in Israel and in Judah, concerning the words of the book that has been found. For great is the wrath of the LORD that is poured out on us, because our fathers have not kept the word of the LORD, to do according to all that is written in this book." (*2 Chronicles 34:21*)

How did the Lord respond? Did He agree with Josiah's sentiments?

- "Thus says the LORD, Behold, I will bring disaster upon this place and upon its inhabitants, all the curses that are written in the book that was read before the king of Judah. Because they have forsaken me and have made offerings to other gods, that they might provoke me to anger with all the works of their hands, therefore my wrath will be poured out on this place and will not be quenched. But to the king of Judah, who sent you to inquire of the LORD, thus shall you say to him, Thus says the LORD, the God of Israel: Regarding the words that you have heard, because your heart was tender and you humbled yourself before God when you heard his words against this place and its inhabitants, and you have humbled yourself before me and have torn your clothes and wept before me, I also have heard you, declares the LORD." (*2 Chronicles 34:24-27*)

According to the Lord's admonition, when Josiah had humbled himself before the Lord, it was the same thing as honoring the *His* Words, the very thing that the rabbis fail to do. The way that Israel was required to love God was by keeping His Words and commandments (*Deuteronomy 5:10; 6:5; 7:9; 10:12; 11:1, 22; 30:16, 20*) and by confessing their sins.

From the prophecies of Jeremiah, the Prophet Daniel knew that the time of Israel's return to their promised land was approaching along with another chance to prove their faithfulness to God's Words, His covenant. Therefore, He too confessed the sins of Israel before the Lord:

- We have sinned and done wrong and acted wickedly and rebelled, turning aside from your commandments and rules. We have not listened to your servants the prophets, who spoke in your name to our kings, our princes, and our fathers, and to all the people of the land. To you, O Lord, belongs righteousness, but to us open shame, as at this day, to the men of Judah, to the inhabitants of Jerusalem, and to all Israel, those who are near and those who are far away, in all the lands to which you have driven them, because of the treachery that they have committed against you. (*Daniel 9:5-7*)

We too must never sugar-coat sin by disregarding God's Words or by placing our traditions on equal footing with Scripture, as the Pharisees of Jesus's day continued to do. However, Jesus denounced them, quoting Isaiah:

- "...So for the sake of your tradition you have made void the word of God. You hypocrites! Well did Isaiah prophesy of you, when he said: 'This people honors me with their lips, but their heart is far from me; in vain do they worship me, teaching as doctrines the commandments of men.'" (*Matthew 15:6-9*)

I grieve that little has changed today among our Orthodox Talmudic Jews. May God hear our prayers!

WORKS CITED

Student, Gil – *The Oral Law*
www.aishdas.org/student/oral.htm

The Babylonian Talmud
www.jewishvirtuallibrary.org/babylonian-talmud-full-text
(Babha Metsia, fol. 33a)
(Sopherim XV, 7, fol. 13b)
(Sanhedrin X, 3, f.88b)
(Pirke Avot 1:1)

The Quran (Koran) - Hasan al-Fatih Qaribullah and Ahmad
Darwish – *(Surah 3:110)*
www.alquranenglish.com/quran-surah-ali-imran-110-qs-3-110-
in-arabic-and-english-translation

The Quran (Koran) - Hasan al-Fatih Qaribullah and Ahmad
Darwish – *(Surah 98:6)*
www.alquranenglish.com/quran-surah-al-bayyinah-6-qs-98-6-
in-arabic-and-english-translation

Chapter 2

RABBIS DO NOT UNDERSTAND THEIR BIBLE

Jesus had accused the scribes, lawyers and Pharisees of distorting the Hebrew Scriptures with esoteric interpretations only accessible to the leaned. This effectively removed it from the common man:

- "Woe to you lawyers! For you have taken away the <u>key of knowledge</u>. You did not enter yourselves, and you hindered those who were entering." (*Luke 11:52*)

In *Why the Jews Rejected Jesus*, David Klinghoffer criticizes Jesus for dismissing the "Tradition of the Elders," which he calls the "Oral Law." Orthodox Jews maintain that the "Oral Law" was given to Moses on Mt. Sinai along with the Written Law (the Torah). It was then orally passed down through the Prophets and then the Rabbis until it was given written form in the Mishnah (200 AD) and then in the Talmud (550 AD).

Orthodox Jews also claim that it is essential for properly understanding the Torah. In this regard, Klinghoffer writes that a proper interpretation of the Torah depends an accurate knowledge of the "Oral Law":

- The more you read it [the Torah] in its original language, the more you realize how in need of interpretation it is--not just any interpretation [but that of the Oral Law]. Any new religious sect, like that of the earliest followers of Jesus, would have to explain where it stood in relationship to the inherited tradition of interpretation: the oral Torah. (Klinghoffer, 24)

Therefore, if the NT's interpretation of the Torah does not accord with the "Oral Law," it is wrong. However, there are numerous problems with this position. For one thing, there is no indication anywhere within the pages of the Old Testament that an Oral Law exists. Nor is there any early testimony (either during New Testament times or before) that Moses had received any additional revelation beyond what he had written.

The Hebrew Scriptures even explicitly tell us that *everything* that Moses had received from God had been written down:

- "And there, in the presence of the people of Israel, he wrote on the stones a copy of the law of Moses, which he had written...And afterward he read all the words of the law, the blessing and the curse, according to all that is written in the Book of the Law. There was not a word of all that Moses commanded that Joshua did not read before all the assembly of Israel, and the women, and the little ones, and the sojourners who lived among them." (*Joshua 8:32, 33-35*)

Joshua *read* everything that God had given to Moses. It was *all* written down! This precludes the existence of an unwritten "Oral Law." Likewise, the Law was often read, but there was never any indication that an "Oral Law" was recited:

- So Ezra the priest brought the Law before the assembly, both men and women and all who could understand what they heard, on the first day of the seventh month. And he read from it facing the square before the Water Gate from early morning until midday, in the presence of the men and the women and those who could understand. And the ears of all the people were attentive to the <u>Book of the Law</u>. (*Nehemiah 8:2-4*)

If the "Oral Law" had been so necessary to the understanding of the Scriptures, why then isn't it ever mentioned? Instead, it seems that the *Book of the Law* was all that was needed.

Scripture assures us that the knowledge of God is within reach of all, without any need for an "Oral Law":

- "Does not wisdom call? Does not understanding raise her voice? On the heights beside the way, at the crossroads she takes her stand; beside the gates in front of the town, at the entrance of the portals she cries aloud: "To you, O men, I call, and my cry is to the children of man. O simple ones, learn prudence; O fools, learn sense." (*Proverbs 8:1-5*)

The problems don't stop here. The Mishnah and Talmud represent a compendium of rabbinic opinions, some of which are contradictory. In a footnote, Klinghoffer admits:

- "Where the sages are on record as disagreeing with one another, it is assumed that there is truth in all their opinions. God communicates paradoxical truths through such seemingly contradictory statements." (Klinghoffer, 223-224)

It's no secret that we rely on commentaries and teachers to reconcile the "seemingly contradictory statements" found within the Scriptures. However, if the commentary itself contains "paradoxical truths" and "seemingly contradictory statements," what good is it? Its purpose is to reconcile the paradoxical statements, not to multiply them.

Let's return to Klinghoffer's claim that the meaning of the Hebrew Scriptures was inaccessible without the "Oral Law," eventually written down by the rabbis:

- Scripture is cryptic…The Pentateuch contained innumerable textual difficulties…The Rabbis taught that what looked like editing glitches in almost every verse were really allusions to esoteric teachings. (Klinghoffer, 224)

25

How then do the rabbis interpret Scripture? They have their own keys – Gematria, for one – taking the numerical value of each letter and deriving meaning from the patterning of these numbers. However, by doing this, Gematria rejects the plain meaning of the Scriptures. Besides, this method of interpretation finds *no* support within the Scriptures.

Instead of the Hebrew Scriptures warning that it couldn't be understood by the common man, it claims the very opposite thing. Therefore, it was able to hold the Israelite to account for not understanding and obeying its instructions:

- "For this commandment which I command you today is not too mysterious for you, nor is it far off. It is not in heaven, that you should say, 'Who will ascend into heaven for us and bring it to us, that we may hear it and do it?' Nor is it beyond the sea, that you should say, 'Who will go over the sea for us and bring it to us, that we may hear it and do it?' But the word is very near you, in your mouth and in your heart, that you may do it." (*Deuteronomy 30:11-14*)

While the Bible does contain deep, secret, and esoteric messages, these do not conflict with its plain teaching:

- "I did not speak in secret, in a land of darkness; I did not say to the offspring of Jacob, 'Seek me in vain.' I the LORD speak the truth; I declare what is right. Assemble yourselves and come; draw near together, you survivors of the nations! They have no knowledge who carry about their wooden idols, and keep on praying to a god that cannot save." (*Isaiah 45:19-20*)

The Lord had been straightforward. He claimed that having "no knowledge" was not the result of having no education or the "Oral Law." Instead, it was the result of hearts hardened in sin and rebellion:

- "My people are destroyed for lack of knowledge; because you have rejected knowledge, I reject you from being a priest to me. And since you have forgotten the law of your God, I also will forget your children." (*Hosea 4:6*)

Why did they reject the knowledge of God? Because they hated it:

- "Because they hated knowledge and did not choose the fear of the LORD, would have none of my counsel and despised all my reproof, therefore they shall eat the fruit of their way, and have their fill of their own devices. For the simple are killed by their turning away…" (*Proverbs 1:29-32*)

Why do we reject this knowledge? Simply because it doesn't tell us what we want to hear. We want our religious writings to make us feel good about ourselves and not to strip us of our pride and sense of entitlement. However, the Bible does not indulge our pride. Instead of being human-centered, it is clearly God-centered.

For example, the Bible presents Israel's greatest king – David – as an adulterer and a murderer, even though he is also known as "a man after God's own heart." However, an orthodox Jew informed me that the Talmud had so sanitized David that his adultery with Bathsheba and the murder of her husband Uriah were both regarded as righteous acts. This is precisely how we humans write our religious books! This tendency also reflects the Talmud and other writings of the rabbis. Here are some examples:

1. **THE PATRIARCHS**: Abraham, Isaac and Jacob, the forefathers of Judaism, were certainly not role-models. Instead, the Bible reveals that they were cowards, deceivers, liars, and worse. We humans ordinarily don't create or select

such role models, least of all those who we identify as the Fathers of our faith.

Instead, the human tendency is to fashion them into the saints with whom others would want to identify. This is exactly what the Talmud did with all of the Patriarchs. It sanitized the Bible's depiction of them, and made them virtually sinless. In contrast, the Bible's portraits sharply conflict with what we'd create – so much so, that we feel compelled to modify them.

For instance, the Bible gives us the portrait of a spineless Abraham who routinely passed off his beautiful wife Sarah as his sister so that no one would kill him in order to have her. Abraham shamefully admitted that he had customarily required this of his lovely wife:

- And Abimelech said to Abraham, "What did you see, that you did this thing?" Abraham said, "I did it because I thought, 'There is no fear of God at all in this place, and they will kill me because of my wife.' Besides, she is indeed my sister, the daughter of my father though not the daughter of my mother, and she became my wife. And when God caused me to wander from my father's house, I said to her, 'This is the kindness you must do me: at every place to which we come, say of me, "He is my brother."'" (*Genesis 20:10-13*)

Our Patriarchal forefathers, Abraham, Isaac, and Jacob, are portrayed in Genesis as scoundrels, pimps, cheats and liars – not the heroes that the Jewish commentaries portray them to be. For instance:

- The Kuzari (Rabbi Judah HaLevi, 1075-1141) states that Abraham was gifted with high intelligence; and, as Maimonides describes, Abraham didn't blindly accept the ubiquitous idolatry. The whole populace had been duped, but the young Abraham contemplated the matter relentlessly, finally arriving at the conclusion that there is One God.

According to this perspective, God chose Abraham because he was more deserving – more virtuous than others:

- Abram tried to convince his father, Terach, of the folly of idol worship. One day, when Abram was left alone to mind the store, he took a hammer and smashed all of the idols except the largest one. He placed the hammer in the hand of the largest idol. When his father returned and asked what happened, Abram said, "The idols got into a fight, and the big one smashed all the other ones." His father said, "Don't be ridiculous. These idols have no life or power. They can't do anything." Abram replied, "Then why do you worship them?" (www.jewfaq.org/origins.htm)

- Abraham…was so successful that he converted thousands to monotheism. His method was one of kindness—he set up a motel and after feeding and watering wayfarers they were introduced to the true belief and blessed G-d the Provider. Abraham converted the men and Sarah the women, and together they successfully brought many souls under the wings of the Shechinah, hence resensitizing the world to G-dliness. (www.chabad.org/library/article_cdo/aid/361874/jewish/Abraham.htm)

More specifically, here's how the rabbis understand the sins of our Patriarchs:

- Abraham asked his wife Sarah to lie and say that she was his sister because he was traveling with her to ancient Egypt, a place known for its lack of morality (*Genesis 12:10-13*). Ramban believes that Abraham unintentionally committed a "great sin" and endangered his wife's virtue because he should have had faith that God would save him and his family. After all, it was God who told Abraham to leave the land of his birthplace. However, even the Ramban would have to agree that, where one does not have the personal assurance of God, one should be permitted to lie. In fact, Abraham used the same ruse again when sojourning in Gerar (*Genesis 20:1-3*). Isaac also used the same lie when traveling in lands where the morality of the inhabitants is questionable and claims that his wife Rebeccah is his sister (*Genesis 26:7*).

In other words, lying is permissible when you're in a situation you regard as threatening. However, in defense of their Patriarchs, the rabbis ruled that deception was even legitimate:

- Jacob's deception of his blind father, Isaac (*Genesis 27*). Was Jacob permitted to deceive his father and pretend to be Esau? Some commentaries take the approach that Jacob did not actually lie. When asked by his father who he was (*Genesis 27:18*), he replied: "I am Esau your firstborn." Rashi and other commentators try to show that this was not really a falsehood. (www.ou.org/torah/parsha/rabbi-sacks-on-parsha/covenant_and_conversation_land/)

2. MOSES: Even the "greatest" of all Israelites had been forbidden entry into the Promised Land because he had sinned. Aaron also is presented in the Torah as a humiliated sinner. What hope therefore could the average Israelite entertain about his own future welfare if even his role models had been disqualified from entering the Promised Land? Not much! Such a revelation could not have been the invention of humans who'd naturally want to maintain a zealous following.

As a young seeker, my favorite book of the Hebrew Scriptures had been the *Book of Joshua*, where we Jews were portrayed as victorious. It made me feel proud of my people. The rabbis are no exception:

- Almost forty years earlier, in similar circumstances, G-d had told him to take his staff and strike the rock [*Exodus 17*]. Now too, G-d told him to take his staff. Evidently Moses inferred that he was being told to act this time as he had before, which is what he does... Moses' inability to hear this distinction was not a failing, still less was it a sin. It was an inescapable consequence of the fact that he was mortal.

- If this interpretation is correct, then Moses did not sin, nor was he punished. To be sure, the Torah uses language expressive of sin ("You did not believe in Me", "You rebelled against Me", "You trespassed against Me", "You did not sanctify Me"). But these phrases may refer, as several commentators suggest ... not to Moses and Aaron but to the people and the incident as a whole. The fact that Moses was not destined to enter the promised land was not a punishment but the very condition of his (and our) mortality. (www.ou.org/torah/parsha/rabbi-sacks-on-parsha/covenant_and_conversation_land/)

After I had finished the *Book of Joshua*, I eagerly went on the next book, *Judges*, the very opposite of the *Book of Joshua*. In Judges, my people suffered one painful defeat after another. Finally, I just had to put it down. However, the rabbis found another solution. They would merely reinterpret the Bible to make a defeat appear to be a victory. Moses simply "was not destined" to enter the Promised Land," rather than it being a "punishment." It was just a "condition of his mortality."

However, the text of the Bible will not allow such a self-serving distortion:

- And the LORD said to Moses and Aaron, "Because you did not believe in me, to uphold me as holy in the eyes of the people of Israel, therefore you shall not bring this assembly into the land that I have given them." (*Numbers 20:12*)

3. THE ISRAELITES: They are not portrayed as faithful to God, but as stubborn and unfaithful. On numerous occasions, Moses warned the Israelites to not think of themselves better or more deserving than others. Meanwhile, the Talmud characterizes the Jewish people as spiritually superior, the very thing that the Bible warns against (*Deuteronomy 9:4-6*).

- "The Jews are human beings, but the goyim [Gentiles] are not human beings; they are only beasts." (Baba Mezia 114a-114b)

Although many verses claim that God had placed His love upon Israel everlastingly (*Isaiah 43:4; 63:9; Jeremiah 31:3; Hosea 11:1; Malachi 1:2*), there is not a single verse in the Hebrew Scriptures that suggests that the Israelites were superior to or more deserving than others.

On the contrary, almost all the prophets denounce Israel, so much so that if we didn't know better, we might conclude that these Scriptures represent the height of anti-Semitism. Often, Israel is indicted more extensively than any other people. Here is just a small sampling of this:

- *Isaiah 64:7* - And there is no one who calls on Your name, who stirs himself up to take hold of You; for You have hidden Your face from us, and have consumed us because of our iniquities.

- *Isaiah 65:2-3* - I have stretched out My hands all day long to a rebellious people, who walk in a way that is not good, according to their own thoughts; 3A people who provoke Me to anger <u>continually</u> to My face; who sacrifice in gardens, and burn incense on altars of brick;

- *Isaiah 66:4* - So will I choose their delusions, and bring their fears on them; because, when I called, <u>no one answered</u>, when I spoke they did not hear; but they did evil before My eyes, and chose that in which I do not delight."

- *Jeremiah 5:3* - O Lord, *are* not Your eyes on the truth? You have stricken them, but they have not grieved; You have consumed them, but they have <u>refused</u> to receive correction. They have made their faces harder than rock; they have <u>refused to return</u>.

- *Jeremiah 8:5-6* - "Why has this people slidden back, Jerusalem, in a <u>perpetual</u> backsliding? They hold fast to deceit, they <u>refuse to return</u>. I listened and heard, b*ut* they do not speak aright. No man repented of his wickedness, saying, 'What have I done?' Everyone turned to his own course."

- *Ezekiel 5:7* - "Therefore thus says the Lord God: 'Because you have multiplied disobedience <u>more than the nations</u> that are all around you, have not walked in My statutes nor kept My judgments, nor even done according to the judgments of the nations that are all around you...'"

- *Ezekiel 16:46-47* - "Your elder sister is Samaria, who dwells with her daughters to the north of you; and your younger sister, who dwells to the south of you, is Sodom and her daughters. You did not walk in their

33

ways nor act according to their abominations; but, as if that were too little, you [Judah] became more corrupt than they in all your ways"

We humans don't characteristically write such disparaging things about ourselves and our people, especially if these writings form the core of our self-identity, significance, and reason-for-being. How is it that the Jewish people would canonize such thoroughly condemning writings? They must have been convinced that they had no other choice. Perhaps it was because God's miraculous presence was simply too close to do otherwise.

4. MOSAIC THREATS: The warnings against disobedience were severe. If an Israelite failed to keep the law in just one respect, he was under a curse:

- "Cursed be anyone who does not confirm the words of this law by doing them. And all the people shall say, 'Amen.'" (*Deuteronomy 27:26*)

This curse damns all Israel as it was intended. We humans would not accept such a threatening religion; nor would the rabbis, who qualified this teaching in several ways. For instance, Gerald Sigal, *The Jew and the Christian Missionary*, wrote,

- [*Deuteronomy 27:26*] does not refer to the breaking of the Law by an ordinary individual. It is, as the Rabbis explain, a reference to the authorities in power who fail to enforce the rule of the Law in the land of Israel (J.T. Sotah 7:4). The leadership of the nation is thus charged, under pain of the curse, to set the tone for the nation and make the Law the operative force in the life of the nation. (Sigal,18)

34

Instead, this verse damns *every* Israelite, as do so many other verses (*Exod. 20:6; 23:21-22; 24:3; Lev. 26:14-16; Deuteronomy 5:29; 6:24-25; 8:1; 10:12; 11:8, 26-28, 32; 12:28*). For this reason, the Psalms repeatedly inform Israel that their *only* hope was in the mercy of God (*Psalm 143:2; 32:1-5; 130:3-8*)!

Consistent with this, there is no verse in the OT that even gets close to applauding Israel in this manner: "You Israelites are doing a great job! Keep up the good work!" Instead, the OT is consistently degrading of God's chosen people!

The Torah's teachings are so humanly degrading and so counter to our human agendas that anyone who wanted to gain a following would *never* invent such a religion. Instead, we tend to come to religion for its benefits and *not* for its curses! No wonder the Torah occupies a rabbinic back-seat.

5. PROPHECIES: The Prophets uniformly prophesied Israel's future failure (*Deuteronomy 29:4; Joshua 24:19*). Moses even taught Israel a song that would serve to continually indict them. Israel would reject their God, and God would bring destruction upon them (*Deuteronomy 32:15-35*). No one would invent a religion foretelling such negative consequences for its own people. And who would follow such a religion! Certainly not the rabbis!

Perhaps even more offensive to the rabbis, the Prophets also envisioned the hated Gentile nations enjoying abundant blessings with Israel in the end. However, the Jews are regarded as clean by the rabbinic writings ~ whereas the Gentiles are not:

- "Why are the Goim [Gentiles] unclean? Because they were not present at Mount Sinai. For when the serpent entered into Eve he infused her with uncleanness. But the Jews were cleansed from this when they stood on

35

Mount Sinai; the Goim, however, who were not on Mount Sinaim were not cleansed." (*Abodah Zarah*, 22b)

- "And he created every living thing, that is, the Israelites, because they are the children of the Most High God, and their holy souls come out from Him. But where do the souls of the idolatrous gentiles come from? Rabbi Eliezer says: from the left side, which makes their souls unclean. They are therefore all unclean and they pollute all who come in contact with them." (*Zohar* I, 46b, 47a)

All of this is, of course, contrary to the Hebrew Scriptures. Yet, we are told that we cannot understand the Hebrew Scriptures without the "Oral Law." This charge also disqualifies the NT's understanding of the Hebrew Scriptures. The next chapter will address this charge.

***

Pride demands a costly payment. I had allowed the lust for pride to control my spiritual quest. The rabbis have been following the same dead end. As a result, instead of enjoying the blessings as God's chosen people, they have pursued the "blessings" of pride to their own destruction – the consistent testimony of Jewish history.

WORKS CITED

Klinghoffer, David, *Why the Jews Rejected Jesus*, (New York: Doubleday, First Edition, 2005)

Sigal, Gerald, *The Jew and the Christian Missionary: A Jewish Response to Missionary Christianity,* (New York: KTAV Publishing House, Inc., 1981)

www.jewfaq.org/origins.htm

www.chabad.org/library/article_cdo/aid/361874/jewish/Abraham.htm

www.ou.org/torah/parsha/rabbi-sacks-on-parsha/covenant_and_conversation_land/

The Babylonian Talmud - (*Baba Mezia* 114a-114b)
www.come-and-hear.com/babamezia/babamezia_114.html

The Babylonian Talmud - (*Abhodah Zarah*, 22b)
http://halakhah.com/zarah/zarah_22.html

The Zohar, Pritzker Edition, Vol. 1, (Stanford University Press, 1st Edition, 2003) (*Zohar* I, 46b, 47a)

Chapter 3

DID PAUL WRONGLY IMPUGN THE MOSAIC LAW?

According to the rabbis, Paul misunderstood the Hebrew Scriptures and attempted to impugn Judaism by alleging that the Mosaic Law inevitably placed everyone under a curse (*Galatians 3:10-12*). To support their claim, the rabbis correctly point out the many positive effects of the Law: that it imparts wisdom and conversion (*Psalm 19*) and that it delights the soul and imparts blessing and peace (*Psalm 119*). In light of this, it seems that Paul is missing the boat when he proclaims that the Law kills.

Did the Law really bring death (*Romans 3:19-20; 11:32; Galatians 3:22*) as Paul alleges? Didn't the Apostle Paul misconstrue the Hebrew Scriptures? Didn't he erroneously impugn the Law of Moses as the inevitable source of condemnation and death, rather than a source of wisdom, blessing, and conversion (*Psalm 19:7-8*)? In *Why the Jews Rejected Jesus*, David Klinghoffer, a columnist for the *Jewish Forward*, offers a resounding "yes!" He charges that Paul so badly twisted the Hebrew Scriptures that he became "the first person to imagine the essence of what would become Christian theology." Klinghoffer contends that Paul's interpretation was so novel and distorted, that no one else would have come up with it, not even Jesus. More specifically, Klinghoffer alleges:

- Paul had misunderstood the verse just quoted from Deuteronomy: 'Cursed be every one who does not *abide* by all things written in the book of the law, and do them.' The Hebrew word he took to mean 'abide by' really means 'uphold.' In other words, the Jew was expected to *uphold* all the Torah's commandments, affirming that they were God's will. But there was no expectation of perfect conformity in his actions. The rabbis made this clear. (Klinghoffer,112)

While Paul understood the Law to teach that any infraction resulted in a curse, Klinghoffer insists that the Law requires Israel to merely, *"uphold* all the Torah's commandments." Mustn't Israel also actually *perform* all the laws? Not according to Klinghoffer! For him, it seems that to *uphold* them simply means "affirming that they were God's will." From where does he derive this piece of sophistry? From the Talmud! His endnote cites *B. Sanhedrin 81A*:

- This citation reads, "When R. Gamaliel read this verse he wept, saying, 'Only he who does all these things shall live, but not merely one of them!' Thereupon R. Akiba said to him, 'If, so, defile not yourselves in all these things is the prohibition against all [combined] only, but not against?' [Surely not!] But it means, in one of these things; so here too, for doing one of these things [shall he live]." While R. Gamaliel was disturbed by the obvious interpretation that an Israelite had to perform each command in order to live, R. Akiba felt that this couldn't be the right interpretation. Instead, he suggested that by "doing one of these things" [commands of God], it would be sufficient to "live."

Clearly, Klinghoffer is not alone in this assessment. The thirteenth century sage and Talmudic jurist, Rabbi Mosheh ben Nachman (Nachmanides), wrote regarding Deuteronomy 27:26, "This refers to a person who denies the Divine origin of any commandment of the Torah and considers its fulfillment valueless." (*The Socino Chumash*, A.Cohen (ed.), 1947, pg. 1123)

Conspicuously absent was any acknowledgement that Israel had to *obey* all God's commands, and that they would fall under His curse if they failed to do so. Similarly, Gerald Sigal wrote,

- [*Deuteronomy 27:26*] does not refer to the breaking of the Law by an ordinary individual. It is, as the Rabbis explain, a reference to the authorities in power who fail to enforce the rule of the Law in the land of Israel (J.T. Sotah 7:4). The leadership of the nation is thus charged, under pain of the curse, to set the tone for the nation and make the Law the operative force in the life of the nation. (Sigal, 18)

As appealing as it might be to the ordinary Israelite that the curses would only apply to the "leadership," the context rules against this interpretation. Instead of addressing the "leadership," the curses are explicitly addressed to "all":

- And the Levites shall speak with a loud voice and say to all the men of Israel: "Cursed is the *one* who makes a carved or molded image." (*Deuteronomy 27:14-15*)

Nevertheless, Klinghoffer is correct that Paul did maintain that the Law brings condemnation. Paul had often asserted that the Mosaic Law kills, and that it is removed through the Messiah's atoning work:

- For as many as are of the works of the law are under the curse; for it is written, 'Cursed is everyone who does not continue in all things which are written in the book of the law, to do them' (quoting *Deuteronomy 27:26*). But that no one is justified by the law in the sight of God is evident, for "the just shall live by faith." Yet the law is not of faith, but "the man who does them shall live by them" (quoting *Leviticus 18:5*). (*Galatians 3:10-12; also Colossians 2:13-14; Romans 7:9-11; 3:19-20; 2 Corinthians 3:6, 9*)

40

According to Paul, the Law is strictly about performance. One violation brought guilt and its consequences. Did Paul misread Jesus in this respect?

Paul's interpretation matched Jesus' and His Apostles' interpretation. Jesus also taught that a single infraction was enough to bring condemnation. One wrong motive or word could open the mouth of hell:

- "You have heard that it was said to those of old, 'You shall not murder, and whoever murders will be in danger of the judgment.' But I say to you that whoever is angry with his brother without a cause shall be in danger of the judgment. And whoever says to his brother, "Raca!" shall be in danger of the council. But whoever says, "You fool!" shall be in danger of hell fire." (*Matthew 5:21-22*)

A portfolio of sins wasn't required for condemnation; a single word was enough! Even looking at a woman lustfully established candidacy for the fires of hell (*Matthew 5:27-30*). James wrote similarly:

- For whoever keeps the whole law but fails in one point has become accountable for all of it. (*James 2:10*)

For all the Apostles, the commission of the slightest sin provided grounds for concern. Peter wrote that our model is perfection Himself (*1 Peter 1:15-16*). Nothing short of this is adequate. In order to support his claim, he cited *Leviticus 11:44-45*, affirming that the Law represented an uncompromising standard. John assured his readership that any sin was damning, but more importantly, that Christ had trumped them all. (*1 John 1:9; 2:1-2; 3:4*)

Uniformly, the Apostles maintained that the Law is about *doing* as opposed to merely *acknowledging* that it is God's will.

Nowhere in the Bible do we find any excuse for a cavalier attitude about the commission of even one sin!

Did Paul misconstrue the Hebrew Scriptures?

If *Deuteronomy 27:26 alone* had posited that a single infraction was enough to bring down a curse, we might have grounds to attempt to reinterpret this verse to bring it into line with other teachings on the subject. But this verse is part of a much greater chorus. Throughout the Law, Israel is repeatedly warned that they had to *obey* and not just to *acknowledge* every command. (*Leviticus 26:14-16; Exodus 20:6; 23:21-22; 24:3; Deuteronomy 5:29; 6:24-25; 8:1; 10:12; 11:8, 26-28, 32; 12:28; Jeremiah 11:3-5; 7:22-23*)

This truth is poignantly illustrated by God's first law: "Of the tree of the knowledge of good and evil you shall not eat, for in the day that you eat of it you shall *surely die*" (*Genesis 2:17*). In contrast to Klinghoffer's position, Adam's problem was never that he had failed to *acknowledge* that this command had come from God. This was never an issue.

Of course, sins could be forgiven, but this is a far cry from Klinghoffer's assertion that merely *acknowledging* that the Law came from God was enough. The damning reality of just one sin is brought home graphically by Ezekiel:

- But when a righteous man turns away from his righteousness and commits iniquity, and does according to all the abominations that the wicked man does, shall he live? All the righteousness which he has done shall not be remembered; because of the unfaithfulness of which he is guilty and the *sin* which he has committed, because of them he shall die. (*Ezekiel 18:24*)

It's important to note that punishment never had to wait until sin reached a certain quantity. There is no "wait-and-see" policy; nor does grace *require* God to extend a second or third chance. Ezekiel simply mentions "the unfaithfulness of which he is guilty and the sin which he has committed." This could be a matter of just one sin! In other words, it was presumptuous for any Israelite to think, "With my perfect record, I've got it made and now can afford to relax!"

The reality of the sacrificial system further enforced the idea that every Israelite had to make payment for *every* offense. It wasn't enough to merely acknowledge a lapse; a sacrificial offering had to be made. Nowhere in Hebrew Scriptures can we find any justification for the idea that it was acceptable to renege on any law. Instead, every transgression carried with it a penalty.

Hebrew narratives also demonstrate the damning power of even one sin. Even more problematic for Klinghoffer's thesis that "there was no expectation of perfect conformity in his [the Israelite's] action," are the numerous Old Testament narratives that show just how damning a single infraction could be.

Moses *struck* the rock instead of speaking to it, as the Lord had directed. Consequently, the Lord informed him that "Because you did not believe Me, to hallow Me in the eyes of the children of Israel, therefore you shall not bring this assembly into the land which I have given them" (*Numbers 20:12*). It would have been ludicrous for Moses to protest, "Lord, since you don't require perfect conformity to Your Word but rather my *acknowledgement* that this Word is indeed Your Word, You are acting a bit heavy-handed in my regards."

Klinghoffer would have had a better case had Moses habitually transgressed, but this was Moses' only recorded sin during his forty desert years with Israel. In *Leviticus 24*, during

43

a fight, one Israelite cursed God. The Lord determined that he should be put to death. Clearly, the Lord did expect *perfect conformity* to His Law and not just an *acknowledgement* that it was God's Law. The punishments for Adam's sin, Cain's sin, and Achan's sin also speak eloquently in support of this fact.

Klinghoffer's interpretation fails to accord with the Hebrew Scriptures, but is the New Testament interpretation reasonable? At first glance it seems both severe and unjust.
Besides, it's easy to wrongly conclude that God had set up Israel for failure. Who was righteous enough to avoid the curse? Nobody (*Psalm 130:3; 143:2; Ecclesiastes 7:20; Isaiah 64:6*)! However, this seems to contribute to our perception that God had set up Israel for failure, right?

No! Uniformly, the Bible holds Israel accountable, *not* God. However, God was always merciful (*Psalm 103:10; Ezra 9:13; Nehemiah 9:31; Daniel 9:18*) when Israel humbled themselves and confessed. However, the condemnation was a necessary piece in the puzzle:

- Scripture [Law] has confined all under sin, that the promise by faith in Jesus Christ might be given to those who believe. But before faith came, we were kept under guard by the law, kept for the faith which would afterward be revealed. Therefore the law was our tutor to bring us to Christ, that we might be justified by faith. (*Galatians 3:22-24*)

According to Paul, the Law and its curse illuminated grace and Messiah. But was Paul merely imposing his own philosophy on the Hebrew Scriptures? No! This same message is *implicit* to the entire body of Scripture. It seems that the Law's curse in regards to his sin with Bathsheba enabled David to see grace even more poignantly:

- Blessed is he whose transgression is forgiven, whose sin is covered. Blessed is the man to whom the LORD does not impute iniquity…I acknowledged my sin to You, and my iniquity I have not hidden. I said, 'I will confess my transgressions to the LORD,' and You forgave the iniquity of my sin. (*Psalm 32:1-5*)

In contrast, Klinghoffer's distinction between *obeying* the Law and *upholding* the Law (merely "affirming that they are God's will") will not produce the desired results. Such a law will not convict or condemn anyone! Why should it, as long as we have the recourse of easily acknowledging that the law is "God's will?" If no one is convicted, then no one needs to be forgiven. No one will cry out for mercy, and therefore receive mercy. Grace is then irrelevant—so too the sacrificial system, Christ, and His New Covenant, and the need for a circumcised heart (*Deuteronomy 30:6*).

Besides, a legal code that only requires *affirmation* is absurd. Imagine a police officer stopping you for going 60 in a 25 MPH zone. Would you say to the officer, "I didn't violate the law, because I *affirm* that the law is the will of the state? The state doesn't expect perfection from me." It would be equally ridiculous to say, "Officer, I have been driving for 20 years without a speeding ticket. Therefore, I don't deserve one now." If such illogical reasoning had prevailed in Israel, any violation of Mosaic Law could be easily dismissed.

OT/NT Harmony

Rather than finding contradiction between Paul and the Scriptures of Israel, we find a glaring chasm between Klinghoffer, the rabbis, and the Scriptures they claim to represent. In spite of Klinghoffer's allegations, a rich and illuminating consistency emerges among Jesus and the Apostles on the one hand, and the Scriptures they embraced on the other.

How then is it that the learned Jewish establishment could be so wrong, while a handful of renegades led by a condemned Rebel would be so consistently right—unless, of course, they had Divine guidance?

WORKS CITED

Cohen, A. (ed.), *The Socino Chumash*, (Hindhead, Surrey: The Soncino Press, 1947)

Klinghoffer, David, *Why the Jews Rejected Jesus,* (New York: Doubleday, First Edition, 2005)

Sigal, Gerald, *The Jew and the Christian Missionary*: *A Jewish Response to Missionary Christianity,* (New York: KTAV Publishing House, Inc., 1981)

Chapter 4

"SOLA SCRIPTURA" - THE GUIDING PRINCIPLE OF THE BOTH THE OLD AND THE NEW TESTAMENTS

The doctrine of "Sola Scriptura" (SS) states that the Bible teaches that God's words must prevail over all other words, statements of truth, and moral imperatives. His words had to take precedence over everything. In the NT, Jesus responded to Satan, "Man does not live by bread alone but by <u>every</u> Word that proceeds from the mouth of God" (*Matthew 4:4*). However, this was a teaching that Jesus had drawn from God's instructions to the Israelites:

- "The whole commandment that I command you today you shall be careful to do, that you may live and multiply, and go in and possess the land that the LORD swore to give to your fathers. And you shall remember the whole way that the LORD your God has led you these forty years in the wilderness, that he might humble you, testing you to know what was in your heart, whether you would keep his commandments or not. And he humbled you and let you hunger and fed you with manna, which you did not know, nor did your fathers know, that he might make you know that man does not live by bread alone, but man lives by every word that comes from the mouth of the LORD." (*Deuteronomy 8:1-3*)

We find in both Testaments that life and well-being were a matter of keeping God's every Word. God's first warning to Adam revealed this essential truth:

- And the LORD God commanded the man, saying, "You may surely eat of every tree of the garden, but of the tree of the knowledge of good and evil you shall not

eat, for in the day that you eat of it you shall surely die."
(*Genesis 2:16-17*)

The first couple's welfare depended on whether or not they would put God's Word above everything else, above every temptation and every fear. This doctrine of SS didn't mean that they couldn't learn from other sources, like their observations and feelings, but God's Word would have to take precedence over everything else.

Abraham passed this test when he placed God's Word even above the life of his son, Isaac, and was ready to sacrifice him, according to God's commands. And God rewarded him for his obedience (*Genesis 22:15-18*). Previously, God had revealed that all the wonderful promises he had made to Abraham depended upon his response to the Word of God:

- "For I have chosen him, that he may command his children and his household after him to keep the way of the LORD by doing righteousness and justice [God's commands], so that the LORD may bring to Abraham what he has promised him." (*Genesis 18:19*)

The imperative to follow all of God's commands had characterized Israel's relationship with God. If they would love God by following them, He would bless Israel; if they turned away from them, they would be cursed (*Deuteronomy 28, 29*). This is what had defined their entire history. The Lord had sent many prophets to His people to warn them of the consequences of their rebellion against His Word:

- The LORD, the God of their fathers, sent persistently to them by his messengers, because he had compassion on his people and on his dwelling place. But they kept mocking the messengers of God, despising his words and scoffing at his prophets, until the wrath of the

LORD rose against his people, until there was no remedy. (*2 Chronicles 36:15-16*)

Israel's response to the Word of God meant life and death. It was also an expression of Israel's faithfulness to their Redeemer. It therefore had to be protected against any alterations or additions at the threat of death (*Deuteronomy 4:2; 12:32*). Even a worker of miracles had to be put to death if he was preaching a message contrary to the Word Israel had already received (*Deuteronomy 13:1-5; 18:20-22*). How was Israel to know which prophets came with God's Words? Their prophecies had to be fulfilled 100% of the time (*Deuteronomy 18:22*).

However, the rabbis seem to have little taste of "sola scriptura," the principle that maintains the supremacy of the Word of God. They have not only added to the Word of God through their inclusion of the Mishna, Talmud, and, much later, the Kabbalah. The rabbis have generally enthroned the Talmud *above* all else. *The Jewish Study Bible* comments that:

- Premodern communal Jewish life was based not on the Bible but on laws, customs, and traditions derived in the main from the Babylonian Talmud...The 17th century Rabbi Joseph Hahn of Franfurt (d. 1637 wrote, "In our generation there are rabbis who never studied the Bible." (Jewish Study Bible, 1908)

Even later, the predominance of the Talmud had remained unchanged:

- ...In Germany, and all the more in Russia and Poland, talmudical study carried greater prestige than biblical. (Jewish Study Bible, 1908)

While the centrality of the Talmud might have eroded in the modern era, it did not cede ground to the Bible but to modern biblical criticism.

In contrast, the NT validated the preeminence of the Words of God. Nothing was allowed to rival the Scriptures. They alone constituted the Word of God:

- "Knowing this first of all, that no prophecy of Scripture comes from someone's own interpretation. For no prophecy was ever produced by the will of man, but men spoke from God as they were carried along by the Holy Spirit." (*2 Peter 1:20-21*)

John invoked the OT warning against tampering with God's Words:

- "I warn everyone who hears the words of the prophecy of this book: If anyone adds anything to them, God will add to him the plagues described in this book." (*Revelation 22:18*)

As was the case in the Hebrew Scriptures, God's Word was to judge everything else, while nothing was to judge His Words. Scripture had to sit in judgment over *all* other truth claims:

- "The weapons we fight with are not the weapons of the world. On the contrary, they have divine power to demolish strongholds. We demolish arguments and every pretension that sets itself up against the knowledge of God, and we take captive every thought to make it obedient to Christ." (*2 Corinthians 10:4-5*)

Scripture was also meant to give God's people everything they needed in order to relate to Him.

- "All Scripture is God-breathed and is useful for teaching, rebuking, correcting and training in righteousness, so that the man of God may be thoroughly equipped for every good work." (*2 Timothy 3:16-17*)

Therefore, Paul reasoned that the Church should not go beyond what had already been given them in the Scriptures:

- "Learn from us the meaning of the saying, 'Do not go beyond what is written.' Then you will not be puffed up in being a follower of one of us over against the other. For who makes you different from anyone else? What do you have that you did not receive? And if you did receive it, why do you boast as though you did not?" (*1 Corinthians 4:6-7*)

This too was the message of the OT. All truth claims had to be consistent with God's Words. There was nothing higher or more authoritative. Scripture was the Supreme Court where the buck stopped:

- "When someone tells you to consult mediums and spiritists, who whisper and mutter, should not a people inquire of their God? Why consult the dead on behalf of the living? Consult God's instruction and the testimony of warning. If anyone does not speak according to this word, they have no light of dawn." (*Isaiah 8:19-20*)

In regards to the things that Scripture taught, it was the brightest light and the source of blessing. In view of this, God had commissioned Joshua:

- "Be careful to obey all the law my servant Moses gave you; do not turn from it to the right or to the left, that you may be successful wherever you go. Keep this Book of the Law always on your lips; meditate on it day and night, so that you may be careful to do everything written in it. Then you will be prosperous and successful." (*Joshua 1:7-8*)

God warned Joshua that his response to His Word would determine blessing and curse. If he failed to follow it, he and Israel would suffer, if he meditated on it to do it, he would prosper. There was no other activity that could compete in importance with Israel's response to the word of God. It occupied an unrivaled position. No amount of philosophizing, painting, poetry writing, or practicing spiritual disciplines could even come close. Scripture was in a league of its own. This was the uniform teaching of Scripture, not just a handful of verses.

All the Apostles recognized that God worked through the understanding of His word to accomplish great things (*Psalm 1*). Paul therefore recited this benediction over the Ephesian elders:

- "Now I commit you to God and to the word of his grace, which can build you up and give you an inheritance among all those who are sanctified." (*Acts 20:32*)

How do we please God? We abide in His word above all else. Peter insisted that:

- "If anyone speaks, they should do so as one who speaks the very words of God... so that in all things God may be praised through Jesus Christ." (*1 Peter 4:11*).

Our church traditions should never be in competition with God's word. This was the problem with the religious leadership of Jesus' day. They valued their own traditions above Scripture. Against this lethal tendency:

- Jesus replied, "And why do you break the command of God for the sake of your tradition?... Thus you nullify the word of God for the sake of your tradition. You hypocrites! Isaiah [*Isaiah 29:13*] was right when he prophesied about you: 'These people honor me with their lips, but their hearts are far from me. They worship me in vain; their teachings are merely human rules.'" (*Matthew 15:3-9*)

Our traditions or institutions cannot be placed on par with Scripture. The resulting worship is of *no* value! God had always intended for His Word to rule over all else. Jesus had been totally sold out for the Scriptures, claiming that it could "not be broken" (*John 10:35*). Everything else could be changed but not Scripture (*Matthew 24:35*). It stood over everything else – sola scriptura! Even Jesus would not do away with Scripture:

- "Do not think that I have come to abolish the Law or the Prophets; I have not come to abolish them but to fulfill them. For truly I tell you, until heaven and earth disappear, not the smallest letter, not the least stroke of a pen, will by any means disappear from the Law until everything is accomplished. Therefore anyone who sets aside one of the least of these commands and teaches others accordingly will be called least in the kingdom of heaven, but whoever practices and teaches these commands will be called great in the kingdom of heaven." (*Matthew 5:17-19*)

Because Scripture came from God, it could not just be set aside. Instead, our standing in the Kingdom depended upon our response to Scripture. However, Jesus would fulfill it, according to Divine intention.

Jesus had such a high regard for Scripture that He continually brought His disciples back to this wellspring of blessing. When

53

Jesus encountered His disheartened disciples after His crucifixion, He could have spoken His own words to encourage them, but instead, He pointed them back to Scripture:

- "'Did not the Messiah have to suffer these things and then enter his glory?'" And beginning with Moses and all the Prophets, he explained to them what was said in all the Scriptures concerning himself. (*Luke 24:26-27*)

Scripture is so central to our lives that Jesus opened their minds to understand it:

- He said to them, "This is what I told you while I was still with you: Everything must be fulfilled that is written about me in the Law of Moses, the Prophets and the Psalms." Then he opened their minds so they could understand the Scriptures. (*Luke 24:44-45*)

Never once do we see any indication that Jesus regarded Scripture as merely a human document. Instead, He copiously quoted Scripture, *always* as maximally authoritative.
Besides, because Scripture is God's authoritative word, we are not free to interpret it in any manner we choose:

- "Above all, you must understand that no prophecy of Scripture came about by the prophet's own interpretation. For prophecy never had its origin in the will of man, but men spoke from God as they were carried along by the Holy Spirit." (*2 Peter 1:20-21; 1 Corinthians 2:12-13*)

Although under both covenants, God had ordained teachers to teach His Words, it was also intended to be so plain that all would be held to account for violating it:

- "For this commandment that I command you today is not too hard for you, neither is it far off. It is not in heaven, that you should say, 'Who will ascend to heaven for us and bring it to us, that we may hear it and do it?' Neither is it beyond the sea, that you should say, 'Who will go over the sea for us and bring it to us, that we may hear it and do it?' But the word is very near you. It is in your mouth and in your heart, so that you can do it." (*Deuteronomy 30:11-14*)

The Word was so approachable that no one had an excuse to not perform it. Paul even quoted these verses to demonstrate the continuity between the Old and the New Covenants (Romans 10:6-8) and that God's Word had to be at the center of the life of God's people. There is nothing higher than Scripture. Consequently, we never are free to *not* obey it:

- Jesus answered him, "If anyone loves me, he will keep my word, and my Father will love him, and we will come to him and make our home with him. Whoever does not love me does not keep my words. And the word that you hear is not mine but the Father's who sent me. (*John 14:23-24*)

To love Him is to place His Word above all else. This is the message of "Sola Scriptura" in both covenants. This should lead us to ask the question, "Why do religious Jews venerate the Talmud, the collected writings of their rabbis, above their own Bible?" I will try to address this question later in this book.

WORKS CITED

The Jewish Study Bible, Jewish Publication Society, TANAHK Translation, Editors: Adele Berlin and Marc Zvi Brettler, (New York: Oxford University Press, 2004)

Chapter 5

EVOLUTION, CREATION, AND THE FALL ~ THEIR HISTORICITY

How should we regard *Genesis 1-3*, which describe the creation and the Fall of humanity into sin and death? Is it historical or non-historical, as the theistic evolutionists (TEs) maintain? If these chapters of Genesis are teaching history, along with theology, they contradict evolution, which regards death and the survival-of-the-fittest as God's original plan for evolving us from one-celled life.

Not only do we *not* find any evidence for evolution – gradualism, random mutation, natural selection through the survival-of-the-fittest – in these chapters, we find the exact opposite thing. God spoke creation into existence and each species as a separate creation.

Genesis 3 claims that there was no sin and death until Adam and Eve disobeyed God and ate the fruit. This is consistent with the creation account in which God states that everything He had created was "very good" (*Genesis 1:31*).

Did this creation include sin and death? Not according to the Biblical account! The creation account is explicitly claims that animals were not intended to eat other animals (*Genesis 1:29-30*), and that there had been such a state of comfort and peace that Adam and Eve were naked and not ashamed (*Genesis 2:25*), because they had not yet sinned. But once the rebellion against the Word of God came, so too did shame and death:

- "By the sweat of your face you shall eat bread, till you return to the ground, for out of it you were taken; for you are dust, and to dust you shall return." (*Genesis 3:19*)

Sin and death entered the world together, contrary to the evolutionary account. The NT also affirms the historicity of Genesis:

- "For the creation was subjected to futility [corruption – the Fall] not willingly, but because of him [God], who subjected it, in hope that the creation itself will be set free from its bondage to corruption and obtain the freedom of the glory of the children of God. For we know that the whole creation has been groaning together in the pains of childbirth until now." (*Romans 8:20-22*)

The TE narrative undermines the teachings of the Bible. The "groaning" and death hadn't been part of God's original design but of our sin.

The genealogies, including *Genesis 5*, also proclaim the historicity of Genesis. If Adam and Eve weren't historical, then there would be no reason to regard others in Adam's genealogy, like Abraham and Jesus as historical.

Besides, *all* of the subsequent Biblical commentary regard these chapters of Genesis as historical. Here is a sampling from the NT affirming the historicity of the creation account:

- When they heard this, they raised their voices together in prayer to God. "Sovereign Lord," they said, "you made the heaven and the earth and the sea, and everything in them." (*Acts 4:24* citing *Genesis 1* as history; *2 Kings 19:15; 2 Chronicles 2:12; Nehemiah 9:6*)

- He also says, "In the beginning, O Lord, you laid the foundations of the earth, and the heavens are the work of your hands." (*Hebrews 1:10* citing *Genesis 1* as history; *Psalm 102:25*)

- "By faith we understand that the universe was formed at <u>God's command</u>, so that what is seen was not made out of what was visible." (*Hebrews 11:3* citing *Genesis 1* as history)

- "Through him all things were made; <u>without him nothing was made that has been made</u>." (*John 1:3* citing *Genesis 1* as history)

By denying the historicity of Genesis, the TE has placed the present consensus of science above the plain teachings of the Bible and even the ancient rabbinic commentaries:

- "Why was only a single specimen of man created first? To teach us that he who destroys a single soul destroys a whole world and that he who saves a single soul saves a whole world; furthermore, so no race or class may claim a nobler ancestry, saying, 'Our father was born first'; and, finally, to give testimony to the greatness of the Lord, who caused the wonderful diversity of mankind to emanate from one type. And why was Adam created last of all beings? To teach him humility; for if he be overbearing, let him remember that the little fly preceded him in the order of creation." (Talmud tractate *Sanhedrin* viii. 4-9, as quoted by *JewishEncyclopedia.com* - on "ADAM")

Adam is consistently regarded as the first man instead of a primate gradually evolved from lower primates:

- "For Adam was <u>formed first</u>, then Eve." (*1 Timothy 2:13* citing G*enesis 2:7* as historical; *Hosea 6:7; Job 31:33; Isaiah 43:27* – in some verses, the Hebrew word for "Adam" is translated as "earth" or "mankind")

- "Created in the image and likeness of God." (*1 Corinthians 11:7; Colossians 3:10; Ephesians 4:24; 2*

Peter 3:9; Genesis 5:1; 9:6; each citing *Genesis 1:26-27* as history)

- So it is written: "The first man <u>Adam</u> became a living being"; the last Adam, a life-giving spirit. (*1 Corinthians 15:45* citing *Genesis 2:23* as history)

- "[Jesus] the son of Enosh, the son of Seth, the son of <u>Adam</u>, the son of God." (*Luke 3:38* citing *Genesis 5:1*-ff as history)

- "Enoch, the seventh from <u>Adam</u>." (*Jude 1:14* citing *Genesis 5* as history)

- Jesus replied, "But <u>at the beginning of creation God 'made them male and female</u>.' 'For this reason a man will leave his father and mother and be united to his wife, and the two will become one flesh.' So they are no longer two, but one. Therefore what <u>God has joined together</u>, let man not separate." (*Mark 10:5-9* citing *Genesis 1:26 and 2:24* as history; *Matthew 19:4-6*)

- "From <u>one man</u> he made every nation of men, that they should inhabit the whole earth; and he determined the times set for them and the exact places where they should live." (*Acts 17:26* alluding to *Genesis 1* as actual history; *Malachi 2:10*)

- "For man did not come from woman, but <u>woman from man</u>; neither was man created for woman, but woman for man." (*1 Corinthians 11:8-9* citing *Genesis 2:18, 23* as history)

Adam as the original sinner and the cause of the Fall:

- "For as in <u>Adam</u> all die, so in Christ all will be made alive." (*1 Corinthians 15:22* alluding to *Genesis 3* as actual history)

- "<u>Death</u> reigned from the time of <u>Adam</u> to the time of Moses, even over those who did not sin by breaking a command, as <u>did Adam</u>, who was a pattern of the one to come." (*Romans 5:14* alluding to *Genesis 3* as history)

If Adam's work had merely been a matter of myth or parable, likewise should we regard the work of Jesus, the second Adam. All of these verses demonstrate that it is not enough to merely strip the first several chapters of Genesis of what God had historically accomplished, the rest of the subsequent Biblical commentary affirming their historicity must also be forcibly stripped away.

Other verses regard even the serpent/Satan as historical:

- "You [Pharisees] are of your father the devil, and your will is to do your father's desires. He was a murderer <u>from the beginning</u>, and does not stand in the truth, because there is no truth in him. When he lies, he speaks out of his own character, for he is a liar and the father of lies." (*John 8:44*; Jesus affirms that the devil was the originator of lies, alluding to *Genesis 3; 1 John 3:8*)

- "And the God of peace will <u>crush Satan under your feet shortly</u>." (*Romans 16:20* alluding to *Genesis 3:15*)

To deny the historicity of *Genesis 3* is to undermine the integrity of the entire Bible. It is to disregard the Bible's own commentary in favor of an alien evolutionary worldview imposed on the text. It is also to add and to subtract the historicity from God's Word:

- "You shall not add to the word that I command you, nor take from it, that you may keep the commandments of the LORD your God that I command you." (*Deuteronomy 4:2; 12:32; Revelations 22:18-19*)

When the TE denies the historicity of *Genesis 1-11*, he takes away from God's Word. When he imposes evolution upon it, he adds to God's Word.

The TE claims that he is salvaging the "Christian faith" for the educated who find themselves in conflict once introduced to the theory of evolution (ToE). However, even atheist Dale McGowan, Managing Editor of the *Atheist Channel* at Patheos, and author of *Atheism For Dummies*, is skeptical. He quotes Tullio Gregory who expresses his concern:

- "Once you cast doubt on man's place in creation, the entire Biblical story of salvation history, from original sin to Christ's incarnation, is also threatened."

Even though he is a strong advocate for evolution, McGowan confesses that he is "conflicted" and troubled by message of *The BioLogos Foundation*, a TE organization peddling evolution to the church:

- In a *BioLogos* video titled, "Adam and Eve: Engaging the Tough Questions," an advisor notes that there are "a lot of proposals out there of when the first sin might have happened, what it might have looked like… we don't have a simple answer on the question of the historical Adam…who were Adam and Eve, when did they live?"

- "This is always the first step in a crumbling theology – the suggestion that the answer is out there, it's just very, very complicated. The problem is our ability to grasp the answer. But no worries, there are a lot of proposals. It all makes for an impressive simulacrum of rigor, an army of question marks in search of meaningful questions."
  (www.patheos.com/blogs/secularspectrum/2015/03/how-to-reconcile-god-and-evolution-and-how-not-to/)

As McGowen points out, *Biologos* has undermined both the clarity of the biblical message and the church's assurance about it. When we cite Scriptures against TE, they warn that "we must be humble about our interpretations of Scripture." However, they are not at all humble about their dismissal of the first eleven chapters of Genesis as history. Nor are they humble about dismissing the NT's clear assertions that Genesis is history.

What happens when Christians bite into the ToE apple?
Kreeft and Tacelli have written:

- "If the Fall really didn't happen in history, then God rather than humanity is to blame for sin, for God must have created us as sinners rather than as innocents. If there was never any real unfallen state, then we were sinners from the first moment of our creation, and God was wrong to declare everything he made 'good.'"
  (*Handbook of Christian Apologetics*, 213)

TE overturns the theology of the Bible. If the survival-of-the-fittest had been part of God's glorious plan, then who can blame Cain for killing Adam, the least fittest of the two, or even Adam and Eve for eating the forbidden fruit so that they could become more adaptive, as God! Perhaps, then, we too should live according to God's initial plan and to attempt to prevail over any opponents, even to rape so that our superior genome will more generously be passed on!

In light of this – imposing an evolutionary worldview upon the Bible – sin and death were God's doing, and He is to blame. However, the destruction of the Biblical worldview is far more extensive.

TE is also the destruction of apologetics, the defense of the faith. How? Since the TE denies that the Bible is about history and science – the physical world – it has deprived the faith of any evidential support. Proof applies what is generally known and certain about the physical world to what is disputed or uncertain, especially in regards to the spiritual. Consequently, we apply the historical evidence that Jesus died on the Cross to the theological – the Bible's assertion that Jesus died for us. However, since the TE removes theological assertions from their necessary historical and physical underpinning, theology is becomes no more than a vapor hanging on nothing. Consequently, TE Ron Choong, the head of *Academy for Christian Thought* in New York City, has written in his publication " Origin of Life" 2006 (pg 36):

- "We cannot know who caused life to live scientifically but we can believe by rational reflection of reasonable faith that it was God who created life to live."

The implication of the above quote is that there is no scientific evidence to support the existence of God. Choong's words parallel those of many other TEs. However, can we take such a stance in light of the Scriptures, which teach us that we are "without excuse" if we deny the plain physical evidences for God's existence?

- "The wrath of God is being revealed from heaven against all the godlessness and wickedness of men who suppress the truth by their wickedness, since what may be known about God is <u>plain</u> to them, because <u>God has made it plain to them</u>. For since the creation of the world God's invisible qualities--his eternal power and divine nature--have been <u>clearly seen, being understood from what has been made</u>, so that men are <u>without excuse</u>." (*Romans 1:18-20*)

Besides, there is no basis to believe in the theological message of the Cross and the Resurrection apart from the fact that Jesus was historically crucified and rose. His disciples had needed to be convinced of His resurrection if they were to continue in the faith. However, the Lord provided physical evidences:

- "He presented himself alive to them after his suffering by many proofs, appearing to them during forty days and speaking about the kingdom of God." (*Acts 1:3*)

TE leads to the destruction of the Christian faith. In "Saving Darwin: How to be a Christian and an Evolutionist," the former co-head of *The Biologos Foundation*, Karl Giberson, was candid about the impact of evolution on his faith:

- "Acid is an appropriate metaphor for the erosion of my fundamentalism, as I slowly lost confidence in the Genesis story of creation and the scientific creationism that placed this ancient story within the framework of modern science. [Darwin's] universal acid dissolved Adam and Eve; it ate through the Garden of Eden; it destroyed the historicity of the events of creation week. It etched holes in those parts of Christianity connected to the stories—the fall, "Christ as the second Adam," the origins of sin, and nearly everything else that I counted sacred." (Giberson, 9-10)

However, Giberson assured his readers that Darwin's acid of evolution would cease to dissolve anything further. However, Giberson had stepped onto a slippery slope and wrote a few short years later that he believed that the God of the Old Testament, Jesus' "Father," was a "monster." This was the result of Giberson having made evolution his guiding light. No wonder Jesus warned against having two masters (*Matthew 6:24*).

TE also leads to the destruction of any confidence about the teachings of the Bible. How? To eliminate all possible conflict, TEs claim that the Bible isn't about the physical world but the spiritual, while evolution is about the physical and not the spiritual.

However, the physical and the spiritual cannot be divorced. Consequently, to deny the historicity of Christ dying for our sins on the Cross (the physical) is also to deny the theological or spiritual messages of the Cross. No historical death of Jesus, no atonement and payment for sins!

Many doctrines depend upon what God has done historically. Consequently, when Jesus was asked about the permissibility of divorce, He based His answer on what God had historically accomplished, the historicity of *Genesis 1 and 2*:

- He answered, "Have you not read that he who created them from the beginning made them male and female [*Genesis 1:26-27*], and said, 'Therefore a man shall leave his father and his mother and hold fast to his wife, and the two shall become one flesh' [*Genesis 2:24*]? So they are no longer two but one flesh. What therefore God has joined together, let not man separate." (*Matthew 19:4-6*)

If God had not historically joined Adam and Even together, then divorce does not violate God's work and Jesus' argument

65

falls apart. Based upon God's actual and historical past judgments, Peter argued that the promised future judgment would *also* be actual:

- "For if God did not spare angels when they sinned, but cast them into hell and committed them to chains of gloomy darkness to be kept until the judgment; if he did not spare the ancient world, but preserved Noah, a herald of righteousness, with seven others, when he brought a flood upon the world of the ungodly; if by turning the cities of Sodom and Gomorrah to ashes he condemned them to extinction, making them an example of what is going to happen to the ungodly...then the Lord knows how to rescue the godly from trials, and to keep the unrighteous under punishment until the day of judgment." (*2 Peter 2:4-9*)

If these historical judgments had not actually happened, there would be no reason to believe that the future judgment would also be actual. However, Peter claimed that these prior judgments had been a matter of actual history. Therefore, the promised future judgment would also be actual and not a metaphor for something else. If the world had been destroyed during the worldwide flood, then we have to seriously consider the promise of a future destruction. However, if the flood had merely been a parable used to make a theological point, then we might also assume that the promised future judgment was also parabolic.

If all of Peter's citations were not actual historical events, what interpretation can we take away from Peter's warning? Who knows! When we are deprived of the grounding historical context, interpretation becomes uncertain. Perhaps Peter's citations merely served as a scare tactic? Perhaps then the Cross was also no more than a scare tactic or a comfort to the guilty-of-heart? Perhaps, also, the threat of eternal punishment is just God's way to keep us in line? In any event, we are left with Biblical agnosticism, a slide into uncertainty regarding the teachings of the entire Bible.

Am I exaggerating the effects of the ToE upon the Church? I don't think so. My many dialogues with TEs have shown me:

- They don't know the Scriptures very well; nor have they derived a systematic worldview based upon the Scriptures. And why should they if the interpretation of the entire Bible is up-for-grabs!

- They are always cautioning me that we have to be humble about our interpretation of the Scriptures. Why? Because they are uncertain about them! (If only they were equally uncertain about Darwin!)

- Their views are almost indistinguishable from the professional or university communities to which they belong. Why? Being agnostic about the teachings of Scripture, they have no defense against competing worldviews and the pressures for peer acceptance.

Unsurprisingly, in a day when pastors and priests embraced the theory of evolution, we should not be surprised that many rabbis have also taken the same route. Jesus had charged the rabbis of His day:

- "For if you believed Moses, you would believe me; for he wrote of me. But if you do not believe his writings, how will you believe my words?" (*John 5:46-47*)

It seems that little has changed. For example, *The Jewish Study Bible* of the *Jewish Publication Society*, "a committee of esteemed biblical scholars and rabbis from the Orthodox, Conservative, and Reformed movements," has written in their introduction to the *Book of Genesis*:

- "How much history lies behind the story of Genesis? Because the action of the primeval story is not represented as taking place on the plane of ordinary human history and has so many affinities with ancient mythology, it is very far-fetched to speak of its narratives as historical at all." (Jewish Study Bible, 11)

However, this statement represents a gross disregard for how the rest of the Hebrew Bible regards the Genesis accounts as historical. Before, the Talmud had been the lens through which to understand the Bible. More recently, the rabbis have adopted the lens of the Bible critics. In either case, it represents a rejection of the Word of God.

WORKS CITED

Choong, Ron,
www.actministry.org/ "The Origin of Life" (2003)

Biologos Video, *Adam and Eve, Engaging the Tough Questions*
www.youtube.com/watch?v=wr5iT5dhaz4

Giberson, Karl, *Saving Darwin: How to Be a Christian and Believe in Evolution* (New York: HarperOne, Reprint edition, 2009)

The Jewish Study Bible, Jewish Publication Society, TANAHK Translation, Editors: Adele Berlin and Marc Zvi Brettler, (New York: Oxford University Press, 2004)

The Jewish Encyclopedia
www.jewishencyclopedia.com/

Kreeft, Peter & Tacelli, Ronald K., *Handbook of Christian Apologetics* (Wheaton: IVP Academic; Reprint edition,1994)

McGowan, Dale,
www.patheos.com/blogs/secularspectrum/2015/03/how-to-reconcile-god-and-evolution-and-how-not-to/

Chapter 6

ABRAHAM AND THE NATURE OF FAITH

If you have seen *Fiddler on the Roof*, you will probably leave with the impression that Judaism is about tradition rather than a faith or belief. If so, you've gotten the right idea, as this representative statement indicates:

- "Judaism does not require faith statements as a sign of legitimacy…Torah goes to great lengths to reassure the searching Jew that skepticism is healthy, legitimate, and even celebrated in Jewish life. Fundamentalists [of other religions] may regard anything short of absolute faith as religiously insufficient; Jewish tradition does not share their reliance on certainty…Synagogue sermons tend either to speak of God as obvious fact or to avoid the issue of God altogether…the question 'Do you believe in God?' is not the central Jewish spiritual question." (www.myjewishlearning.com/article/from-belief-to-faith/)

What brings Jews together if not common beliefs? Tradition! However, today even tradition is not providing the necessary glue. Instead, Judaism seems to have more to do with just a vague and uncertain sense of identification.

This raises the question, "What was the required glue for the Israelite, if there was any at all?" The life of Abraham answers this question. After about ten years of sojourning in the Promised Land, Abraham had lost faith in God's promise that if he would leave his family and go to a land that God would show him, He would give him many descendants (*Genesis 12:1-3, 7*). Since his wife Sarah had been barren, this promise spoke volumes to this grieving couple.

70

However, after ten years of waiting for its fulfillment, Abraham had lost faith in God's promise and had resigned himself to the disappointing likelihood that his servant Eliezer would be his heir. However, once again, the Lord came to him:

- And behold, the word of the LORD came to him: "This man shall not be your heir; your very own son shall be your heir." (*Genesis 15:4*)

When the Lord came to Abraham it was the same as the Word of the Lord with His teachings, a necessary preamble to the faith. The Lord then led Abraham outside to look at the sky and told him that his offspring would be as numerous as the stars, and Abraham believed the Word of the Lord:

- "And he <u>believed</u> the LORD, and he counted it to him as righteousness." (*Genesis 15:6*)

God was pleased that Abraham believed and hadn't remained in disbelief. This doesn't mean that Abraham's faith was now filled with a glowing and unquenchable *feeling* of confidence. It certainly wasn't. Even though Abraham believed, he asked God to reassure him regarding this Word:

- But he said, "O Lord GOD, how am I to know that I shall possess it?" (*Genesis 15:8*)

God granted Abraham his request by pledging Himself to His Word through a formal Covenant. What then is faith? It is not exactly peace of mind and glowing emotions, although these might result from faith. There is no indication in this account that Abraham's faith was accompanied by a glowing, warm, and fuzzy experience. Instead, God's covenantal pledge to Abraham was associated with a "dreadful and great darkness" which came down upon him (*Genesis 15:12*). Besides, the presence of God was accompanied by symbols of His wrath as He made this pledge to Abraham. Why was it that such a

71

great promise was associated with dread? I think that this was indicating that, in order to fulfill His pledge, the Son would have to die for the sins of the world (*2 Corinthians 1:20*). Thus, God was giving Abraham a foretaste of the Gospel.

What then is faith? It is fundamentally a willingness and a commitment to take God at His Word, even when it hurts and doesn't make any sense to us. It is a matter of believing and trusting in the Word rather than in ourselves or our traditions and rituals.

A few years later, Abraham again lost faith in the Word of the Lord, God's promise. Instead of believing God, he placed his trust in his own ill-advised devices and impregnated their servant girl, Hagar, in order to produce his heir. Although this didn't thwart the plan of God, the birth of Ishmael did produce a ton of domestic strife.

God returned to Abraham, when he was 99 years old and Sarah was 90, after she had ceased having her periods, and announced that next year Sarah would give birth to Isaac, the long-awaited promised child (*Genesis 18*). Abraham believed God, but succumbed to fear, when sojourning in Gerar (*Genesis 20*). He lied, claiming that Sarah was merely his sister. Consequently, the king received his still beautiful wife into his harem. However, God returned Sarah to her humiliated husband.

However, Abraham was learning to believe in the Word of God, rather than in resorting to his own devices or in performing a household tradition. When God asked Abraham to offer his treasured son Isaac as a burnt offering, he had learned that he had to trust in God rather than in traditions:

- "By faith Abraham, when he was tested, offered up Isaac, and he who had received the promises was in the act of offering up his only son, of whom it was said,

72

'Through Isaac shall your offspring be named.' He considered that God was able even to raise him from the dead…" (*Hebrews 11:17-19*)

Abraham had grown in faith in his God and understood that, somehow, he would rescue Isaac. After perhaps 50 years of sojourning in the Promised Land, God had proven Himself trustworthy, the very thing He has always intended to do. His Word had never failed him, and Abraham was convinced that His Word wouldn't fail this time, even if he had to put his son to death.

What does God want from us? To always remain critical and skeptical of the Word of God, as the rabbis suppose? No! Instead, He wants us to trust in His Word, with or without traditions. How did God achieve this? He intervened before Abraham sacrificed Isaac:

- "Do not lay your hand on the boy or do anything to him…By myself I have sworn, declares the LORD, because you have done this and have not withheld your son, your only son, I will surely bless you, and I will surely multiply your offspring as the stars of heaven and as the sand that is on the seashore. And your offspring shall possess the gate of his enemies." (*Genesis 22:12,16-17*)

Obedience to God's Word, rather than to our own interests or to considerations of tribal solidarity, is only possible once we have learned to have faith in *Him*. It was a lesson that Israel had to repeatedly learn:

- "And he humbled you and let you hunger and fed you with manna, which you did not know, nor did your fathers know, that he might make you <u>know</u> that man does not live by bread alone, but man lives by every word that comes from the mouth of the LORD. Your clothing did not wear out on you and your foot did not swell these forty years. Know then in your heart that, as a man disciplines his son, the LORD your God disciplines you. So you shall keep the commandments of the LORD your God by walking in his ways and by fearing him." (*Deuteronomy 8:3-6*)

Faith and belief didn't require a blind leap. Nor did it require the Israelite to shelve both mind and skepticism. However, Israel's God was intent on remold their skepticism into an evidence-based faith. He, therefore, provided many evidences of His love for His people – His deliverance from slavery through ten supernatural plagues, the splitting of the sea, and His provisions during the 40 years sojourn in the desert. Based upon God's miraculous confirmations, Moses advised Israel to believe in their God and to obey Him:

- "To you it was shown, that you might <u>know</u> that the LORD is God; there is no other besides him. Out of heaven he let you hear his voice, that he might discipline you. And on earth he let you see his great fire, and you heard his words out of the midst of the fire. And because he loved your fathers and chose their offspring after them and brought you out of Egypt with his own presence, by his great power, driving out before you nations greater and mightier than you, to bring you in, to give you their land for an inheritance, as it is this day, <u>know</u> therefore today, and lay it to your heart, that the LORD is God in heaven above and on the earth beneath; there is no other. Therefore you shall keep his statutes and his commandments, which I command you today, that it may go well with you and with your children after you, and that you may prolong your days in the land that the LORD your God is giving you for all time." (*Deuteronomy 4:34-40*)

By His miraculous works, God deprived Israel of any basis for skepticism. In place of skepticism, He gave Israel a solid evidential foundation. Consequently, any disobedience would not result from the lack of evidence but from a stubborn refusal to have faith in their God. If they weren't certain that He existed and loved them, there would be no reason for them to obey God or to even celebrate their Biblically-derived traditions. Consequently, a Judaism without some degree of certainty and assured knowledge of God is unthinkable, a perversion of God's will and workings.

In the midst of Israel's continued rebellion against God's Word, God sought to win their faith and allegiance to His Word. Even after seeing God's many miracles, Israel rebelled against God as they heard the Egyptian chariots approaching them.

- [Israel] said to Moses, "Is it because there are no graves in Egypt that you have taken us away to die in the wilderness? What have you done to us in bringing us out of Egypt? Is not this what we said to you in Egypt: 'Leave us alone that we may serve the Egyptians'? For it would have been better for us to serve the Egyptians than to die in the wilderness." (*Exodus 14:11-12*)

At God's command, Moses instructed them to not fear but to have faith in Him:

- And Moses said to the people, "Fear not, stand firm, and see the salvation of the LORD, which he will work for you today. For the Egyptians whom you see today, you shall never see again. (*Exodus 14:13*)

Moses knew that God would deliver Israel. He therefore counseled them to trust in Him based upon what He had already done for them and what He had promised to do. This is a theme echoed throughout the Scriptures:

- "Trust in the LORD with all your heart, and do not lean on your own understanding. In all your ways acknowledge him, and he will make straight your paths. Be not wise in your own eyes; fear the LORD, and turn away from evil. It will be healing to your flesh and refreshment to your bones." (*Proverbs 3:5-8*)

How do we "trust in the Lord?" By not trusting in our own understanding but in His! However, in order to trust in someone, we need to believe that he is trustworthy. In other words, we need to know who he is and how he has rescued us in the past.

However, even Moses had slipped. Israel was once again rebelling against the Word of God. Therefore, God instructed Moses to speak to a rock instead of what He had instructed Moses to do previously when Israel thirsted and rebelled. Before, God had instructed Moses to strike the rock so that water would come forth (*Exodus 17*). However, Moses disobediently struck the rock (God certainly wasn't creating a tradition of striking rocks but of trusting in His Word):

- And the LORD said to Moses and Aaron, "Because you did not believe in me, to uphold me as holy in the eyes of the people of Israel, therefore you shall not bring this assembly into the land that I have given them." (*Numbers 20:12*)

To not believe in God's Word was to not believe in God. It was also to dishonor God before all Israel. God also deemed this lack of believe as worthy of punishment. In contrast to this, the rabbis say, "Jewish tradition does not share their reliance on certainty." This is absurd. It would also have been absurd for Moses to retort, "God, you celebrate uncertainty. Therefore, I was uncertain about your instructions."

Resisting our fears and desires, requires a confident knowledge of God through His Word. This was the basis of Joshua's trust in the Lord. God had been with him in many tangible ways and promised to never leave him:

- "This Book of the Law shall not depart from your mouth, but you shall meditate on it day and night, so that you may be careful to do according to all that is written in it. For then you will make your way prosperous, and then you will have good success. Have I not commanded you? Be strong and courageous. Do not be frightened, and do not be dismayed, for the LORD your God is with you wherever you go." (*Joshua 1:8-9*)

Being "*strong and courageous*" was a matter of believing in God's Word, which promised great blessing. Therefore, we cannot separate belief in doctrine and God's Words from obedience, blessings, and even from the traditions that the rabbis value. If the truth of God's Word does not underlie our traditions, our traditions are baseless and will not endure the storms.

God would be Joshua's strength and hope, and God had provided him with evidence and a knowledge of God as a foundation for this faith, contrary to the rabbis – "Torah goes to great lengths to reassure the searching Jew that skepticism is healthy, legitimate, and even celebrated in Jewish life." Joshua never celebrated skepticism. While there is a place for skepticism to lead us to truth, we never find anyone in the Bible celebrating skepticism. Job had become skeptical of God's goodness and justice. However, in the midst of his trials, he never celebrated his skepticism.

Jonah, and many of the other Prophets of Israel, had been skeptical about God's judgments. However, they were chastened for their skepticism. Even the most righteous of men, Job, was corrected: "And the LORD said to Job: 'Shall a faultfinder contend with the Almighty?'" (*Job 40:1-2*)

Unlike our rabbis, Moses understood the value of proof and evidences, rather than skepticism, and so did God. At the burning bush, God instructed Moses to return to Egypt to lead His people out of bondage. Understandably, the reluctant Moses retorted that the Israelites had no reason to believe that God had spoken to him. However, God was not like the rabbis, who glory in skepticism and simply affirm tradition:

- The LORD said to him [Moses], "What is that in your hand?" He said, "A staff." And he said, "Throw it on the ground." So he threw it on the ground, and it became a serpent, and Moses ran from it. But the LORD said to Moses, "Put out your hand and catch it by the tail"—so he put out his hand and caught it, and it became a staff in his hand—"that they may believe that the LORD, the God of their fathers, the God of Abraham, the God of Isaac, and the God of Jacob, has appeared to you." Again, the LORD said to him, "Put your hand inside your cloak." And he put his hand inside his cloak, and when he took it out, behold, his hand was leprous like snow. Then God said, "Put your hand back inside your cloak." So he put his hand back inside his cloak, and when he took it out, behold, it was restored like the rest of his flesh...If they will not believe even these two signs or listen to your voice, you shall take some water from the Nile and pour it on the dry ground, and the water that you shall take from the Nile will become blood on the dry ground." (*Exodus 4:2-9*)

These miraculous signs were intended to combat any possible skepticism among His people Israel. The rabbis make a mistake when they insist that faith and certainty are unnecessary and associate them with a rigid fundamentalism. In contrast to the rabbis, Moses wanted to remove from his people any grounds for skepticism. He, therefore, warned them of the great price that they had paid for their skepticism. Because they had rebelled against the Word of God, they would have to wonder 40 years in the desert:

- "Yet you would not go up [into the Promised Land], but rebelled against the command of the LORD your God. And you murmured in your tents and said, 'Because the LORD hated us he has brought us out of the land of Egypt, to give us into the hand of the Amorites, to destroy us.'" (*Deuteronomy 1:26-27*)

After all of the miracles that Israel had seen, their skepticism was as warranted as an air conditioner in the North Pole. Moses, therefore, also reminded them:

- "Did any people ever hear the voice of a god speaking out of the midst of the fire…Or has any god ever attempted to go and take a nation for himself from the midst of another nation, by trials, by signs, by wonders, and by war, by a mighty hand and an outstretched arm, and by great deeds of terror, all of which the LORD your God did for you in Egypt before your eyes? To you it was shown, that you might know that the LORD is God; there is no other besides him." (*Deuteronomy 4:33-35)*

All of these things happened to replace skepticism with the knowledge of God and faith in God. However, the rabbis claim, "the question 'Do you believe in God?' is not the central Jewish spiritual question." However, this claim violates Scripture at every turn. Moses reminded Israel that their entire identity was based upon their God:

- "I am the LORD your God, who brought you out of the land of Egypt, out of the house of slavery. You shall have no other gods before me. You shall not make for yourself a carved image…You shall not bow down to them or serve them; for I the LORD your God am a jealous God, visiting the iniquity of the fathers on the children to the third and fourth generation of those who hate me." (*Deuteronomy 5:6-9*)

When Israel would periodically reject this faith, they suffered greatly, as Biblical history abundantly details. Should we then not cry out "repent and return!"

WORKS CITED

Gordis, Rabbi Daniel, *"From Belief to Faith - Can the skeptic embark on a Jewish spiritual journey?"* www.myjewishlearning.com/article/from-belief-to-faith/

Chapter 7

SALVATION, HEAVEN, AND THE MERCY OF GOD

How do we get to heaven? Christians and Jews come up with different answers. While the rabbis do not dismiss the idea of the necessity of grace, they emphasize following the commandments – the performance of mitzvot – to secure them a place in heaven:

- "Therefore, when we study Torah and keep the Mitzvot we are in absolute communion with G-d... When Man observes the Mitzvot in deed, discusses the Mitzvot in speech, and concentrates and grasps all that his intellect is able to grasp of the Torah in thought, then Man's soul is fully clothed in the Mitzvot and is in perfect unity with G-d."
(www.myjewishlearning.com/article/mitzvot-a-mitzvah-is-a-commandment/)

For the rabbis, mitzvot-keeping is not a *hypothetical* pathway to union with God but *actual*. According to them, many are actually achieving this union. Meanwhile, the entire Mosaic system yells "foul." It informed the Israelite that no one could enter into the Presence of God in the Temple – only the High Priest once a year on Yom Kippur – without suffering death. However, the rabbis claim that the Israelite could not only enter into His Presence but into a oneness with Him.

Contrary to this, Kabbalistic theology, which began to arise in the 13th century, claims that humanity can work their way up into the Presence of God, even into "perfect unity with G-d.

- "When a critical mass of people are taking part in this war [against sin and doubt] then the Moshiach [Messiah] has arrived...Contrary to much thought, we are not waiting for the Moshiach to come, but rather,

WE are the ones and WE are the only ones that through our efforts are capable of creating this state of being."
(www.jewishmag.com/66mag/kabbalah/kabbalah.htm)

Other Kabbalistic exponents claim that since we had been created in the image of God, we are already perfect and simply have to realize it. All of this would have been a surprise to Abraham who believed God, and his belief alone became the pathway to receiving mercy and the gift of imputed righteousness (*Genesis 15:6*), without any mention of his keeping the mitzvot.

In contrast to the rabbis, the Hebrew Scriptures prove:

  ➤ No one is deserving before God.
  ➤ Israel certainly wasn't deserving.
  ➤ Grace will come to the penitent (repentant), not to the "deserving."
  ➤ It is the penitent, not the deserving, who will unilaterally be given the grace of God in the end.

1. *No one is deserving before God:*

Instead of blessing, we deserve cursing as a result of our performance in obeying the mitzvot. This had been Moses' judgment:

  • "Cursed is anyone who does not uphold the words of this law by carrying them out." Then all the people shall say, "Amen!" (*Deuteronomy 27:26*)

This stipulation placed a curse on everyone, demonstrating that blessing could not be earned or deserved but would be conferred on Israel by God's mercies alone. We cannot earn anything from God but curses. Instead, Israel needed His mercy, as so many of the Psalms attest:

82

- "If you, O LORD, kept a record of sins, O Lord, who could stand? But with you there is forgiveness; therefore you are feared." (*Psalm 130:3-4*)

- "Do not bring your servant into judgment, for no one living is righteous before you." (*Psalm 143:2*)

We are all sinners in desperate need of the mercy of God. In contrast to this dismal assessment, one rabbi wrote:

- "Kabbalah states that the community of Israel, comprising 600,000 souls, is the general source of vitality for the world as a whole, for the world was created for the sake of these souls."

However, this directly contradicts everything in the Hebrew Scriptures. In fact, Moses warned the people against thinking that they were more righteous and deserving than others:

- "After the Lord your God has driven them out before you, do not say to yourself, 'The Lord has brought me here to take possession of this land because of my righteousness.' No, it is on account of the wickedness of these nations that the Lord is going to drive them out before you. It is not because of your righteousness or your integrity that you are going in to take possession of their land; but on account of the wickedness of these nations, the Lord your God will drive them out before you, to accomplish what he swore to your fathers, to Abraham, Isaac and Jacob. Understand, then, that it is not because of your righteousness that the Lord your God is giving you this good land to possess, for you are a stiff-necked people." (*Deut. 9:4-6*)

At times Israel had even morally descended beneath the other nations:

- "Therefore thus says the Lord GOD: 'Because you have multiplied disobedience more than the nations that are all around you, have not walked in My statutes nor kept My judgments, nor even done according to the judgments of the nations that are all around you...'" (*Ezekiel 5:7*)... "Your elder sister is Samaria, who dwells with her daughters to the north of you; and your younger sister, who dwells to the south of you, is Sodom and her daughters. You did not walk in their ways nor act according to their abominations; but, as if that were too little, you became more corrupt than they in all your ways" (*Ezekiel 16:46-47*).

Scripture also teaches the impossibility of earning anything from God, as He revealed to the contrite Job:

- "Who has a claim against me that I must pay? Everything under heaven belongs to me." (*Job 41:11*)

In contrast, the rabbis claim:

- "[Man] has the capacity to elevate and transform all of creation for a higher purpose. When one fulfills one's duty [mitzvot-keeping] and mission in life, not only is the one's goal in the scheme of Creation reached, but also helps the rest of the world attain perfection."

What hubris! Humanity fulfills nothing, and the law should have made this clear to Israel. Israel had been repeatedly warned against such arrogance. God had even taught Moses a song, which the Israelites were to sing perpetually to testify against them and their future hubris (*Deuteronomy 32*).

Instead, we consistently fail to fulfill our "duty and mission in life," as Paul's quotations from the Hebrew Scriptures attest:

- "As it is written: 'There is none righteous, no, not one; there is none who understands; there is none who seeks after God. They have all turned aside; they have together become unprofitable; there is none who does good, no, not one.'" (Roma*ns 3:10-12* quoting *Psalm 14, 53; Rom. 3:19-20*)

According to Job, it is delusional to suppose that we will ever be in a position to *earn* God's mercy:

- "What is man, that he could be pure, or one born of woman, that he could be righteous? If God places no trust in his holy ones, if even the heavens are not pure in his eyes, how much less man, who is vile and corrupt, who drinks up evil like water!" (*Job 15:14-16*)

In light of this, the rabbinic assertion that we can lift ourselves up is absurd:

- "The beauty of Torah and Mitzvot is that through simple everyday actions that are well within the reach of normal individuals, every person can connect with the Divine and transform this world into an abode for G-d."

Instead, the Mosaic Temple communicated that Israel fell far short of God's standards and dwelt under His wrath. Therefore, substitutionary blood sacrifices had to be *continually* offered to secure God's forgiveness.

2. Israel certainly wasn't deserving of any of God's blessings:

Almost all of the Prophets of Israel denounced Israel:
- "The ox knows its owner and the donkey its master's crib; but Israel does not know, My people do not consider. Alas, sinful nation, a people laden with

iniquity, a brood of evildoers, children who are corrupters! They have forsaken the LORD, they have provoked to anger the Holy One of Israel, they have turned away backward." (*Isaiah 1:3-4*)

Israel didn't know God because they did not seek Him:

- "For the people do not turn to Him who strikes them, nor do they seek the LORD of hosts". (Isai*ah 9:13*)

- "And there is no one who calls on Your name, who stirs himself up to take hold of You; for You have hidden Your face from us, and have consumed us because of our iniquities." (*Isaiah 64:7*)

Israel did not seek God because they didn't want God:

- "So will I choose their delusions, and bring their fears on them; because, when I called, <u>no one answered</u>, when I spoke they did not hear; but they did evil before My eyes, and chose that in which I do not delight." (*Isaiah 66:4*)

- "I have stretched out My hands all day long to a <u>rebellious</u> people, who walk in a way that is not good, according to their own thoughts; people who provoke Me to anger continually to My face; who sacrifice in gardens, and burn incense on altars of brick." (*Isaiah 65:2-3*)

- "Do not be like your fathers, to whom the former prophets preached, saying, 'Thus says the LORD of hosts: 'Turn now from your evil ways and your evil deeds. But they did <u>not hear nor heed Me</u>,' says the LORD." (Ze*chariah 1:4*)

Israel's "obedience" had been superficial and hypocritical:

- "The multitude of your sacrifices— what are they to me?" says the Lord. "I have more than enough of burnt offerings, of rams and the fat of fattened animals... Stop bringing meaningless offerings! Your incense is detestable to me. New Moons, Sabbaths and convocations— I cannot bear your worthless assemblies. Your New Moon feasts and your appointed festivals I hate with all my being. They have become a burden to me; I am weary of bearing them. When you spread out your hands in prayer, I hide my eyes from you; even when you offer many prayers, I am not listening. Your hands are full of blood!" (*Isaiah 1:11-15*)

If obedience is necessary to receive God's blessings, then Israel and all humanity are without hope. All fell under a curse that only mercy could address! However, the rabbis have an inflated estimation of Israel's faithfulness to their God:

- "It is necessary to fulfill the practical Mitzvot performed by the body itself in deed. In this way the actual power of the body engaged in this act is absorbed into the Divine Light and will and unites with Him in perfect unity."

However, Israel's failures were far worse than simply failing to be obedient. Instead, Israel utterly *rejected* their God:

- "LORD, are not Your eyes on the truth? You have stricken them, but they have not grieved; You have consumed them, but they have <u>refused</u> to receive correction. They have made their faces harder than rock; they have <u>refused to return</u>." (*Jeremiah 5:3*)

- "Why has this people slidden back, Jerusalem, in a perpetual backsliding? They <u>hold fast to deceit</u>, they <u>refuse to return</u>. I listened and heard, but they do not

87

speak aright. <u>No man repented</u> of his wickedness, saying, 'What have I done?' Everyone turned to his own course." (*Jeremiah 8:5-6*)

- "My people are destroyed for lack of knowledge. Because you have <u>rejected</u> knowledge, I also will reject you from being priest for Me; because you have forgotten the law of your God, I also will forget your children." (*Hosea 4:6*)

In light of these, how can the rabbis confidently insist that our deeds will unite us "with Him in perfect harmony?" Instead, almost all of the Prophets testify that Israel's deeds have *separated* them from their God, something that Jewish history has made very clear. There is not even one verse in the entirety of the Hebrew Bible that claims that Israel deserves the blessings of God.

Was there ever a Prophet who assured Israel, "You are doing a great job! Keep up the good work!" No! However, Scripture does make many promises that those who keep the commandments will be blessed. This, of course, is true, but Israel's unfaithfulness disqualified them from this promise and qualified them for only the curse (*Deuteronomy 28-29*)! Consequently, Israel could only hope for the mercy of God, but so often, their hope was focused elsewhere.

3. Grace and blessedness will come to the penitent (repentant), not to the "deserving":

King David had committed adultery and murder. He deserved to die and he knew it, but he found God's mercy:

- "Blessed is he whose transgression is forgiven, whose sin is covered. Blessed is the man to whom the LORD does not impute iniquity, and in whose spirit there is no deceit…I acknowledged my sin to You, and my iniquity

88

I have not hidden. I said, 'I will confess my transgressions to the LORD,' and You forgave the iniquity of my sin." (*Psalm 32:1-5*)

The Temple and the offerings symbolized the fact that blessedness depended not on what Israel *earned* but on *whom they trusted*. After Solomon commemorated the Temple, the Lord assured him that His mercy depends not a successful record of keeping the mitzvot, but on a repentant heart:

- "If my people, who are called by my name, will humble themselves and pray and seek my face and turn from their wicked ways, then will I hear from heaven and will forgive their sin and will heal their land." (*2 Chronicles 7:14*)

God would "freely pardon" Israel's sins. It didn't depend on Israel's moral virtue:

- "Let the wicked forsake his way and the evil man his thoughts. Let him turn to the LORD, and he will have mercy on him, and to our God, for he will freely pardon." (*Isaiah 55:7*)

God demanded that Israel repent without having to first build up their portfolio with good deeds:

- "Therefore, O house of Israel, I will judge you, each one according to his ways, declares the Sovereign LORD. Repent! Turn away from all your offenses; then sin will not be your downfall. Rid yourselves of all the offenses you have committed, and get a new heart and a new spirit. Why will you die, O house of Israel? For I take no pleasure in the death of anyone, declares the Sovereign LORD. Repent and live!" (*Ezekiel 18:30-32*)

Having a change of heart was critical. If they truly repented, there would also be evidence of this. They would "Turn away from all your offenses."

4. *It is the penitent, not the deserving, who will unilaterally be given the grace of God in the end:*

What do we find in the end when Messiah returns? Do we find Israel waiting expectantly, having fulfilled the mitzvot? Not at all! Instead, Israel will mourn for having rejected their Messiah:

- "And I will pour out on the house of David and the inhabitants of Jerusalem a spirit of grace and supplication. They will look on me, the one they have pierced, and they will mourn for him as one mourns for an only child, and grieve bitterly for him as one grieves for a firstborn son." (*Zechariah 12:10*)

There is no indication that Israel will wake up on their own and perform the required mitzvot, as the rabbis suggest:

- There are a number of ways conducive to hasten the Messianic redemption prior to its final date. Generally speaking these involve the observance of some special mitzvot which constitute comprehensive principles of the Torah.
  (www.chabad.org/library/moshiach/article_cdo/aid/1016 81/jewish/Hastening-Mashiach.htm)

There is no prophecy in the entire body of the Hebrew Scriptures that suggests that Israel will hasten the coming of their Messiah through their "observance of some special mitzvoth." Instead, their Messiah will *unilaterally* open their darkened eyes:

- "They shall be My people, and I will be their God; then I will give them one heart and one way, that they may fear Me forever, for the good of them and their children after them. And I will make an everlasting covenant with them, that I will not turn away from doing them good; but I will put My fear in their hearts so that they will not depart from Me. Yes, I will rejoice over them to do them good, and I will assuredly plant them in this land, with all My heart and with all My soul.' (*Jeremiah 32:38-41*)

In fact, there is not a single prophecy that even suggests that God will re-establish Israel based on Israel's worthiness:

- "For I will take you from among the nations, gather you out of all countries, and bring you into your own land. Then I will sprinkle clean water on you, and you shall be clean; I will cleanse you from all your filthiness and from all your idols. I will give you a new heart and put a new spirit within you; I will take the heart of stone out of your flesh and give you a heart of flesh. I will put My Spirit within you and cause you to walk in My statutes, and you will keep My judgments and do them. Then you shall dwell in the land that I gave to your fathers; you shall be My people, and I will be your God. I will deliver you from all your uncleannesses." (*Ezekiel 36:24-29*)

- "My people are bent on backsliding from Me. Though they call to the Most High, none at all exalt Him..." (*Hosea11:7*) "I will heal their backsliding, I will love them freely, for My anger has turned away from him." (*Hosea 14:4*)

- "Behold, I will bring it health and healing; I will heal them and reveal to them the abundance of peace and truth...I will cleanse them from all their iniquity by which they have sinned against Me, and I will pardon all their iniquities by which they have sinned and by which they have transgressed against Me." (*Jeremiah 33:6-8*)

Israel will be transformed apart from any mitzvot-keeping. Instead of God restoring Israel because Israel is worthy of His mercy, God will restore despite Israel's ubiquitous unworthiness.

Does this mean that Israel would be forgiven and blessed without any need to be obedient? Obedience would be the necessary *consequence* of His saving work, *not its cause*:

- "...And I will give them one heart, and a new spirit I will put within them. I will remove the heart of stone from their flesh and give them a heart of flesh, that they may walk in my statutes and keep my rules and obey them. And they shall be my people, and I will be their God." (*Ezekiel 11:18-20*)

Therefore, Rabbi Gerald Sigal wrote:

- The fulfillment of all the promises God made to Abraham, both those made before circumcision and those made after, is contingent upon obedience to God's will, not simply faith alone. (Sigal, 274)

There is some truth in Sigal's statement. Blessing is contingent upon faithful obedience to God. "We reap what we sow" is a principle found throughout the Bible. It was also true for Abraham. God confided in Abraham, reasoning:
- "For I have chosen him, that he may command his children and his household after him to keep the way of the LORD by doing righteousness and justice, so that the LORD may bring to Abraham what he has promised him." (*Genesis 18:19*)

The fulfillment of God's gracious promises depended upon Abraham's obedience. However, obedience is a byproduct of God choosing and establishing Abraham.

Israel will live in obedience to God in His heavenly Kingdom, not because of their uprightness but because God will give them a new heart. They would be born-from-above. Consequently, Israel's obedience would be the fruit of being born-again, and not its root (cause):

- "And I will give you a new heart, and a new spirit I will put within you. And I will remove the heart of stone from your flesh and give you a heart of flesh. And I will put my Spirit within you, and cause you to walk in my statutes and be careful to obey my rules." (*Ezekiel 36:26-27*)

God's gift of a new heart would "cause" Israel to walk in obedience to the commands of their Savior:

- "I will make with them an everlasting covenant, that I will not turn away from doing good to them. And I will put the fear of me in their hearts, that they may not turn from me. I will rejoice in doing them good, and I will plant them in this land in faithfulness, with all my heart and all my soul." (*Jeremiah 32:40-41*)

This new heart would bring about such a faithfulness towards God that Israel would *never* again "turn from" God into disobedience. As a result, He would *never* cease "doing them good."

Do any of us ever merit salvation and our Savior's future blessings? Not at all! They are all given as a result of His love and mercy. To deny this is to claim credit for God's blessings – a great affront to the grace of God (*Romans 5:8-10; John 3:16*).

Consequently, even the best examples of Israel's establishment where called "whitewashed tombs" by the Messiah:

- "Woe to you, scribes and Pharisees, hypocrites! For you are like whitewashed tombs, which outwardly appear beautiful, but within are full of dead people's bones and all uncleanness. So you also outwardly appear righteous to others, but within you are full of hypocrisy and lawlessness." (*Matthew 23:27-28*)

This same indictment can be brought against all of us. However, the Pharisees were convinced that the charges of the Prophets of Israel didn't pertain to them. Such is the awesome power of self-righteousness!

WORKS CITED

Kellman, Raphael, *"Is Kabbalah our Savior?"*
www.jewishmag.com/66mag/kabbalah/kabbalah.htm

Robinson, George*, Mitzvot: "Contemporary Understandings"*
www.myjewishlearning.com/article/mitzvot-contemporary-understandings/

Schochet, J. Immanuel, *"Hastening the Coming of Mashiach"*
www.chabad.org/library/moshiach/article_cdo/aid/101681/jewish/Hastening-Mashiach.htm

Sigal, Gerald, *The Jew and the Christian Missionary: A Jewish Response to Missionary Christianity*, (New York: KTAV Publishing House, 1981)

Chapter 8

LEGALISM, SELF-RIGHTEOUSNESS, AND THE RABBIS

When I was a young Christian, I was uncertain about what I should believe and where I should place my trust. I concluded that the safe thing to do was to cover-all-the-bases and to place my trust in both Jesus and my good deeds. However, I later realized that to place my trust in anything in addition to the Savior and His dying for me on the cross would disqualify me:

- "Therefore let no one pass judgment on you in questions of food and drink, or with regard to a festival or a new moon or a Sabbath. These are a shadow of the things to come, but the substance belongs to Christ. Let no one disqualify you, insisting on asceticism and worship of angels, going on in detail about visions, puffed up without reason by his sensuous mind." (*Colossians 2:16-18 ESV*)

Here, Paul warned about two things that could disqualify us from salvation – trusting in asceticism (a severe form of self-denial or self-punishment) and the worship of angels. I began to see that, to some extent, I too had been trusting in myself and my moral merit to earn me salvation. I too had believed that I could make myself worthy of God by denying myself. This is common in perhaps all religions and even in sects of Christianity. However, self-punishment is a denial of the fact that Christ had paid the price for all of our sins forever. Instead, asceticism insists that *we* have to pay the price.

We do this in subtle ways. I would only indulge in a milkshake if I felt deserving. Getting an "A" on a test would make me feel deserving. Otherwise, indulging would make me feel anxious and unworthy. If I spent more than two minutes in the shower, I would also feel anxious.

Masochism is a form of asceticism. We hurt ourselves as a way to reduce stress and feel entitled to enjoy ourselves. Why? Our conscience correctly tells us that there is something wrong with us and that we have to pay a price for our unworthiness. However, once I learned that Jesus paid the price for my sins in full, the need to prove myself worthy of His love and mercy began to decrease.

Some Christians value asceticism in another way. They believe that the discipline of self-denial is transferrable to spiritual matters. If we learn to discipline our bodies as an athlete or a soldier, we can then transfer this discipline to combat the temptations of sin. However, Paul had argued against such reasoning:

- "If with Christ you died to the elemental spirits of the world, why, as if you were still alive in the world, do you submit to regulations—'Do not handle, Do not taste, Do not touch' [referring to things that all perish as they are used]—according to human precepts and teachings? These have indeed an appearance of wisdom in promoting self-made religion and asceticism and severity to the body, but they are of <u>no value</u> in stopping the indulgence of the flesh." (*Colossians 2:20-23*)

Paul denied that physical training would help us resist sin. While he didn't dismiss the value of bodily discipline and exercise, he refused to prescribe it for spiritual matters:

- "Have nothing to do with irreverent, silly myths. Rather train yourself for godliness; for while bodily training is of some value, godliness is of value in every way, as it holds promise for the present life and also for the life to come." (*1 Timothy 4:7-8*)

The "worship of angels" is a matter of placing our trust in anyone – even in ourselves – in addition to Jesus. Therefore, Paul had warned:

- "Look: I, Paul, say to you that if you accept circumcision [to become a Jew in order to trust in Law-keeping], Christ will be of no advantage to you. I testify again to every man who accepts circumcision that he is obligated to keep the whole law. You are severed from Christ, you who would be justified [or made righteous] by the law; you have fallen away from grace." (*Galatians 5:2-4*)

When we trust anyone in addition to Jesus, we are not truly trusting Jesus but in ourselves or someone else. To worship angels is to trust in angels.

Trusting in anything in addition to God is forbidden, even in the Hebrew Scriptures:

- "He alone is my rock and my salvation, my fortress; I shall not be greatly shaken...For God alone, O my soul, wait in silence, for my hope is from him. He only is my rock and my salvation, my fortress; I shall not be shaken. On God rests my salvation and my glory; my mighty rock, my refuge is God. Trust in him at all times, O people; pour out your heart before him; God is a refuge for us." (*Psalm 62:2, 5-8*)

Israel was to trust in God alone and not in themselves, foreign gods, or in their own righteousness:

- "Thus says the LORD: 'Cursed is the man who trusts in man and makes flesh his strength, whose heart turns away from the LORD. He is like a shrub in the desert, and shall not see any good come. He shall dwell in the parched places of the wilderness, in an uninhabited salt land. Blessed is the man who trusts in the LORD, whose trust is the LORD.'" (*Jeremiah 17:5-7; Psalm 2:12; 25:2; 34:8; 71:5; 125:1*)

To trust in our own abilities, strengths, or righteousness represented a failure to trust in God. To trust in anything in addition to our Savior is spiritual adultery. It is as acceptable as having an adulterous relationship. However, we commit spiritual adultery when we place unqualified trust in anyone else. When we go to spiritualists for answers, we are no longer trusting in God:

- And when they say to you, "Inquire of the mediums and the necromancers who chirp and mutter," should not a people inquire of their God? Should they inquire of the dead on behalf of the living? To the teaching and to the testimony! If they will not speak according to this word, it is because they have no dawn. (*Isaiah 8:19-20*)

Trusting in God was always a matter of putting trust in His Words and in doing them, the way to fulfill His Covenant. However, Israel consistently added to the law, in opposition to the commands of God:

- "You shall not add to the word that I command you, nor take from it, that you may keep the commandments of the LORD your God that I command you." (*Deuteronomy 4:2; 12:32*)

These became known as the "*Traditions of the Elders*" in Jesus' time. There is nothing the matter with traditions as long as they are not elevated to a status equivalent to the Word of God. There is nothing wrong with a family tradition of celebrating birthdays as long as it is not elevated and made mandatory as if from God. Jesus castigated the religious leadership for doing this:

- "You hypocrites! Well did Isaiah prophesy of you, when he said: 'This people honors me with their lips, but their heart is far from me; in vain do they worship me, teaching as doctrines the commandments of men.'" (*Matthew 15:7-9, citing Isaiah 29:13*)

Consequently, their heart-less worship was for naught. It reflected the fact that they didn't really trust in God but in their own doctrines. When the heart is right towards God, we place *His* Word above all else. Unless our heart is right towards the Lord, all of our external piety is also for naught. It is merely a grotesque show. Even our prayers were unacceptable to God if we are not devoted to Him through His Word:

- "The ox knows its owner and the donkey its master's crib; But Israel does not know, My people do not consider...Bring no more futile sacrifices; Incense is an abomination to Me. The New Moons, the Sabbaths, and the calling of assemblies--I cannot endure iniquity and the sacred meeting. Your New Moons and your appointed feasts My soul hates; They are a trouble to Me, I am weary of bearing them. When you spread out your hands [in prayer], I will hide My eyes from you; even though you make many prayers, I will not hear. Your hands are full of blood. Wash yourselves, make yourselves clean; put away the evil of your doings from before My eyes." (*Isaiah 1:3, 13-16*)

Even today, superficial law-keeping is extoled among some Orthodox groups. The Lubavitchers, one sect of the Hasidic community, have often stopped me on the street to ask if I am Jewish and to invite me into their van to put on the prayer shawl to perform a ritual. When I'd explain that I cannot do it because I do not believe in it, they respond, *"It doesn't matter. You will be blessed if you do it."* I then refer them to Isaiah's warnings against superficial, faithless law-keeping.

For them, God's blessings can be earned apart from a faith-filled relationship with God. Instead, we must believe and trust in God:

- "But without faith it is impossible to please Him, for he who comes to God must believe that He is, and that He is a rewarder of those who diligently seek Him." (*Hebrews 11:6*)

This is also a principle deeply embedded within the Hebrew Scriptures:

- "For You do not desire sacrifice, or else I would give it; You do not delight in burnt offering. The sacrifices of God are a broken spirit, a broken and a contrite heart-- these, O God, You will not despise…Then You shall be pleased with the sacrifices of righteousness, with burnt offering and whole burnt offering; then they shall offer bulls on Your altar." (*Psalm 51:16-19*)

To have a contrite and broken heart is to grieve over our sins (*Matthew 5:3-6*) and to humbly confess them to God. If one's heart is right towards God, then the prayers and offerings would be gladly received. However, this required that God had to be Israel's first concern:

- "You will seek me and find me, when you seek me <u>with all your heart</u>. I will be found by you, declares the LORD, and I will restore your fortunes and gather you from all the nations and all the places where I have driven you, declares the LORD, and I will bring you back to the place from which I sent you into exile." (*Jeremiah 29:13-14; Matthew 6:33*)

A relationship with God was always intended to arise from a sincere heart, as David had counseled his son Solomon:

- "And you, Solomon my son, know the God of your father and serve him with a <u>whole heart and with a willing mind</u>, for the LORD searches all hearts and understands every plan and thought. If you seek him, he will be found by you, but if you forsake him, he will cast you off forever." (*1 Chronicles 28:9*)

However, the Lubavitchers have rejected this all-important principle. Paul had explained that the Jews of Jesus' day were convinced that they could attain the righteousness of God on their own:

- "…Gentiles who did not pursue righteousness have attained it, that is, a righteousness that is by faith; but that Israel who pursued a law that would lead to righteousness did not succeed in reaching that law. Why? Because they did not pursue it by faith, but as if it were based on works. They have stumbled over the stumbling stone [Christ]." (*Romans 9:30-32*, alluding to *Psalm 118*)

Faith in our own righteousness actually reflects the entire history of humankind. Why? Although wisdom, even self-knowledge of our need for a Savior, is available but we reject:

- "Blessed is the one who listens to me [wisdom], watching daily at my gates, waiting beside my doors. For whoever finds me finds life and obtains favor from the LORD, but he who fails to find me injures himself; all who hate me love death." (*Proverbs 8:34-36*)

Although wisdom is within the reach of all, we hate it. Why? It reveals the truth about us. It shows us that we are not the people we want to believe we are. Instead, we are sinners who are in desperate of the Savior, without Whom we can do nothing of any value (*John 15:4-5*). Wisdom humbles us and strips us of the drug of pride. It rebukes our arrogance:

- "Wisdom cries aloud in the street, in the markets she raises her voice...If you turn at my reproof, behold, I will pour out my spirit to you; I will make my words known to you. Because I have called and you refused to listen, have stretched out my hand and no one has heeded, because you have ignored all my counsel and would have none of my reproof... Because they hated knowledge and did not choose the fear of the LORD, would have none of my counsel and despised all my reproof, therefore they shall eat the fruit of their way, and have their fill of their own devices. For the simple are killed by their turning away, and the complacency of fools destroys them." (*Proverbs 1:20, 23-24, 29-32*)

Pride is our designer-cloak. It hides our twisted motives. We cling to self-righteousness as our supreme treasure. We kill to preserve our honor and respect, but will forgive the thief for stealing our car. Any wise counsel that might undermine our self-righteousness is seen as an enemy. We therefore run from the light that might expose us and choose the darkness which promises to not disclose our lies (*John 3:19-20*).

Therefore, wisdom and self-awareness is in our crosshairs and our gun is loaded. It murdered the Prophets of Israel. Consequently, Jesus lamented:

- "O Jerusalem, Jerusalem, the city that kills the prophets and stones those who are sent to it! How often would I have gathered your children together as a hen gathers her brood under her wings, and you were not willing!" (*Matthew 23:37*)

Jesus offered life, forgiveness, and reconciliation with our righteous God. However, the religions of man offer us means to establish our own righteousness. They claim that we can ascend to God, experience Him, and earn His mercies. However, Scripture consistently forbids such hubris, as God had informed Job:

- "Who has first given to me, that I should repay him? Whatever is under the whole heaven is mine." (*Job 41:11*)

King David came to understand that there was no way that he could buy God off:

- "For you will not delight in sacrifice, or I would give it; you will not be pleased with a burnt offering. The sacrifices of God are a broken spirit; a broken and contrite heart, O God, you will not despise." (*Psalm 51:16-17*)

Our God desires a broken and repentant heart, one that cries out for the Lord's forgiveness (*Luke 18:9-14*). This is the very antithesis of the expectation of self-righteousness – that it has earned the right to the mercies of God.

It is this attitude of entitlement or moral superiority that our Lord finds contemptible:

- "Everyone who is arrogant in heart is an abomination to the LORD; be assured, he will not go unpunished…Pride goes before destruction, and a haughty spirit before a fall. It is better to be of a lowly spirit with the poor than to divide the spoil with the proud. Whoever gives thought to the word will discover good, and blessed is he who trusts in the LORD." (*Proverbs 16:5,18-20*)

While the humble submit to the Word, the self-righteous have lifted themselves above the Word. They see little need submit.

This would only bring them down. Jesus acknowledged that the rabbis studied the Word, not to submit to it, but to use it climb up an entitlement ladder:

- "You search the Scriptures because you think that in them you have eternal life; and it is they that bear witness about me…But I know that you do not have the love of God within you." (*John 5:39, 42*)

From where does the love of God come? From the understanding that He has forgiven our sins even though we don't deserve it, as Jesus had explained regarding a prostitute's love for Him:

- "Therefore, I tell you, her sins, which were many, have been forgiven; hence she has shown great love. But the one to whom little is forgiven, loves little." (*Luke 7:47 NRSV*)

Those who think that they have successfully climbed the ladder of spirituality do not think that they have been forgiven much. Instead, they are convinced that they deserve much.

The more we misunderstand the sinful status of humanity, the more we will misunderstand God and His ways. Also, the more highly we esteem man, the less highly will we esteem God. The *Jewish Study Bible* exhibits an inordinately high estimation of man, especially of Job, and this has led them to misinterpret the *Book of Job* by concluding that Job's suffering was undeserved and unjust:

- There is no way of understanding the meaning of suffering. That is, in the Lord's argument, the reasons for suffering—if there are any—are simply beyond human comprehension…Human suffering is not necessarily deserved…When…God says to Job's three friends, "You have not spoken the truth about Me as did

My servant Job" (*Job 42:8*), God is in effect agreeing with Job's contention, among others, "He destroys the blameless and the guilty (*Job 9:22*)."

While it is true that Job was the most righteous man in all the earth, he too was a sinner who required the undeserved mercy of God. However, the self-righteous are unable to see this.

After God confronted Job about his irrational and malicious charges against Him (*Job 38:1-3; 40:7-8*), Job repented twice (*Job 40:4-5; 42:3-6*). He realized that he had sinned and affirmed God's charge against him:

- "I have uttered what I did not understand, things too wonderful for me, which I did not know...I had heard of you by the hearing of the ear, but now my eye sees you; therefore I despise myself, and repent in dust and ashes." (*Job 42:3-6*)

Even though the rabbis regard Job as a "mensch," Job would have disagreed with their assessment that "There is no way of understanding the meaning of suffering." He would have also disagreed with them about the truth of his charge against God, "He destroys the blameless and the guilty (*Job 9:22*)." God also agreed with Job's confession of his self-righteous confidence:

- "After the LORD had spoken these words to Job, the LORD said to Eliphaz the Temanite: "My anger burns against you and against your two friends, for you have not spoken of me what is right, as my servant Job has." (*Job 42:7*)

Job had confessed his sins, and all was forgiven, as if Job's irresponsible charges had never been uttered. However, Job's three friends were still dominated by their self-righteous lens and also needed to confess their sins.

The rabbis also have a well-entrenched case of self-righteousness. If they understood Scripture and their own need for divine discipline, they would have known something about the meaning of suffering.

NO WORKS CITED

Chapter 9

WAS SALVATION IN THE OLD TESTAMENT SAME AS THAT OF THE NEW TESTAMENT?

Salvation under the Old Covenant resembled the New. Throughout, it was a matter of the mercy of God. However, the earliest revelations of salvation left out many crucial features. Conspicuously absent was any promise of an afterlife, of a heaven or hell. In a comprehensive list of the ways that God would bless Israel for their adherence to His commandments, there was no promise of a salvation from sins or of an eternal life (*Deuteronomy 28*). Instead, the blessing was for a long life, as promised for honoring father and mother (*Exodus 20:12; Deuteronomy 5:16*) and for obedience in general. *Deuteronomy 4:40; 22:7*).

Consequently, we read in the New Testament about the ongoing debate between Pharisee and Sadducee regarding whether eternal life even existed. In *Ecclesiastes*, we read that King Solomon, who had everything, had hated life, because, even with all of his wisdom, he could not perceive through the curtain of death into the next world:

- "For of the wise as of the fool there is no enduring remembrance, seeing that in the days to come all will have been long forgotten. How the wise dies just like the fool! So I hated life, because what is done under the sun was grievous to me, for all is vanity ["incomprehensible"] and a striving after wind." (*Ecclesiastes 2:16-17*)

Without the knowledge of the afterlife, the meaning of life remained hidden from even Solomon's wisdom:

- "For what happens to the children of man and what happens to the beasts is the same; as one dies, so dies

108

the other. They all have the same breath, and man has no advantage over the beasts, for all is vanity...Who knows whether the spirit of man goes upward and the spirit of the beast goes down into the earth?" (*Ecclesiastes 3:19, 21*)

How blessed we now are to see beyond the horizon! However, in a dialogue with the Sadducees, Jesus, referring to Moses' encounter with God in the burning bush (*Genesis 3*), revealed that, even in the Torah, eternal life, the salvation of God's people, had been revealed:

- "And as for the resurrection of the dead, have you not read what was said to you by God: 'I am the God of Abraham, and the God of Isaac, and the God of Jacob'? He is not God of the dead, but of the living." "And when the crowd heard it, they were astonished at his teaching." (*Matthew 22:31-33*)

Weren't there plainer texts in the Torah from which Jesus might have made His case in favor of eternal life? This silence illustrates the fact that God kept many secrets. One of them was the *source* of His mercy and salvation, symbolized by the one object that Israel could not look upon without being struck dead – the mercy seat of God (*Leviticus 16:13; Romans 3:25*), which covered the Ten Commandments within the Ark.

Nevertheless, God would reveal it to those who hungered and thirsted to understand His ways (*Psalm 25:14*). In fact, God was always preaching the Gospel. He preached it to Abraham and his offspring (*Galatians 3:8*). On one occasion, God had commanded Abraham to sacrifice his only son Isaac. However, before Abraham could accomplish this task, God intervened and gave Abraham a ram to sacrifice in place of Isaac. But this was far more than a test of Abraham's obedience. It was also a revelation of the heart of God:

- "And Abraham lifted up his eyes and looked, and behold, behind him was a ram, caught in a thicket by his horns. And Abraham went and took the ram and offered it up as a burnt offering instead of his son. So Abraham called the name of that place, 'The LORD will provide'; as it is said to this day, "On the mount of the LORD it shall be provided." (*Genesis 22:13-14*)

Why didn't Abraham name Mount Moriah, "The Lord <u>has</u> provided," as He had, instead of "The LORD <u>will</u> provide?" It had evidently been revealed to Abraham that what he had experienced was prophetic of something that the Lord would do – provide a Son as Abraham had provided with Isaac.

It was also revealed to the Apostle Paul that the Lord had revealed the means of His salvation through Abraham:

- "For if Abraham was justified by works, he has something to boast about, but not before God. For what does the Scripture say? 'Abraham believed God, and it was counted to him as righteousness.'" (*Romans 4:2-3*; quoting *Genesis 15:6*)

This was a righteousness that God had reckoned to Abraham apart from any merit that Abraham might have achieved. Instead, it was mercifully given because Abraham had merely "believed God." Did it also consist of God's gift of eternal life? Paul was convinced that it did:

- "For the promise to Abraham and his offspring that he would be <u>heir of the world</u> did not come through the law but through the righteousness of faith." (*Romans 4:13*)

They would live again, and the world would be their inheritance. Quoting *Psalm 32:1-2*, Paul also used King David as an example of this gift of salvation:

- …David also speaks of the blessing of the one to whom God counts righteousness apart from works: "Blessed are those whose lawless deeds are forgiven, and whose sins are covered; blessed is the man against whom the Lord will not count his sin." (*Romans 4:6-8*)

In both cases, Paul had demonstrated that salvation was a matter of the mercy of God in forgiving sin. This is the revelation of the OT, as well as the New. The entire sacrificial system was a revelation of the mercy of God. It taught that each sin deserved death but that an animal could be sacrificed in the place of Israel's sins, and the mercy of God would receive it in place of the death of the Israelites.

Could any Israelite ever be good enough so that he would not deserve death? Not according to the Scriptures:

- "Enter not into judgment with your servant, for no one living is righteous before you." (*Psalm 143:2; Job 9:2; 15:14; 25:4*)

- "If you, O LORD, should mark iniquities, O Lord, who could stand?" (*Psalm 130:3*)

No one could stand before God apart from His mercy (*Psalm 15, 24*). Similarly, at King Solomon's consecration the Temple, God affirmed that Israel's hope had to be in His mercy alone:

- "When I shut up the heavens so that there is no rain, or command the locust to devour the land, or send pestilence among my people, if my people who are called by my name humble themselves, and pray and seek my face and turn [repent] from their wicked ways, then I will hear from heaven and will forgive their sin and heal their land." (*2 Chronicles 7:13-14; 1 Kings 8:46*)

No one would ever be able to successfully plead that their good works entitled them to God's forgiveness or salvation:

- "When iniquities prevail against me, you atone for our transgressions. Blessed is the one you choose and bring near, to dwell in your courts! We shall be satisfied with the goodness of your house, the holiness of your temple! By awesome deeds you answer us with righteousness, O God of our salvation, the hope of all the ends of the earth and of the farthest seas." (*Psalm 65:3-5*)

God had to be the Source of Israel's salvation. There was no other hope. King David certainly understood this:

- "Great salvation he brings to his king, and shows steadfast love to his anointed, to David and his offspring forever." (*2 Samuel 22:51*)

The truth of the need for the mercy of God was illustrated before Israel in many ways. They had rebelled against the Lord repeatedly:

- "And the people spoke against God and against Moses, 'Why have you brought us up out of Egypt to die in the wilderness? For there is no food and no water, and we loathe this worthless food.' Then the LORD sent fiery serpents among the people, and they bit the people, so that many people of Israel died. And the people came to Moses and said, 'We have sinned, for we have spoken against the LORD and against you. Pray to the LORD, that he take away the serpents from us.' So Moses prayed for the people. And the LORD said to Moses, 'Make a fiery serpent and set it on a pole, and everyone who is bitten, when he sees it, shall live.' So Moses made a bronze serpent and set it on a pole. And if a serpent bit anyone, he would look at the bronze serpent and live." (*Numbers 21:5-9*)

Jesus understood that this had been a demonstration of the mercy of God, which also pertained to His atonement on the Cross:

- "And as Moses lifted up the serpent in the wilderness, so must the Son of Man be lifted up, that whoever believes in him may have eternal life." (*John 3:14-15*)

Jesus illustrated that fact that salvation in the OT prefigured salvation in the New. Both depended upon faith in the mercy of God. However, His salvation was dimly perceived in the midst of the Old. However, it should have been clear that salvation didn't depend on their merit:

- "The salvation of the righteous is from the LORD; he is their stronghold in the time of trouble." (*Psalm 37:39*)

This is the way it had been from the beginning:

- "But if they confess [changing their mind about sin – repentance] their iniquity and the iniquity of their fathers in their treachery that they committed against me, and also in walking contrary to me, so that I walked contrary to them and brought them into the land of their enemies—if then their uncircumcised heart is humbled and they make amends for their iniquity [a demonstration of faith/repentance], then I will remember my covenant with Jacob, and I will remember my covenant with Isaac and my covenant with Abraham, and I will remember the land." (*Leviticus 26:40-42*)

This highlights the fact that the Biblical faith had always been opposed to other religions where the faithful had to earn their way up to their deities, through obedience, knowledge, or by gaining spiritual insight. However, the Biblical faith reveals that becoming worthy of God through human efforts was impossible (*Romans 3:19-20; 11:35; Galatians 2:16*). Instead, Israel had to humble themselves by confessing their sins, and God would reach down to them:

- "Go, and proclaim these words toward the north, and say, 'Return, faithless Israel, declares the LORD. I will not look on you in anger, for I am merciful, declares the LORD; I will not be angry forever. Only acknowledge your guilt, that you rebelled against the LORD your God and scattered your favors among foreigners under every green tree, and that you have not obeyed my voice, declares the LORD.'" (*Jeremiah 3:12-13*)

Many verses simply indicate that "God is our salvation." Consequently, salvation is in a *Person* and *not by our own deeds*:

- "Truly the hills are a delusion, the orgies on the mountains. Truly in the LORD our God is the salvation of Israel." (*Jeremiah 3:23; Psalm 68:19-20; 98:3*)

Other verses refer to God as "The LORD is our righteousness" (*Jeremiah 23:6; 33:16*), indicating that our hope of righteousness and salvation doesn't depend on our performance but upon His. He Himself would clothe us "with the garments of salvation; he has covered me with the robe of righteousness" (*Isaiah 61:10*). All of our good deeds could not adequately clothe us to come into His presence.

The Prophets of Israel had consistently revealed that salvation was of the Lord not of themselves:

- "And it shall come to pass that everyone who calls on the name of the LORD shall be saved. For in Mount

Zion and in Jerusalem there shall be those who escape, as the LORD has said, and among the survivors shall be those whom the LORD calls." (*Joel 2:32*; also *Romans 10:12-13*)

No one would ever be able to say, "I am entitled to salvation!" Instead, Israel had to seek out the Lord's mercy by calling upon Him as He had directed, "Seek the Lord and live" (*Amos 5:4, 6*).

- "I will go away *and* return to My place until they acknowledge their guilt and seek My face; In their affliction they will earnestly seek Me." (*Hosea 5:15, NASB*)

- "Return, Israel, to the Lord your God. Your sins have been your downfall! Take words [of confession] with you and return to the Lord. Say to him: "Forgive all our sins and receive us graciously." (*Hosea 14:1-2, NASB*)

Israel had to confess and repent of their sins. They only had to come to their Savior with their sincere and broken hearts. All of this demonstrated that salvation is a matter of the mercy of God (*Isaiah 44:3; 45:17; 46:12-13; 51:4-5; 52:10; 57:18-19; 61:1-8; 63:9; 66:22*). God would unilaterally regenerate His people so that they would never again rebel against Him:

- "I will give them one heart and one way, that they may fear Me forever, for the good of them and their children after them. And I will make an everlasting covenant with them, that I will not turn away from doing them good; but I will put My fear in their hearts so that they will not depart from Me. Yes, I will rejoice over them to do them good, and I will assuredly plant them in this land, with all My heart and with all My soul." (*Jeremiah 32:39-41; Isaiah 59:21; Ezekiel 34:25-26*)

115

Salvation is all about God. Notice how many times He declares, "I will." *God* will perform major heart surgery upon Israel, removing from them any reason for boasting:

- "Then I will sprinkle clean water on you, and you shall be clean; I will cleanse you from all your filthiness and from all your idols. I will give you a new heart and put a new spirit within you; I will take the heart of stone out of your flesh and give you a heart of flesh. I will put My Spirit within you and cause you to walk in My statutes, and you will keep My judgments and do them." (*Ezekiel 36:25-27; 16:59-63*)

How will God accomplish this? In a manner prefigured by the Old Testament sacrificial system! However, God cryptically promised that it would be *He*, not the priesthood, who would make atonement for the people:

- "Rejoice, O Gentiles, with His people; for He will avenge the blood of His servants, and render vengeance to His adversaries; He will provide atonement for His land and His people." (*Deuteronomy 32:43, Psalm 79:9*)

However, many Jewish sources teach a form of self-salvation, for example:

- "Judaism has always held that we do not need that [Christian] sort of salvation...Quite the contrary. The Torah says: "If you do good, won't there be special privilege? And if you do not do good, sin waits at the door. It lusts after you, but you can dominate it." (*Genesis 4:7*) In other words, you can do good, and if you do, things will be better for you. If you do not do good, sin wants to be partners with you. But you can

116

control sin, you can control your evil desires, and you can be good."
(www.beingjewish.com/toshuv/salvation.html)

The trouble was that Israel could never be *good enough* and would always be in need of the mercy of God. The rabbis have turned away from the Biblical hope in the Messiah. He would be their Redeemer:

- "No lion shall be there, nor shall any ravenous beast go up on it; it shall not be found there. But the redeemed shall walk there, And the ransomed of the LORD shall return, and come to Zion with singing, with everlasting joy on their heads." (*Isaiah 35:9-10; Psalm 19:14*)

The "redeemed" were to be "ransomed of the Lord." He would have to pay the redemption price as He had foreshadowed with His payment of the price of the Egyptian firstborn sons. However, the rabbis see no need for a Redeemer. According to many of them, Israel is *already* righteous:

- "But if they [Christians] choose to say that all people, including Jews, are sinful and cannot be righteous, I have to strongly disagree, because the Torah says quite the opposite: "All your nation [Israel] is righteous, they will inherit the earth eternally; the shoot that I have planted, the work of My hands, something to be proud of" (*Isaiah 60:21*). So we are righteous, and Hashem is proud of us."
(www.beingjewish.com/toshuv/salvation.html)

However, this very text from Isaiah does *not* claim that Israel *is already righteous*. Instead, they will eventually be made righteous:

- "The sun shall be no more your light by day, nor for brightness shall the moon give you light; but the LORD will be your everlasting light, and your God will be your glory. Your sun shall no more go down, nor your moon withdraw itself; for the LORD will be your everlasting light, and your days of mourning shall be ended. Your people shall all be righteous; they shall possess the land forever, the branch of my planting, the work of my hands, that I might be glorified." (*Isaiah 60:19-21*)

Israel should have realized their hope was in promised Messiah:

- "Behold, I send my messenger, and he will prepare the way before me. And the Lord whom you seek will suddenly come to his temple; and the messenger of the covenant in whom you delight, behold, he is coming, says the LORD of hosts. But who can endure the day of his coming, and who can stand when he appears? For he is like a refiner's fire and like fullers' soap. He will sit as a refiner and purifier of silver, and he will purify the sons of Levi and refine them like gold and silver, and they will bring offerings in righteousness to the LORD. (*Malachi 3:1-3; Isaiah 42:6; 49:8; Isaiah 9:6-7; 11:1-10*)

However, the role of the Messiah was also carefully concealed (*Isaiah 49:2; 51:16*) until God could not contain Himself anymore:

- "Surely he [the Messiah] has borne our griefs and carried our sorrows; yet we esteemed him stricken, smitten by God, and afflicted. But he was pierced for our transgressions; he was crushed for our iniquities; upon him was the chastisement that brought us peace, and with his wounds we are healed. All we like sheep have gone astray; we have turned—every one—to his own way; and the LORD has laid on him the iniquity of us all." (*Isaiah 53:4-6; Psalms 22, 40; 69*)

God is the Savior! His salvation and eternal life are progressively revealed throughout the Old and New Testaments. The portrait is so consistent, even breathtaking, so that we can conclude that it represents the single plan of One surpassingly intelligent Being who has worked seamlessly through many authors, cultures, and epochs.

WORKS CITED

How Does a Jew Attain Salvation?
www.beingjewish.com/toshuv/salvation.html

Chapter 10

PROPHETS OF GOD AND
THEIR PROBLEMS WITH GOD

While I was living in Israel as a Zionist, someone gave me a copy of the Hebrew Scriptures. My favorite book quickly became the *Book of Joshua*. Why? Because, in this book, my people were triumphing militarily! It felt like I too was triumphing. However, *Joshua* soon gave way to the *Book of Judges*, where I was plunged into defeat along with each Israelite defeat. Consequently, I put the Bible down.

Years later, reading the Bible with a Christian lens, *Joshua* was replaced by *Genesis* as my favorite book. I came to realize that this book wasn't about exalting Abraham, Isaac, and Jacob as role-models but *God* Himself, who never gave up on His fearful and highly tainted Patriarchs but persevered with them. Consequently, they were a great encouragement to me. They were far from perfect and so was I. I began to realize that I didn't have to be perfect but rather, His child, and He would patiently do the heavy lifting for me.

However, the rabbis do not regard the Patriarchs in this way. According to one of many rabbinic sources:

- "Prophets and prophecy are integral to Judaism. Abraham, Isaac and Jacob, the forefathers of the Jewish people, were prophets...As the wife of Abraham, Sarah was an equal partner in his efforts to spread monotheistic beliefs and morality. Abraham led the men, and Sarah shepherded the women...Sarah was so holy that her bread would remain fresh all week, her Shabbat candles would burn until the following Friday, and a cloud would hover above her tent. In telling Sarah's age at the time of her passing, the verse states that her life was "100 years, and 20

years, and 7 years." The sages explain that when she was 100, she was as pure of sin as a maiden of 20; and when she was 20, she was as beautiful as an innocent seven-year old."
(www.chabad.org/library/article_cdo/aid/4058906/jewish/21-Jewish-Prophets-Everyone-Should-Know.htm)

The rabbis generally regard the Patriarchs and their other Prophets as super-spiritual. Without warrant, they embellish the Biblical text with their own inventions. However, the NT regards the Patriarchs and Prophets as human as the rest of us:

- "Elijah was a man with a nature like ours, and he prayed fervently that it might not rain, and for three years and six months it did not rain on the earth." (*James 5:17*)

We too tend to regard the Prophets and Apostles as spiritual giants. However, they struggled as we do. It also seems that they had issues with God. For a while, Elijah's presence had brought blessing upon a widow of Zeraphath and her son, but her son suddenly died. Elijah, therefore, accused God:

- "O LORD my God, have you brought calamity even upon the widow with whom I sojourn, by killing her son?" (*1 Kings 17:20*)

Nevertheless, the Lord healed the son through Elijah.

The Prophet Jonah's issues with God were even more severe. He rejected God's calling to preach to Nineveh and fled. It even seems that he preferred death over his heavenly calling. Nevertheless, after being swallowed by a great fish, Jonah agreed to preach to Nineveh. However, the very thing that Jonah had feared came to pass. They repented and God relented from His promise to destroy Nineveh.

121

However, instead of rejoicing with the Lord, Jonah became angry (*Jonah 4:1*) and wanted to die, but God tried to teach him that he was his own worst enemy:

- "Therefore now, O LORD, please take my life from me, for it is better for me to die than to live." And the LORD said, "Do you do well to be angry?" (*Jonah 4:3-4*)

Of course, Jonah's anger wasn't serving him well. However, God didn't give up on Jonah and continued to provide object lessons to expose his anger and rebellion for what they were. Overnight, He provided Jonah with a plant to shade him from the intense sun. God then destroyed the plant, and Jonah foolishly became angry at it – another teachable moment:

- "When the sun rose, God appointed a scorching east wind, and the sun beat down on the head of Jonah so that he was faint. And he asked that he might die and said, "It is better for me to die than to live." But God said to Jonah, "Do you do well to be angry for the plant?" And he said, "Yes, I do well to be angry, angry enough to die." And the LORD said, "You pity the plant, for which you did not labor, nor did you make it grow, which came into being in a night and perished in a night. And should not I pity Nineveh, that great city, in which there are more than 120,000 persons who do not know their right hand from their left, and also much cattle?" (*Jonah 4:8-11*)

God reasoned with Jonah to win his heart through his mind. Without any clear resolution, the *Book of Jonah* ends abruptly with these verses. Did Jonah learn God's lessons? Did he repent of his anger, his self-centered worldview, and his rebellion against the Word of God? We are not told. However, we do see the patience and graciousness of God on his behalf. Despite, Jonah's rebellion, God remained faithful to His Prophet.

To win the mind is also to win the heart. Once our heart has been opened, faithfulness to our Savior must be secured by reason through our minds. This becomes the seat of transformation (*Romans 12:2; Colossians 3:10*). We too have our issues with God, and He also has to instruct and humble us.

However, we tend to think that we are miles away from the example of Elijah, who had raised the dead child. However, it is evident that this child was healed not because of Elijah's great faith, but because of God's faithfulness.

We despair of having faith like Elijah who had prayed for a drought, and there was drought, and who prayed for rain, and there was rain. However, we often fail to see that Elijah had accomplished what he did not by virtue of His great faith, but in accordance with the Word, the instructions of God (*1 Kings 17:1, 9; 18:1, 36*). He merely did what God had told him to do:

- "And at the time of the offering of the oblation [in his confrontation with the priests of Baal], Elijah the prophet came near and said, "O LORD, God of Abraham, Isaac, and Israel, let it be known this day that you are God in Israel, and that I am your servant, and that I have done all these things at your word." (*1 Kings 18:36*)

As a result, fire came down from heaven to consume Elijah's offering. This convinced Israel that Elijah was of God and the prophets of Baal were deceivers.

We wrongly conceive of great faith as a matter of intense effort to rid from our minds any doubts or feelings that might betray a lack of confidence, and Elijah was the expert. However, Elijah had merely learned to take God at His Word. God had told him to pray, and Elijah prayed, and God provided the increase. Did he believe that he was accruing brownie-points in heaven or that he had become super-spiritual? Perhaps? However, even if he was beginning to believe this way, his God would not allow such conceit to stand. Immediately after Elijah's great victory over the prophets of Baal on Mt. Carmel, Elijah lost heart at the threats of King Ahaz' wife and fled like a coward.

ISAIAH'S PROBLEM WITH GOD

Isaiah didn't seem to have any illusions about Israel's lack of merit or righteousness. If he did have any illusions, God promptly dispelled them:

- "Children have I reared and brought up, but they have rebelled against me. The ox knows its owner, and the donkey its master's crib, but Israel does not know, my people do not understand." Ah, sinful nation, a people laden with iniquity, offspring of evildoers, children who deal corruptly! They have forsaken the LORD, they have despised the Holy One of Israel, they are utterly estranged." (*Isaiah 1:2-4*)

However, Isaiah had a different issue with God. He correctly understood that God is omnipotent and could do anything He wanted to do:

- "All of us have become like one who is unclean, and all our righteous acts are like filthy rags; we all shrivel up like a leaf, and like the wind our sins sweep us away. No one calls on your name or strives to lay hold of you; for you have hidden your face from us and made us waste away because of our sins. Yet, O LORD, you are our Father. We are the clay, you are the potter; we are all the work of your hand." (*Isaiah 64:6-8*)

Yes, Israel was rebellious and deserved judgment. However, if God is the potter – and Isaiah was convinced that He is – He should be able to mold Israel into anything He wanted, even into righteous children:

- "Do not be angry beyond measure, O LORD; do not remember our sins forever. Oh, look upon us, we pray, for we are all your people... After all this, O LORD, will you hold yourself back? Will you keep silent and punish us beyond measure?" (*Isaiah 64:9,12*)

Isaiah was perplexed why God was holding Himself back from molding His clay into a faithful people and upset that God would "punish beyond measure," at least according to Isaiah's reckoning. However, God's answer must have been less than satisfying:

- "All day long I have held out my hands to an obstinate people, who walk in ways not good, pursuing their own imaginations-- a people who continually provoke me to my very face, offering sacrifices in gardens and burning incense on altars of brick [to false gods]... I will destine you for the sword, and you will all bend down for the slaughter; for I called but you did not answer, I spoke but you did not listen. You did evil in my sight and chose what displeases me." (*Isaiah 65:2-3,12*)

God didn't directly answer Isaiah's question. However, in many ways, God had answered. He had already given Israel everything He could:

- "Let me sing for my beloved my love song concerning his vineyard: My beloved had a vineyard on a very fertile hill. He [God] dug it and cleared it of stones, and planted it with choice vines; he built a watchtower in the midst of it, and hewed out a wine vat in it; and he looked for it to yield grapes, but it yielded wild grapes. And now, O inhabitants of Jerusalem and men of Judah, judge between me and my vineyard. What more was there to do for my vineyard, that I have not done in it? When I looked for it to yield grapes, why did it yield wild grapes?" (*Isaiah 5:1-4*)

God insisted that there is nothing more that He could have done for Israel, and that He was not holding-back, as Isaiah had charged. However, if God is omnipotent, it is hard for us to understand why God is not more merciful towards His people. If He changed the heart of some, why could He not change the heart of *all*?

But what is God's omnipotence? Can He not do anything? It doesn't seem so. While He can accomplish *anything He wants*, there are things that He *cannot* do. He cannot sin – a violation of His character. Nor does it seem that He can violate His promises. Perhaps, also, He also cannot violate His internal logic and create a stone that He cannot lift.

Jesus had petitioned the Father for something that pointed to the Father's Self-limitation:

- "Going a little farther, he [Jesus] fell with his face to the ground and prayed, 'My Father, if it is possible, may this cup [the Cross] be taken from me. Yet not as I will, but as you will.'" (*Matthew 26:39*)

While God can do all things He wants to do, He cannot do them in any manner. He was not able to grant Jesus His request. His righteous character prevented the payment of humanity's in any other way. Jesus had to die! Animals certainly weren't able to bring our forgiveness. Nor was anything else able to display His righteousness (*Romans 5:8-10*) to the extent that He desired. Only the supreme price, the death of God the Son could adequately communicate His righteousness and the depth of our sins.
Let me apply this to the question of God saving all Israel. While God wants all to be saved (*2 Peter 3:9*), there might be

a Self-limitation within His very Nature that does not permit this.

Nevertheless, God promised that He would show incredible grace to Israel, but only through his Messiah:

- "The Redeemer [the promised Messiah] will come to Zion, to those in Jacob who repent of their sins," declares the LORD. "As for me, this is my covenant with them," says the LORD. "My Spirit, who is on you, and my words that I have put in your mouth will not depart from your mouth, or from the mouths of your children, or from the mouths of their descendants from this time on and forever," says the LORD." (*Isaiah 59:20-21*)

- "Behold, I will create new heavens and a new earth. The former things will not be remembered, nor will they come to mind. But be glad and rejoice forever in what I will create, for I will create Jerusalem to be a delight and its people a joy. I will rejoice over Jerusalem and take delight in my people; the sound of weeping and of crying will be heard in it no more..." (*Isaiah 65:17-19*)

In the end, there will be a great salvation. All those left in the end will be rescued:

- "From one New Moon to another and from one Sabbath to another, all mankind will come and bow down before me," says the LORD." (*Isaiah 66:23*)

This is an indication that, in the end, our Lord will open the floodgates of heaven:

- "Turn to me and be saved, all you ends of the earth; for I am God, and there is no other... Before me every knee will bow; by me every tongue will swear. They will say of me, 'In the LORD alone are righteousness and strength.'" All who have raged against him will come to him and be put to shame. But in the LORD all the descendants of Israel will be found righteous and will exult." (*Isaiah 45:22-25; 60:14; also Romans 11:12-27; James 2:13*)

But God made us this way, right? Isn't he also to blame? This is one charge that the Prophets never brought against God. Instead, they accepted what He had revealed – that the fault is all ours, and that God had done for Israel everything that He could do (*Isaiah 5:2-5; Jeremiah 2:21*).

Isaiah merely charged that God could correct Israel's heart. However, he probably never received a complete and satisfactory answer, but perhaps what had been revealed to him was enough. Hopefully, it will be enough for us.

JEREMIAH'S PROBLEM WITH GOD

How can we believe in a God of the holocausts, who annihilated the Canaanites and the Amalekites? In our eyes, except for a few bad apples, our fellow human beings do not appear so evil, certainly not so evil that they deserve to die.

This is the most common challenge to our faith. We are troubled by it, but it was also troubling to the prophets of Israel. *Habakkuk (1:12-17)* had objected that, although his people were sinners, they weren't bad enough to warrant the coming Babylonian destruction of their homeland! Jeremiah had a similar complaint—God's indictment against Jerusalem was just too extreme! Therefore, God prepared for His prophet a challenge and an object lesson:

- "Go up and down the streets of Jerusalem, look around and consider, search through her squares. If you can find but one person who deals honestly and seeks the truth, I will forgive this city. Although they say, 'As surely as the LORD lives,' still they are swearing falsely." (*Jeremiah 5:1-2*).

Jeremiah didn't fault God's gracious offer to forgive. Only *one* honest person needed to be present in Jerusalem. The offer seemed more than gracious! This was because Jeremiah was convinced that there were many righteous Israelites, and that God's displeasure could only reasonably apply to the uneducated rabble. Surely, the leadership knew better and would respond to God and would then spearhead the return to God!

- "O LORD, do not your eyes look for truth? You struck them, but they felt no pain; you crushed them, but they refused correction. They made their faces harder than stone and refused to repent. I thought, 'These are only the poor; they are foolish, for they do not know the way of the LORD, the requirements of their God. So I will go to the leaders and speak to them; surely they know the way of the LORD, the requirements of their God.' But with one accord, they too had broken off the yoke and torn off the bonds [of God]" (*Jeremiah 5:3-5*).

We don't see as God does. Our own people tend to look pretty good to us, especially those of Jeremiah's own priestly clan. The prophets' problem had been much the same as ours. They failed to comprehend the depth of Israel's sin and rebellion against God. As a result, God's punishment seemed extreme and unwarranted. However, Israel's prophets needed a crash course in human depravity if they were going to represent God faithfully, and He was glad to provide it to them. He enlightened Jeremiah regarding the rebellion of even the educated leadership:

- "Why should I forgive you? Your children have forsaken me and sworn by gods that are not gods. I supplied all

129

their needs, yet they committed adultery and thronged to the houses of prostitutes. They are well-fed, lusty stallions, each neighing for another man's wife. Should I not punish them for this?...The house of Israel and the house of Judah have been utterly unfaithful to me...They [the false prophets] have lied about the LORD" (*Jeremiah 5:7-13*).

God is faithful, but Israel had been utterly unfaithful. Seen in this light, our Creator and Redeemer had every reason to judge. However, Jeremiah was still unable to see his people through God's lens.

Holding faith isn't always comfortable. We don't always have the answers that our restless minds crave. Life continues to pose the ultimate question to us: "Are you still willing to follow your God even when things don't make perfect sense?" This had been Jesus' challenge to multitudes that were following Him because of the free meals. He laid down a difficult teaching to separate those merely looking for another handout from the true seekers: "Unless you drink my blood..." (*John 6*). It didn't make sense; it wasn't the Jewish way, and many left.

God posed a similar question to Abraham when He asked him to sacrifice his son, Isaac (*Genesis 22*). It seemed to go against everything God had promised Abraham—that the world would be blessed through Isaac and his seed. Abraham didn't have the answer to this dilemma, but he knew God well enough to know that God did. We too must live with the discomfort of an incomplete puzzle. However, we've hopefully learned where to look for the missing pieces!

Nevertheless, it's amusing to see how quickly our philosophical objections evaporate when we become the object of persecution. Jeremiah's tune changed, once he realized that even his own educated family wanted to kill him:

- "Then the LORD told me about the plots my enemies were making against me. I had been as unaware as a lamb on the way to its slaughter. I had no idea that they were planning to kill me!" (*Jeremiah 11:18-19*)

God revealed to Jeremiah what His prophet could never have imagined:

- "Even your own brothers, members of your own family, have turned on you. They have plotted, raising a cry against you. Do not trust them, no matter how pleasantly they speak." (*Jeremiah 12:6*)

A pleasant facade can be a ploy. Gradually, Jeremiah's experiences changed his attitude and he began to see things through God's holy lens:

- "Avenge me on my persecutors... But you know, O LORD, all their plots to kill me. Do not forgive their crimes or blot out their sins from your sight... let me see your vengeance upon them." (*Jeremiah 15:15; 18:23; 20:12*)

Unless we first learn about the righteousness and justice of God's judgments, we cannot understand His mercy. Jeremiah's opinion about the pervasiveness of sin was beginning to change. He finally declared:

- "The heart is deceitful above all things and beyond cure. Who can understand it?" (*Jeremiah 17:9*)

Only when we understand the depths of human perversity are we prepared to grasp the depths of God's mercy. Otherwise, we will regard it as our just entitlement.

THE PROPHET EZEKIEL'S GRIEVANCE

To prepare His prophet for faithful service, the Lord had taken Ezekiel on a spiritual journey into the heart of His Temple where Ezekiel observed the abominations of the priesthood, which he had never dreamed possible. God then gave Ezekiel a vision of the destruction that He would bring upon Israel. However, Ezekiel was still unconvinced about the justice of God's wrath:

- "So it was, that while they were killing them, I was left alone; and I fell on my face and cried out, and said, "Ah, Lord GOD! Will You destroy all the remnant of Israel in pouring out Your fury on Jerusalem?" Then He said to me, "The iniquity of the house of Israel and Judah is exceedingly great, and the land is full of bloodshed, and the city full of perversity; for they say, 'The LORD has forsaken the land, and the LORD does not see!'" (*Ezekiel 9:8-9; 11:13, 16-20*)

Ezekiel was unable to grasp the extent of Israel's corruption, but God was slowly molding Ezekiel into a son of God, a man after His own heart and mind, unlike his self-righteous brethren. He commanded Ezekiel to put the Words of God above everything else:

- "And if I say to the wicked man, 'You will surely die,' but he then turns away from his sin and does what is just and right-- if he gives back what he took in pledge for a loan, returns what he has stolen, follows the decrees that give life, and does no evil, he will surely live; he will not die. None of the sins he has committed will be remembered against him. He has done what is just and right; he will surely live. "Yet your countrymen say, 'The way of the Lord is not just.' But it is their way that is not just. If a righteous man turns from his righteousness and does evil, he will die for it. And if a wicked man turns away from his wickedness and does what is just and right, he will live by doing so. Yet, O house of Israel, you say, 'The way of the Lord is not just.' But I will judge each of you according to his own ways." (*Ezekiel 33:14-20*)

God's ways never seem just to the self-righteous. Although they might realize that they aren't perfect, they still believe that their good far outweighs their evil, and that this entitles them to God's blessings. They might even feel entitled, by their "good moral record," to do a little evil. However, the reluctant Ezekiel was told to announce that, no matter how good their performance might have been, once they turn to sin, they deserve death. He was also warned that if he proceeded according to his own understanding, instead of God's Word, and did not warn, he too would be guilty (*Ezekiel 33:1-9*).

The self-righteous cannot endure such righteous teaching. They believe they stand by virtue of their esteemed moral record and not by the mercy of God. Therefore, a few sins should not change anything. They, therefore, were convinced that "The way of the Lord is not just" and failed to understand that none of us can stand before our righteous God apart from His mercy or conclude that, "He owes me blessings because of my surpassing righteousness.

Repeatedly, Jesus had to teach His Apostles this same lesson. They too were convinced that the educated elite and those blessed with wealth also deserved to be blessed with eternal life. However, Jesus confounded their thinking:

- "But Jesus said to them again, 'Children, how difficult it is to enter the kingdom of God! It is easier for a camel to go through the eye of a needle than for a rich person to enter the kingdom of God.' And they were exceedingly astonished, and said to him, 'Then who can be saved?' Jesus looked at them and said, 'With man it is impossible, but not with God. For all things are possible with God.'" (*Mark 10:24-27*)

God's ways are not our ways. Forgiveness and reconciliation are a gift from God. Although the entire Bible rests upon this truth, it is still so radical to human ears that Israel failed to get their minds around it. However, when we fail to understand this vital truth, we fail to understand God – His righteousness and His love for His wayward humanity. We also fail to perceive and to understand ourselves.

Nor did Jesus' disciples understand. They saw reality through human eyes, the eyes of their rabbis, and were convinced that the rich and educated were *entitled* to salvation. Therefore, when Jesus told them that even the rich and esteemed could not be saved by their efforts, incredulously, they responded, "Then who can be saved?"

As the rabbis continued to exchange the truth of God (the Scriptures) for their own self-aggrandizing human traditions, which later became codified as the Babylonian Talmud, they also exchanged the veneration of God for the veneration of their own sages.

WORKS CITED

Posner, Menachem,
"*21 Jewish Prophets Everyone Should Know*"
www.chabad.org/library/article_cdo/aid/4058906/jewish/21-Jewish-Prophets-Everyone-Should-Know.htm

Chapter 11

WAS THERE FORGIVENESS UNDER THE MOSAIC COVENANT?

www.mannsword.blogspot.com/2019/03/chapter-11-was-there-forgiveness-under.html

Many Old Testament verses indicate that God had forgiven the Israelites through animal sacrifices (*Leviticus 4, 5*)! In light of this, it would seem that the Cross was unnecessary, according to the rabbis.

However, the Old Testament didn't claim that God's forgiveness under the Mosaic system *eradicated* sin, as we now experience after the Cross. Instead, God merely *passed over* or *covered* the sins of the Hebrew saints:

- "For I will pass through the land of Egypt that night, and I will strike all the firstborn in the land of Egypt, both man and beast; and on all the gods of Egypt I will execute judgments: I am the LORD. The blood shall be a sign for you, on the houses where you are. And when I see the blood, I will <u>pass over</u> you, and no plague will befall you to destroy you, when I strike the land of Egypt." (*Exodus 12:12-13, 27*)

The OT gives us no indication that Israel's sins had been eradicated through the atoning sacrifice of an animal. Nevertheless, it does indicate that this kind of atonement would lead to forgiveness:

- Thus the priest shall make atonement for him for the sin which he has committed in any one of these things, and he shall be forgiven. And the remainder shall be for the priest, as in the grain offering." (*Leviticus 5:13*)

However, from all indications, this "atonement" only brought a *superficial* forgiveness. It only was an *outward* cleansing, little different from the external cleansing of a house:

- "He shall make atonement for the holy sanctuary, and he shall make atonement for the tent of meeting and for the altar, and he shall make atonement for the priests and for all the people of the assembly." (*Leviticus 16:33; Ezekiel 43:20; 45:20*)

It should have been obvious to the Israelites that this kind of atonement was unable to penetrate to their core to give them the renewed heart and spirit as had been promised (*Ezekiel 36:25; 11:19-20; Jeremiah 33:6, 14-16*). It is only through Christ that our sins are cleansed and purified so that we can confidently enter into the presence of God (*Hebrews 10:19-22*). Instead, OT forgiveness was only a matter of God *passing over* sins, not *removing* them:

- "Blessed is the one whose transgression is forgiven, whose sin is <u>covered</u>." (*Psalm 32:1*)

- "Who is a God like you, pardoning iniquity and <u>passing over transgression</u> for the remnant of his inheritance?" (*Micah 7:18*)

The OT saints would only experience a "passing over transgression," but they were also promised a New Covenant through which God would "remember their sins no more" (*Jeremiah 31:34*).

The New Testament also consistently taught that OT forgiveness was not the same as the forgiveness that came through the Cross:

- "For since the law has but a shadow of the good things to come instead of the true form of these realities, it can

136

never, by the same sacrifices that are continually offered every year, make perfect those who draw near. Otherwise, would they not have ceased to be offered, since the worshipers, having once been cleansed, would no longer have any consciousness of sins? But in these sacrifices there is a reminder of sins every year. For it is impossible for the blood of bulls and goats to take away sins." (*Hebrews 10:1-4*)

Instead of the *eradication* of sin, the Old Testament forgiveness merely *covered over* sin:

- "[Jesus] whom God put forward as a propitiation by his blood, to be received by faith. This was to show God's righteousness, because in his divine forbearance he had passed over former sins." (*Romans 3:25*)

Because Israel's sins were merely "passed over," Jesus' atonement had to work retroactively to cleanse the sins of the OT saints:

- "For if the blood of goats and bulls, and the sprinkling of defiled persons with the ashes of a heifer, sanctify for the purification of the flesh, how much more will the blood of Christ, who through the eternal Spirit offered himself without blemish to God, purify our conscience from dead works to serve the living God. Therefore he is the mediator of a new covenant, so that those who are called may receive the promised eternal inheritance, since a death has occurred that redeems them from the transgressions committed under the first covenant." (*Hebrews 9:13-15*)

Because their sins hadn't been eradicated, even the deceased OT saints could not come into the presence of a God, whose righteousness had not yet been satisfied by the Cross:

- "And all these, though commended through their faith, did not receive what was promised, since God had provided something better for us, that apart from us they should not be made perfect." (*Hebrews 11:39-40*)

Consequently, after Jesus proclaimed that "It is finished" and the veil of the Temple was torn in two, symbolizing the fact that the way into presence of God was now opened, there was a great earthquake to reinforce this lesson:

- "And behold, the curtain of the temple was torn in two, from top to bottom. And the earth shook, and the rocks were split. The tombs also were opened. And many bodies of the saints who had fallen asleep were raised, and coming out of the tombs after his resurrection they went into the holy city and appeared to many." (*Matthew 27:51-53*)

Presumably, after their appearances, those saints were enabled to ascend into God's presence. Consequently, Jesus had died for all sins, past, present, and future (*Hebrews 7:19, 25*).

The Old and New Testaments have gradually unveiled God's one plan for humanity, which culminates in our being made one with our Savior? It's a puzzle with Christ as the center piece. It is not a hodge-podge, constructed by 40 different authors over 1500 years, but a single vision that moves irresistibly to take hold of eternity. I think that this says something about Divine authorship, but now we have to turn to the "why" questions.

NECESSARY LESSONS FROM THE CROSS

The rabbis do not believe that God would have required that a human die for the sins of the world. Besides, they claim that any form of human sacrifice was strictly prohibited by God.

Rabbi and debater, Tovia Singer, claims that the Scriptures teach *against* human vicarious (substitutionary) atonement:

- "...nor does Scripture ever tell us that an innocent man can die as an atonement for the sins of the wicked." (www.outreachjudaism.org)

However, Scripture does tell us that one man would die for the sins of the world:

- "Yet it was the will of the LORD to crush him; he has put him to grief; when his soul makes an offering for guilt, he shall see his offspring; he shall prolong his days; the will of the LORD shall prosper in his hand. Out of the anguish of his soul he shall see and be satisfied; by his knowledge shall the righteous one, my servant, make many to be accounted righteous, and he shall bear their iniquities." (*Isaiah 53:10-11*)

The rabbis, prior to the esteemed commentator Rashi (1040-1105 A.D.), were in agreement that *Isaiah 53* taught that the Messiah would die for the sins of the people:

- Rabbi Moshe Alshekh, a famous sixteenth-century scholar, asserted: "[Our] Rabbis with one voice, accept and affirm the opinion that the prophet [*Isaiah 53*] is speaking of King Messiah. (www.jewsforjesus.org/publications/issues/issues-v07-n09/what-the-prophet-said-what-the-rabbis-said/)

- The Talmud tractate *Sanhedrin 98a* states: "The Rabanan [rabbis] say that Messiah's name is The Suffering Scholar . . . for it is written, "Surely He hath borne our grief and carried our sorrows, yet we did esteem him stricken, smitten of God and afflicted." (*Isaiah 53:4*)

139

- "In the hour in which they tell the Messiah about the sufferings of Israel in exile, and about the sinful among them who seek not the knowledge of their Master, the Messiah lifts up his voice and weeps over the sinful among them. This is what is written: He was wounded because of our transgressions, he was crushed because of our iniquities (*Isaiah 53:5*). Those souls then return to their places. In the Garden of Eden there is a Hall which is called the Hall of the Sons of Illness. The Messiah enters that Hall and summons all the disease and all the pains and all the suffering of Israel that they should come upon him, and all of them come upon him." (*The Zohar 2:212a*)

- "The children of the world are members one of another. When the Holy One desires to give healing to the world, he smites one just man amongst them, and for his sake heals all the rest. Whence do we learn this? From the saying, "He was wounded for our transgressions, bruised for our iniquities"' [*Isaiah 53:5*]" (The Zohar; Numbers, Pinchus, *218a*).

- The highly regarded first-century Rabbi Shimon Ben Yochai stated: "The meaning of the words 'Bruised for our iniquities' [*Isaiah 53:5*] is that since the Messiah bears our iniquities, which produce the effect of his being bruised, it follows that whoso will not admit that the Messiah thus suffers for our iniquities, must endure and suffer them for them himself." (Neubauer, p. xl.)

- The Midrash Aseret Memrot states: "The Messiah, in order to atone for them both [for Adam and David] will 'make his soul a trespass offering,'" (*Isaiah 53:10*).

Israel's hope had been in the Messiah who would pay the ultimate price for their sins beyond what the offering of animals could possibly accomplish. Nevertheless, Singer

140

claims that *Scripture* rules out the possibility that one man will die for all. However, God's command to Abraham to sacrifice his son Isaac as a burnt offering (*Genesis 22*) suggests otherwise, but not according to Singer:

- "When Abraham was ready to sacrifice Isaac, the Almighty admonished him that He did not want the human sacrifice…The Almighty's directive—that He only wanted animal sacrifices rather than human sacrifices—was immediately understood. This teaching has never departed from the mind and soul of the faithful children of Israel." (Singer, www.outreachjudaism.org/)

However, God never informed Abraham that He didn't "want the human sacrifice." Instead, God provided Abraham with a substitute offering – a ram. Nor is there any evidence that either Abraham or Israel had derived the understanding that Singer claims to have derived. For one thing, God did not admonish Abraham for offering his son as a sacrificial offering. Instead, He *commended* Abraham:

- But the angel of the Lord called out to him from heaven, "Abraham! Abraham!" "Here I am," he replied. "Do not lay a hand on the boy," he said. "Do not do anything to him. Now I know that you fear God, because you have not withheld from me your son, your only son." Abraham looked up and there in a thicket he saw a ram caught by its horns. He went over and took the ram and sacrificed it as a burnt offering instead of his son. So Abraham called that place The Lord Will Provide. And to this day it is said, "On the mountain of the Lord it will be provided." The angel of the Lord called to Abraham from heaven a second time and said, "I swear by myself, declares the Lord, that because you have done this and have not withheld your son, your only son, I will surely bless you and make your descendants as

141

numerous as the stars in the sky and as the sand on the seashore. Your descendants will take possession of the cities of their enemies, and through your offspring all nations on earth will be blessed, <u>because you have obeyed me</u>." (*Genesis 22:11-18*)

Because Abraham had been faithful, God promised to bless him. Contrary to Singer's assertion, He certainly wasn't chastening Abraham for his willingness to offer his son as a sacrifice, as God had commanded him to do.

Also, it seems that both Israel and Abraham had derived an even greater message about something that God would offer in the future – "The Lord *will* Provide." Ordinarily, this would be a strange way to name Mt. Moriah, since this event described how God *had already* provided an animal substitute for Isaac. Why then wasn't Moriah named, "The Lord *has* Provided?" Evidently, what God would provide in the future would *overshadow* what He had *already* provided. But it would be something akin to what had already been provided – Jesus Himself!

However, this isn't our point, but merely that Singer's assertion – *"that He only wanted animal sacrifices rather than human sacrifices"* – is scripturally unwarranted! Instead, it seems that God instructed Abraham to offer Isaac as a human sacrifice as a foreshadowing of what He would provide by His Son (*Genesis 22*). He also cryptically indicated that this Son would provide the blood for the New Covenant (*Isaiah 42:6; 9:8; Psalms 22; 69*) and would provide Him with a body instead of the bodies of bulls and sheep (*Psalm 40; Hebrews 10:5-7*). More explicitly, this Arm of God would serve as the ultimate and final burnt offering:

Why didn't the omnipotent Father simply eradicate sin without *any* blood offering? Why was it necessary for Jesus to die for our sins? Evidently, there was no alternative to Jesus' horrid and public death for humanity. In the Garden of Gethsemane, Jesus had prayed for an alternative, but none was offered (*Matthew 26:39*). Why then did Jesus have to endure the Cross if God is omnipotent and can do all things?

Our Lord kept many secrets, even the most important ones, including the nature of His glory. Moses had sought the glory of God during a time of great disappointment. He had just spent 40 days with God on Mt. Sinai where he had received the Ten Commandments. Meanwhile, down below, Israel had made the idolatrous Golden Calf and was partying. As a result, for the first time God's anger broke out against Israel, and many died of a plague.

Moses was crushed and requested to see God's glory. God's answer was probably not what Moses had expected:

- "I will make all My goodness pass before you, and I will proclaim the name of the LORD before you. I will be gracious to whom I will be gracious, and I will have compassion on whom I will have compassion." But He said, "You cannot see My face; for no man shall see Me, and live." (*Exodus 33:19-20 NKJV*)

Instead of a visual display of His glory with lightning and thunder, God only partially disclosed Himself to Moses – His back:

- And the LORD passed before him and proclaimed, "The LORD, the LORD God, merciful and gracious, longsuffering, and abounding in goodness and truth, keeping mercy for thousands, forgiving iniquity and transgression and sin, by no means clearing the guilty, visiting the iniquity of the fathers upon the children and the children's children to the third and the fourth generation." (*Exodus 34:6-7*)

143

Moses seemed satisfied with His self-disclosure and worshipped (*Exodus 34:8*). Instead of seeing God's face – and the face best reveals the identity of the person – Moses was only permitted to see the backside of God. Nevertheless, this very partial disclosure had satisfied Moses, and he worshipped God. After all, Moses had earlier requested that he would be given a greater understanding of God:

- "I pray, if I have found grace in Your sight, show me now Your way, that I may know You and that I may find grace in Your sight." (*Exodus 33:13*)

God, therefore, revealed His "way" to Moses but not completely, not His "face," the most revealing part of His Being. This was protected at the threat of death.

What would His face have revealed? Something that Israel was not ready to see. It was hidden away at the threat of death! Why death? Along with this hidden aspect of God, there was also an object concealed within the Holy of Holies that carried the threat of death to anyone who would look upon it.

It was obscured by the massive wings of two cherubim who were mounted above it. The Holy of Holies could be entered only once a year by only the High Priest on Yom Kippur. Even he was warned that if he looked upon this object, he would die. Therefore, when he was permitted to enter, he had to enter with great billows of smoke lest he would be struck dead by inadvertently seeing this object.

Surprisingly, it wasn't the Ark of the Covenant, its contents (including the Ten Commandments), or the Law, which brought death to the one who saw it (*Galatians 3:10-12; Matthew 5:21-22*). Instead, the forbidden object *covered* the Ark and its contents – the "Mercy Seat," also called the "Atonement Cover" (*Romans 3:25*), the thing that symbolized life and mercy (*Leviticus 16:13*), the great and carefully guarded mystery of our Savior!

How are we to understand God's concealment? Jesus' mission had also been concealed. It was only at the end that He began to reveal it more fully:

- But Jesus answered them, saying, "The hour has come that the Son of Man should be glorified. Most assuredly, I say to you, unless a grain of wheat falls into the ground and dies, it remains alone; but if it dies, it produces much grain." (*John 12:23-24; 13:31-32*)

What glory had our Lord been hiding for millennia? That He loved us so much that He would die the most horrid and humiliating death to prove His love for us, even while we were still His enemies.

Why would He conceal the centerpiece of His glory? Evidently, humankind was not ready to receive it. When they saw Christ's crucifixion, they were horrified and ran away, convinced that what they had seen was not the glory of God but the absolute end of hope. Only the Resurrection and Jesus opening their minds to the Scriptures was able to turn them around (*Luke 24:13-47*).

The Law had to precede God's grace. God had to first convince Israel of His holiness and righteousness before they would ever be able to receive His all-surpassing love, a love that we still cannot fathom (*Ephesians 3:19*).

The Cross represented the supreme display of God's glory (*John 12:23-24; 13:31-32*). How strange that the hour of God's greatest glory was also Jesus' painful, humiliating, and disgraceful death on the Cross. However, it *proved* the extent of God's love, as nothing else could. He would die for us while we were still His enemies:

145

- "...but God <u>shows</u> his love for us in that while we were still sinners, Christ died for us. Since, therefore, we have now been justified by his blood, much more shall we be saved by him from the wrath of God. For if while we were enemies we were reconciled to God by the death of his Son, much more, now that we are reconciled, shall we be saved by his life. More than that, we also rejoice in God through our Lord Jesus Christ, through whom we have now received reconciliation." (*Romans 5:8-11*)

This display of God's love and glory it not just a graphic gory show, it is a display that I had vitally needed. One atheist had made a public challenge to all Christians – "How do you know that your faith is not just an elaborate con-job by the greatest con in existence?"

Actually, this had been my question for years. Although I believed in Jesus, I was dogged by the doubt that He might be a sadist who created us merely for His entertainment. This is the way I had felt while undergoing the most intense depression and panic attacks. Eventually, however, it was revealed to me that He couldn't be a sadist if He had willingly endured the Cross for me.

But did He actually die this most excruciating death for us? Many skeptics regard the Cross as an indisputable historical fact:

- NT scholar, John Dominic Crossan: "That He was crucified is as sure as anything historical ever can be." (Strobel,113)

- "Both Gerd Ludemann, an atheistic NT critic, and Bart Ehrman, who's an agnostic, call the crucifixion an indisputable fact." (Strobel,113)

146

- Tacitus, Roman historian (110 AD): "Jesus suffered the extreme penalty under the reign of Tiberius." (Strobel,113)

- "Josephus [the Jewish historian, 90 AD] reports that Pilate 'condemned him to be crucified'...Even the Jewish Talmud reports that 'Yeshu was hanged.'" (Strobel, 113)

- Apologist Michael Licona reports that "Lucian of Samosata also, who was a Greek satirist, mentions the crucifixion, and Mara Bar-Serapion, who was a pagan, confirms Jesus was executed." (Strobel, 113)

The evidence that the Cross of Christ is a thoroughly-proven historical fact set me free from doubts that the God really didn't love me. Instead, I became convinced that His love passes all understanding (*Ephesians 3:16-19*).

The Cross was not only a necessary display of God's love and glory, it also represented the ultimate display of His righteousness. He also had to display to the world that He is so serious about sin that an adequate payment had to be made for it:

- ...Christ Jesus, whom God put forward as propitiation by his blood, to be received by faith. This was to show God's righteousness, because in his divine forbearance he had passed over former sins. It was to show his righteousness at the present time, so that he might be just and the justifier of the one who has faith in Jesus. (*Romans 3:24-26*)

This revelation of God's righteousness at the Cross speaks volumes to us about the seriousness of our sins. They are so serious that no payment could ever suffice apart from the death of God the Son Himself. And if our sins had been so heinous before God that nothing short of the death of His Son could take them away, we need to resist them with all of our might. This means that we cannot simply say, "He just wants us to try our best." Instead, He demands righteous perfection, as Jesus taught: "You therefore must be perfect, as your heavenly Father is perfect" (*Matthew 5:48*). The only thing that protects us from this severe righteousness is His undeserved mercy and the free gift of God (*Romans 6:23*).

Let's return to the question of why the Father didn't answer the pray of the Son. He could have created another being who could die in the place of Jesus. However, this wouldn't prove that God truly loves us. A created being would cost God nothing.

Likewise, a created being or the mere appearance of one couldn't convey the extent of God's righteousness, His hatred of sin. The death of God the Son proved that our sins are so heinous that nothing short of the death of God the Son could have paid the price for them.

These two seemingly opposite truths must be maintained. We are required to be morally perfect, and yet our Lord forgives all whenever we confess our sins (*1 John 1:9*). Let me try to explain the need for both. If you give your wife a black eye, it is not enough to say:

- Don't get so ruffled. This is the first time I've ever done this to you. That's not so bad, is it?

But it is. We have to take *full* responsibility for *all* of our behavior, even if we have had a perfect track-record.

This standard of perfection should also humble us and prevent self-righteousness and the thinking, "I'm more deserving than you," or "I *deserve* heaven." Instead, He shows us repeatedly that it's all about His mercy and not what is owed to us – a source of arrogance.

The Bible continually warns against the evil of pride. Even the Apostle Paul was vulnerable to this poison. Because of this, God allowed Satan to afflict him. (*2 Corinthians 12:7-10*)

However, many rabbis have sidestepped the Biblical warnings and have cleared the way for self-aggrandizement. I was attending the studies of one very learned and charismatic rabbi. He taught what other rabbis and rabbinic literature had been teaching – that the Jews occupy a superior status. We are actually part of the Mind of God.

One of the several lawyers and judges who also attended his studies asked:

- Rabbi, I have been reading that the Bible often describes the Jews as a "stubborn and stiff-necked" people. How do you reconcile this with the fact that we are actually part of the Mind of God?

The rabbi answered that we have to understand what the Bible means by "stubborn and stiff-necked." He explained that the Jews are so "stubborn and stiff-necked" that we stubbornly keep our eyes focused on God.

Such misguided interpretation represents a perfect prescription for pride, and pride is a killer. It kills the possibility of any real gratefulness for God. It so exalts the self to such a height that there remains little room for God at the top and for the forgiveness He achieved through the death of His Son.

Instead, a Biblical knowledge of the extent of God's love produces gratefulness, which is so necessary for our spiritual growth. It also enables us to reciprocate God's love and to cement this eternally nurturing relationship.

WORKS CITED

Alshekh, Rabbi Moshe
www.jewsforjesus.org/publications/issues/issues-v07-n09/what-the-prophet-said-what-the-rabbis-said/

Mann, Daniel, *"Was There Forgiveness Under the Mosaic Covenant"*
www.mannsword.blogspot.com/2019/03/chapter-11-was-there-forgiveness-under.html

Neubauer, Adolf, *The Fifty-Third Chapter of Isaiah: According to Jewish Interpreters,* (New York: KTAV Publishing House, 1969)

Singer, Rabbi Tovia
www.outreachjudaism.org

Strobel, Lee, *The Case for the Real Jesus*, (Grand Rapids: Zondervan, 2007)

The Zohar,
www.zohar.com/article/source-healing

Chapter 12

RABBIS CLAIM THAT THE SHEDDING OF BLOOD WAS UNNECESSARY FOR FORGIVENESS

The Hebrew Scriptures claim that the shedding of blood was necessary for God to forgive sin:

- "For the life of the flesh is in the blood, and I have given it for you on the altar to make atonement for your souls, for it is the blood that makes atonement by the life." (*Leviticus 17:11*)

Many other verses make the same claim in regards to animal sacrifice (substitutionary atonement; *Leviticus 1:4; 4:4, 15, 29, 334:20; 4:26; 4:31; 4:35; 5:4-13; Numbers14:18-20; 15:25*). According to the New Testament, forgiveness also *requires* the sacrifice of a substitute: "The law requires that nearly everything be cleansed with blood, and without the shedding of blood there is no forgiveness" (*Hebrews 9:22*). However, since the destruction of the Temple in 70 AD, Orthodox Judaism has tended to regard the Old Testament sacrifices as *unnecessary*. In favor of this point of view, Rabbi David Rosen writes:

- "Judaism does not accept the idea of vicarious [substitutionary] atonement. We can only atone for our own sins and are responsible for our own actions." (Rosen,109-110)

If animal sacrifice *is* necessary, and the Temple no longer exists, then the Christian claim that Messiah has fulfilled and replaced them becomes embarrassingly compelling. This represents a threat to Judaism. Well, if animal sacrifice wasn't necessary, why then had God commanded it? For its symbolic value! Rosen writes:

- Our ancient sages affirm that… "sincere repentance and works of lovingkindness (charity) are the real intercessors before God's throne" (TB Shabbat 32A) and that "sincere repentance is the equivalent to the rebuilding of the Temple, the restoration of the altar and the offering of *all* the sacrifices" (TB Sanhedrin 43B). In terms of Jewish understanding of the sacrificial rites in the temple, while the blood of the sacrifice did indeed represent life, it was seen precisely in a representational role symbolizing "the complete yielding up of the worshipper's life to God" (Hertz, Pentateuch and Haftorahs) (Rosen, 109)

The New Testament *also* understands the sacrificial system as symbolic (but also *mandatory*), a foreshadowing of the once-and-for-all substitutionary offering of God's Son. Instead, much of Rabbinic Judaism maintains that it represents the yielded life. The Orthodox Jewish columnist, David Klinghoffer, also argues in favor of divine forgiveness without blood:

- …the idea that penitence was not enough would have come as a surprise to the large majority of first-century Jews, who lived in the Diaspora and therefore had no regular access to the Temple rites. In not availing themselves of these rites at all times, they were relying on scripture, which taught that forgiveness could be secured without sacrifice. (Klinghoffer,111)

Klinghoffer supports this claim by citing Solomon's prayer at the consecration of the Temple as proof:

- "…and *when* they return to You with all their heart and with all their soul in the land of their enemies who led them away captive, and pray to You toward their land which You gave to their fathers, the city which You have chosen and the temple which I have built for Your name: then hear in heaven Your dwelling place their prayer and their supplication, and maintain their cause, and <u>forgive</u> Your people who have sinned against You, and all their transgressions which they have transgressed against You; and grant them compassion before those who took them captive, that they may have compassion on them." (*1 Kings 8:48-50*).

For Klinghoffer, this constitutes proof that a sacrificial offering isn't necessary. This is odd. How could Solomon, on the one hand, bless the inauguration of his costly, God-ordained Temple, while, at the same time, preach that the Temple wasn't necessary? Instead, there are other ways to explain the fact that God would forgive the Israelites without an immediate Temple sacrifice. Simply because blood wasn't required at *that* time doesn't mean it wasn't required! A bank will grant a loan, if repayment is guaranteed. The loan doesn't represent a free-ride, but a *postponement* of payment. Similarly, God could postpone payment of the debt in view of the Messianic guarantor (*Genesis 15:8-21, Hebrews 9:26*), even for the sins that had formerly been committed during the first covenant (*Hebrews 9:15*).

Even though the sacrificial system was symbolic, the shedding of blood was also a *requirement* (*Leviticus 16:34*) through which God passed over Israel's sins (*Romans 3:25*). Thus, it couldn't simply be set aside or lose its potency, but had to be *fulfilled* by a once-and-for-all bloody atonement (*Hebrews 10:14*), through which God Himself would make atonement (*Deuteronomy 32:43*).

An Unnecessary System is a Wasteful System. The expenditures underlying the Temple system were tremendous. Add to this the cost of maintaining the priesthood and the lives of multitudes of animals. It seems unreasonable that this was merely as a symbol of Israel's duty to live in submission to God.

It was a Requirement. The sacrificial system had been so central to God's workings with Israel that Moses and Aaron informed Pharaoh,

- "The God of the Hebrews has met with us. Please, let us go three days' journey into the desert and sacrifice to the LORD our God, lest He fall upon us with pestilence or with the sword." (*Exodus 5:3*)

Either Israel would sacrifice animals or they would be sacrificed. Christian apologist, Michael Brown, correctly concludes, "The very reason God gave for calling his people out of Egypt was to offer sacrifices to him." He adds:

- A careful study of the Five Books of Moses indicates that more chapters are devoted to the subject of sacrifices and offerings than to the subjects of Sabbath observance, high holy days, idolatry, adultery, murder, and theft combined. (*Answering Jewish Objections to Jesus*, vol. Two (Grand Rapids, Baker Books, 2007), (Brown,73.)

Indeed, Moses explicitly states that the blood offering was *necessary* to cover or atone for sins (*Leviticus 17:11*). Sacrifice was never optional. When the Angel of Death destroyed the firstborn from the land of Egypt, he passed over and spared those Israelite homes that had the blood of the offering upon them (*Exodus 12:23*). Any firstborn without the blood on his doorposts would have been killed. Blood was also required to cover all the sins of Israel (*Leviticus 16:21-22*) in accordance with the New Testament (*Hebrews 9:22*).

Anti-Christian-Missionary, Rabbi Tovia Singer, also asserts that animal sacrifice was unnecessary: "The prophets loudly declared to the Jewish people that the contrite prayer of the penitent sinner replaces the sacrificial system..." He assumes that since Israel no longer had its Temple, prayer and repentance would now suffice. He cites *Hosea 14:2-3* to prove that the sacrificial system had been replaced by "words":

- Take words with you, and return to the LORD. Say to Him, "Take away all iniquity; Receive *us* graciously, for we will offer the sacrifices ('bulls' in Hebrew) of our lips." (www.outreachjudaism.org/jesusdeath.html)

Singer is correct in pointing out that Hosea foresees "words" replacing the offering of "bulls." However, this change is associated with the Cross and God's declaration that "I will heal their backsliding, I will love them freely, for My anger has turned away from him" (*Hosea 14:4*). Therefore, it wasn't a matter of blood sacrifices being unnecessary, but rather *fulfilled* by the Messianic atonement!

There is no Indication that Sacrificial Offerings were ever Set Aside under the Mosaic Covenant. There is nothing in Moses' Law that suggests that sacrifices were optional (Leviticus 5:12) or that they would be abrogated apart from the Messianic atonement of Jesus. However, there are a number of verses that communicate God's displeasure with the offerings (*Psalm 50:8-15; Proverbs 15:8; 21:3; Isaiah 1:11-17; Jeremiah 7:23; Amos 5:21-27; Hosea 6:6*). However, these in no way indicate that God was doing away with offerings, leaving no substitutionary blood offering in their place. Instead, these verses can be explained in either of two other ways. First, God's displeasure didn't reflect a disdain for the offerings themselves but for the hypocrisy of the offerors. *Psalm 51:16-19* illustrates this:

- "For You do not desire sacrifice, or else I would give it; You do not delight in burnt offering. The sacrifices of God are a broken spirit, a broken and a contrite heart-- these, O God, You will not despise…Then You shall be pleased with the sacrifices of righteousness, with burnt offering and whole burnt offering; then they shall offer bulls on Your altar."

God was "pleased...with burnt offerings" when they were offered with a broken and repentant heart. However, when offered hypocritically, God refused to hear even the prayers of Israel (*Isaiah 1:15*). In this regard, the highly regarded Jewish thinker, Abraham Joshua Heschel, wrote,

- "Of course, the prophets did not condemn the practice of sacrifice in itself; otherwise we should have to conclude that Isaiah intended to discourage the practice of prayer...Men may not drown out the cries of the oppressed with the noise of hymns, nor buy off the Lord with increased offerings. The prophets disparaged the cult [of animal sacrifice] when it became a substitute for righteousness." (Brown, 86)

Second, the other verses that assert that God didn't desire the blood of animals (even though He commanded it) are explained by recognizing that animal blood was merely a symbol of the ultimate Messianic offering. Israel had a dim understanding that something had to take the place of the Mosaic system and that the repeated offering of the same sacrifices only gave Israel a temporary reprieve (*Hebrews 10.1-4*). They had also been graphically instructed by the Temple and offerings that intimacy with God was not yet a reality. They could not enter into God's presence (nor did they dare to!), and yet, they had been promised betrothal to their God (*Hosea 2:18-19*). Furthermore, they had been promised a "New Covenant" through which their sins would truly and permanently be forgiven (*Jeremiah 31:31-34*). Consistent with this understanding, *Psalm 40:6-8* declares that Israel's God was preparing a sacrifice that would put an end to all other sacrifices:

- *"Sacrifice and offering You did not desire*, but a **body** You have prepared for Me. *In burnt offerings and sacrifices for sin You had no pleasure*. Then I said, 'Behold, **I have come**—in the volume of the book it is written of Me—to do Your will, O God.'" (*Hebrews 10:5-7* quoting *Psalm 40:6-8*).

After the two times where *Psalm 40* dismisses animal sacrifice, it then presents a human body, suggesting that the latter sacrifice will take the place of the former. This shouldn't have been foreign to Israelite ears. They had often been promised, starting with Moses (*Deuteronomy 32:43*), that God Himself would ultimately atone for Israel's sins.

It was Never a Matter of *Either* Blood Sacrifice or Repentance. Although Job had never been short on animal sacrifices, Elihu counseled him that a special ransom was required *in addition* to repentance (*Job 33:24-28*). However, Tovia Singer claims that there are three types of atonement (sacrifice, repentance, alms), and that any one will suffice! However, this is contradicted by the fact that any one of them was *incapable* of bringing forgiveness:

> Speak to the children of Israel: "When a man or woman commits any sin that men commit in unfaithfulness against the LORD, and that person is guilty, then he shall (1) confess the sin which he has committed. He shall (2) make restitution for his trespass in full…in addition to the (3) ram of the atonement with which atonement is made for him. (*Numbers 5:6-8; Leviticus 5:5-6*).

Gerald Sigal erroneously writes, "It is clear from the Scriptures that sin is removed through genuine remorse and sincere repentance." In support, he cites Micah 6:8, stating that the Lord requires justice and mercy, (Sigal, 16). However, this also falls short of proving that sacrifice isn't part of the equation.

157

Blood atonement, *without* confession and repentance, never accomplished anything (*Amos 5:21-24*). Nevertheless, it was still *mandatory*. There is no Biblical evidence that it was or could be simply set aside apart from the Messiah's coming. After surveying the rabbinic literature, Michael Brown concludes:

- It was only after the Temple was destroyed [in 70 AD] that the Talmudic rabbis came up with the concept that God had provided other forms of atonement aside from blood. (Brown, 112)

There had to be the payment of a ransom. Even in the midst of God's earliest response to humankind's sin, a ransom was cryptically provided when *He* replaced the first couple's inadequate fig leaves with animal skins (*Genesis 3:21*), foreshadowing His Messianic endgame (*Isaiah 61:10*).

A ransom is inseparably and necessarily connected to Israel's return to God (*Isaiah 35:10; 51:10-11; 48:20*):

- "...He who scattered Israel will gather him, and keep him as a shepherd *does* his flock." For the LORD has redeemed Jacob, and ransomed him from the hand of one stronger than he." (*Jeremiah 31:10-11*).

God Himself would have to pay the ransom. The Israelite couldn't afford it (*Psalm 49:7-9*)! So God Himself would pay the price (*Psalm 49:15*):

- "I have blotted out, like a thick cloud, your transgressions, and like a cloud, your sins. Return to Me, for I have redeemed you." (*Isaiah 44:22*)

Without God's ransom, Israel couldn't return to God (*Psalm 65:3-5; 78:38; 130:7-8; Deuteronomy 32:43; Isaiah 54:5-8; Hosea 13:12-14*). Although repentance is necessary, it isn't sufficient (*Isaiah 59:16-20*). *Psalm 24* offers a graphic, if perhaps cryptic demonstration of this principle. It asks the question, "Who may stand in His holy place!" The answer is discouraging—only the perfect (*Psalm 15*)! Because of this dismal response, even the gates are hanging their heads in despair, until the mysterious appearance of the "King of Glory" entering through the Temple gate into *God's* presence to make intercession!

Messiah would pay with His own blood. Singer asserts, "…nor does Scripture ever tell us that an innocent man can die as an atonement for the sins of the wicked." However, according to the Zohar, the most-esteemed Jewish mystical book:

- The children of the world are members of one another, and when the Holy One desires to give healing to the world, He smites one just man amongst them, and for his sake heals all the rest [according to *Isaiah 53:5*—Zohar]. (Brown, 157)

Israel's salvation depended upon Messiah's substitutionary atoning death and *not* upon the Israelites sufficiently yielding themselves:

- "Break forth into joy, sing together…For the LORD has comforted His people, He has redeemed Jerusalem. The LORD has made bare His holy arm…"(*Isaiah 52:9-10; 59:16; 63:5*).

His "holy arm," the Son (*Isaiah 53:1*), will pay the price:

- "But he was pierced for our transgressions, he was crushed for our iniquities; the <u>punishment that brought us peace was upon him</u>, and by <u>his wounds we are healed</u>. We all, like sheep, have gone astray, each of us has turned to his own way; and the LORD has <u>laid on</u>

159

<u>him the iniquity of us all</u>." (*Isaiah 53:5-7; Psalm 40:6-8; Daniel; 9:24-27; Zechariah 12:10-13:1, 7; Psalm 22, 69*)

Singer maintains that God's provision of a ram in the place of Isaac (*Genesis 22*) proved that He would never accept a human sacrifice:

- "When Abraham was ready to sacrifice Isaac, the Almighty admonished him that He did not want the human sacrifice...The Almighty's directive—that He only wanted animal sacrifices rather than human sacrifices—was immediately understood. This teaching has never departed from the mind and soul of the faithful children of Israel."

This, however, wasn't the lesson that Israel learned, but rather the opposite - that *God* would provide: "And Abraham called the name of the place, The-LORD-Will-Provide; as it is said to this day, 'In the Mount of The LORD it shall be provided'" (*Genesis 22:14*). However, it was more than just a matter of God's faithfulness. It was also prophetic, Gospel-centered! The mountain wasn't named "The Lord-*has*-provided," but that He *will* provide! Nor would God provide *in general*! Instead, God would provide a greater offering (overshadowing what He had already provided), "in the mount of the Lord," a phrase that "referred to the Temple mount in Jerusalem!" (*The NIV Study Bible,* 38) This became the very place that God did provide on the Cross at Calvary.

Rather than symbolizing our yielded lives, the animal sacrifices symbolized the very opposite—our *un*-yielded, condemnation-worthy lives. That's why every Israelite had to confess his sins upon the head of the sacrificial animal, which paid the price for his un-yieldedness. In this way, the Israelite was taught that his hope couldn't be in his own righteousness or virtue (*Deuteronomy 27:26*), but in a perfect substitution.

The rabbis missed the message of their Bible in many regards, while the uneducated writers of the New Testament understood it, but how? Simply this - they had been inspired by the Holy Spirit.

WORKS CITED

Brown, Michael, *Answering Jewish Objections to Jesus*, Vol. Two (Grand Rapids: Baker Books, 2007)

Kendall, R.T and Rosen, David, *The Christian and the Pharisee* (New York: Faith Words, 2006)

NIV Study Bible (Grand Rapids: Zondervan, 1985)

Sigal, Gerald, *The Jew and the Christian Missionary*: *A Jewish Response to Missionary Christianity,* (New York: KTAV Publishing House, Inc., 1981)

Singer, Tovia Rabbi
www.outreachjudaism.org/jesusdeath.html

Chapter 13

HAVE SOME GONE SO FAR THAT THEY ARE NO LONGER ELIGIBLE TO RECEIVE FORGIVENESS?

Jesus was willing to forgive all. Even on the Cross, He prayed: "Father, forgive them, for they know not what they do" (*Luke 23:34*). However, Jewish scholars and rabbis tend to believe that some have just gone too far to be forgiven. For example, when Jews celebrate Purim, they spit when the name of Haman is mentioned. This symbolizes their belief that Haman, who had wanted to destroy the Jewish people, as recorded in the *Book of Esther*, had lost any possibility of receiving forgiveness.

Likewise, Elie Wiesel, winner of the Nobel Peace Prize, admitted that Jews are not willing to forgive all evil-doers. Rabbi Meir Y. Soloveichik also confessed:

- During my weekly coffees with my friend Fr. Jim White, an Episcopal priest, there was one issue to which our conversation would incessantly turn, and one on which we could never agree: Is an utterly evil man—Hitler, Stalin, Osama bin Laden—deserving of a theist's love? I could never stomach such a notion, while Fr. Jim would argue passionately in favor of the proposition. Judaism, I would argue, does demand love for our fellow human beings, but only to an extent. 'Hate' is not always synonymous with the terribly sinful. While Moses commanded us 'not to hate our brother in our hearts,' a man's immoral actions can serve to sever the bonds of brotherhood."
  (*www.firstthings.com/article/2003/02/the-virtue-of-hate*)

Soloveichik offered two examples of people who had crossed the line. Samson had finally been captured by the Philistines, who had cut his hair to deprive him of his strength and had plucked out his eyes. The Philistines had chained him to the pillars of their stadium before a sellout crowd who came to see him tormented. However, Samson prayed:

- "O Lord GOD, remember me, I pray! Strengthen me, I pray, just this once, O God, that I may with one blow take vengeance on the Philistines for my two eyes!" (*Judges 16:28*).

The Lord answered his prayer, and Samson brought down the stadium causing thousands of deaths. Soloveichik reasoned that God had granted his prayer because the Philistines were beyond forgiveness. He therefore wrote:

- Indeed, the contrast between the two Testaments indicates that this is the case: Jesus' words ['Forgive them for they know not what they do'] could not be more different than Samson's."

According to Soloveichik, this proved that the NT had veered far from the Hebrew Scriptures. He then offered the example of King Agag of the Amalekites, who Saul had spared in opposition to God's instructions.

- [The Prophet] Samuel said [to King Saul], "Although you were once small in your own eyes, did you not become the head of the tribes of Israel? The LORD anointed you king over Israel. And he sent you on a mission, saying, 'Go and completely destroy those wicked people, the Amalekites; make war on them until you have wiped them out.' Why did you not obey the LORD? Why did you pounce on the plunder and do evil in the eyes of the LORD?" (*1 Samuel 15:17-19*)

- Then Samuel said, "Bring me Agag king of the Amalekites." Agag came to him confidently, thinking, "Surely the bitterness of death is past." But Samuel said, "As your sword has made women childless, so will your mother be childless among women." And Samuel put Agag to death before the LORD at Gilgal. (*1 Samuel 15:32-33*)

Once again, Soloveichik reasoned that Agag was no longer eligible for forgiveness and was therefore executed. However, Soloveichik wrongly assumes that forgiveness and temporal (earthly) punishment are mutually exclusive. He assumes that if God forgives, He will not also punish. However, there are many Biblical examples that show that God will forgive and still punish. He forgave King David for his adultery and murder of Bathsheba's husband Uriah. However, He would also punish David:

- David said to [the Prophet] Nathan, "I have sinned against the LORD." And Nathan said to David, "The LORD also has put away your sin; you shall not die. Nevertheless, because by this deed you have utterly scorned the LORD, the child who is born to you shall die." (*2 Samuel 12:13-14*)

If God can punish but also forgive upon confession of sins, the fact that He had punished the Philistines and Agag didn't mean that they had gone so far that they could no longer be forgiven. Instead, they never confessed their sins – the necessary requirement to receive forgiveness.

Instead, Israelites were expected to show mercy to even their enemies. There is no indication that these commands excluded really bad enemies:

- "If you meet your enemy's ox or his donkey going astray, you shall surely bring it back to him again. If you see the donkey of one who hates you lying under its burden, and you would refrain from helping it, you shall surely help him with it." (*Exodus 23:4-5*)

164

- If your enemy is hungry, give him food to eat; if he is thirsty, give him water to drink. In doing this, you will heap burning coals on his head, and the LORD will reward you. (*Proverbs 25:21-22*)

If God required mercy for the worst of enemies, then we should expect at least the same from Him. Jesus had commanded us to be perfect as our heavenly Father is perfect (*Matthew 5:48*). Therefore, being merciful to the worst of people would be something that God would do. Jesus also explained:

- "But I say to you, Love your enemies and pray for those who persecute you, so that you may be sons of your Father who is in heaven. For he makes his sun rise on the evil and on the good, and sends rain on the just and on the unjust." (*Matthew 5:44-45*)

(A strange anomaly should be noted. The God had never asked the Israelite to forgive. Perhaps this is because a complete forgiveness had not yet been accomplished on the Cross.)

Soloveichik also seems to overlook the fact that God had forgiven the worst people. King Manasseh had arguably been the worst of Judah's kings. He had reigned in Judah for more than 50 years and killed so many of the righteous as to create a veritable bloodbath:

- "Because Manasseh king of Judah has done these abominations (he has acted *more wickedly* than all the Amorites who were before him, and has also made Judah sin with his idols), therefore thus says the LORD God of Israel: 'Behold, I am bringing such calamity upon Jerusalem and Judah...'" (*2 Kings 21:10-12*).

165

However, after he had been captured and imprisoned by the Assyrians, he repented and the Lord evidently forgave him:

- "Now when he was in affliction, he implored the LORD his God, and humbled himself greatly before the God of his fathers, and prayed to Him; and He received his entreaty, heard his supplication, and brought him back to Jerusalem into his kingdom. Then Manasseh knew that the LORD was God" (*2 Chronicles 33:12-13*).

This would suggest that the Lord would forgive any who would Sincerely call upon Him:

- And it shall come to pass that everyone who calls on the name of the LORD shall be saved. For in Mount Zion and in Jerusalem there shall be those who escape, as the LORD has said, and among the survivors shall be those whom the LORD calls. (*Joel 2:32*)

This is the same hope that the Lord extends to His errant people Israel:

- "O Israel, hope in the LORD; for with the LORD there is mercy, and with Him is abundant redemption. And He shall redeem Israel from *all* his iniquities" (*Psalm 130:7-8*).

- "I will cleanse them from all their iniquity by which they have sinned against Me, and I will pardon *all* their iniquities by which they have sinned and by which they have transgressed against Me" (*Jeremiah 33:8; also 31:34; Isaiah 43:25*).

There were even times that Israel was worse than her pagan neighbors. However, this did not make them ineligible for forgiveness and salvation:

166

- "Therefore thus says the Lord GOD: 'Because you have multiplied disobedience more than the nations that are all around you, have not walked in My statutes nor kept My judgments, nor even done according to the judgments of the nations that are all around you...'" (*Ezekiel 5:7*)... "Your elder sister is Samaria, who dwells with her daughters to the north of you; and your younger sister, who dwells to the south of you, is Sodom and her daughters. You did not walk in their ways nor act according to their abominations; but, as if that were too little, you became more corrupt than they in all your ways" (*Ezekiel 16:46-47*).

Despite the gravity of their sins, God would remain faithful to Israel. Of course, Israel would have to turn from their sins and turn back to God:

- "If my people who are called by my name humble themselves, and pray and seek my face and turn from their wicked ways, then I will hear from heaven and will forgive their sin and heal their land." (*2 Chronicles 7:14; Isaiah 55:7; 59:20*)

Nevertheless, in the end, God will unilaterally change Israel in order to forgive them. He will initiate their return without waiting for Israel to turn to Him:

- "Behold, I will gather them from all the countries to which I drove them in my anger and my wrath and in great indignation. I will bring them back to this place, and I will make them dwell in safety...I will give them one heart and one way, that they may fear me forever, for their own good and the good of their children after them. I will make with them an everlasting covenant, that I will not turn away from doing good to them. And I will put the fear of me in their hearts, that they may not turn from me. I will rejoice in doing them good, and I will plant them in this land in faithfulness, with all my heart and all my soul." (*Jeremiah 32:37-41*)

God will pour out His Spirit and bring Israel to mourning and repentance:

- "And I will pour out on the house of David and the inhabitants of Jerusalem a spirit of grace and pleas for mercy, so that, when they look on me, on him whom they have pierced, they shall mourn for him, as one mourns for an only child, and weep bitterly over him, as one weeps over a firstborn...The land shall mourn, each family by itself." (*Zechariah 12:10,12*)

I don't think that Soloveichik realizes that when he disqualifies the Hamans of this world, he is also disqualifying his own people, contrary to the mercy of God. In contrast to Soloveichik, God pleads with His rebellious and unfaithful people:

- Go, and proclaim these words toward the north, and say, "'Return, faithless Israel, declares the LORD. I will not look on you in anger, for I am merciful, declares the LORD; I will not be angry forever. Only acknowledge your guilt, that you rebelled against the LORD your God and scattered your favors among foreigners under every green tree, and that you have not obeyed my voice, declares the LORD. Return, O faithless children, declares the LORD; for I am your master; I will take you, one from a city and two from a family, and I will bring you to Zion. (*Jeremiah 3:12-14*)

WORKS CITED

Soloveichik, Rabbi Meir Y.
www.firstthings.com/article/2003/02/the-virtue-of-hate

Chapter 14

ARE WE STILL UNDER THE LAW OF MOSES?

Strangely, some groups that believe in Jesus insist that we are still under this Law. One such collection of groups is the *Hebrew Roots Movement*. Although they concede that no one can be saved or made righteous by works of the law, they maintain that believers in Jesus are still required to keep the OT laws for the purpose of fellowship with God:

- We believe that Moshiach Yahshua [Jesus] taught all His true followers both Jew and non-Jew that all the precepts of written Torah are eternally binding. Moshiach Yahshua, never negated Torah, but expects and commands us to follow Torah (Matthew-Mattityahu 5:17-19), so as to continually express and renew our love for Him by our obedience." (www.watchman.org)

Does Jesus teach that we are still under the Law? Not really:

- "Do not think that I have come to abolish the Law or the Prophets; I have not come to abolish them but to <u>fulfill</u> them. For truly, I say to you, until heaven and earth pass away, not an iota, not a dot, will pass from the Law until all is <u>accomplished</u>." (*Matthew 5:17-18; ESV*)

It certainly seems like Jesus "fulfilled" or "accomplished" the Law on the Cross, when He proclaimed that "it is finished," and the veil of the Temple was rent in two, signifying that the Mosaic Law separation between God and His people had been removed.

However, Jesus had been secretive about many things including His Deity, His Messiah-ship, the Atonement, and His instituting the New Covenant, at least until the end:

169

- And he took a cup, and when he had given thanks he gave it to them, saying, "Drink of it, all of you, for this is my blood of the covenant, which is poured out for many for the forgiveness of sins. I tell you I will not drink again of this fruit of the vine until that day when I drink it new with you in my Father's kingdom." (*Matthew 26:27-29; Mark 14:24; Luke 22:20*)

Jesus gave many other indications that the Mosaic Covenant was coming to an end. He had equated His body with a new "temple" of God, the new place that God's people would meet Him:

- So the Jews said to him, "What sign do you show us for doing these things?" Jesus answered them, "Destroy this temple, and in three days I will raise it up." The Jews then said, "It has taken forty-six years to build this temple, and will you raise it up in three days?" But he was speaking about the temple of his body. (*John 2:18-21*)

He even indicated that He was greater than the Temple:

- "I tell you, something greater than the temple is here. And if you had known what this means, 'I desire mercy, and not sacrifice,' you would not have condemned the guiltless. For the Son of Man is lord of the Sabbath." (*Matthew 12:6-8*)

Not only did Jesus declare Himself greater than the Mosaic Temple, but by declaring Himself "lord of the Sabbath," He was also declaring Himself above the Mosaic Law.

Jesus even cryptically dismissed the Mosaic Law, teaching against its stipulations:

- And he said to them, "Then are you also without understanding? Do you not see that whatever goes into a person from outside cannot defile him, since it enters not his heart but his stomach, and is expelled?" Thus he declared all foods clean. (Mark 7:18-19)

This teaching cryptically contradicted Mosaic Law that specified that certain foods would defile when ingested. Defilement also had been caused by contact with the dead, blood and with certain diseases. Mark understood that Jesus had been preparing His disciples for the fact that the Mosaic Law would soon be fulfilled.

It also seemed that Jesus was teaching that people are also clean, despite their health condition. He illustrated this by touching many of the infirmed who, under Mosaic Law, would have defiled Him with their contact.

On one occasion, a woman with a constant issue of blood secretly touched Jesus' garment, hoping that she'd be healed. However, Jesus exposed her. She was frightened and shamed, because He had exposed her sin. However, instead of condemning her, as Mosaic Law required:

- Jesus turned, and seeing her he said, "Take heart, daughter; your faith has made you well." And instantly the woman was made well. (*Matthew 9:20*)

Similarly, when Jesus sent out His disciples to minister, He never instructed them to teach the Law, but rather *His* teachings:

- "Go therefore and make disciples of all nations, baptizing them in the name of the Father and of the Son and of the Holy Spirit, teaching them to observe all that I have commanded you. And behold, I am with you always, to the end of the age." (*Matthew 28:19-20*)

If He had intended that His disciples would have to teach that they were *still* under the Mosaic Law or, at least, had to follow all of its stipulations, it is curious that He hadn't been plain about this.

Instead, in the *Gospel of Luke*, He commissioned His disciples:

- ... "Thus it is written, that the Christ should suffer and on the third day rise from the dead, and that repentance and forgiveness of sins should be proclaimed in his name to all nations, beginning from Jerusalem." (*Luke 24:46-47*)

Again, no instructions to preach Moses! Jesus' commission of His Apostles in the Gospel of John was even more dismissive of the Mosaic Law. Instead of the Levites administering God's forgiveness, it would now be His Apostles:

- Jesus said to them again, "Peace be with you. As the Father has sent me, even so I am sending you." And when he had said this, he breathed on them and said to them, "Receive the Holy Spirit. If you forgive the sins of any, they are forgiven them; if you withhold forgiveness from any, it is withheld." (*John 20:21-23*)

On the Mount of the Transfiguration, the three Apostles were shaken by a radical revelation they had received:

- ..."Jesus took with him Peter and James, and John his brother, and led them up a high mountain by themselves. And he was transfigured before them, and his face shone like the sun, and his clothes became white as light. And behold, there appeared to them Moses and Elijah, talking with him." (*Matthew 17:1-3*)

This passage only indicates that Jesus had been transfigured and *not* Moses and Elijah, who had been regarded as the greatest Israelites. However, the Apostles were blind to its significance. Peter seemed to regard them as equals and suggested that they erect three dwellings, one for each. However, a divine voice from heaven corrected Peter's mistaken assumption:

- He was still speaking when, behold, a bright cloud overshadowed them, and a voice from the cloud said, "This is my beloved Son, with whom I am well pleased; listen to him." (*Matthew 17:5*)

The Apostles were terrified. When they opened their eyes, they saw Jesus standing alone. Undoubtedly, He was the "beloved Son" whom they must obey. This was contrary to their expectations. Instead, the voice should have said, "Listen to Moses and to his covenant" or at least, "Listen to both of them." Evidently, the heavenly voice had been instructing them that Jesus was greater than Moses, and His teachings would soon take precedence over those of Moses. However, since Jesus had not yet made atonement for the sins of the world, Jesus instructed them to tell no one about what they had learned until He had risen. After all, until the Cross, they were still under Moses.

As we advance further into the NT after the Cross, the teachings become more explicit that we are no longer under the Law. This question had become hot:

- "Some believers who belonged to the party of the Pharisees rose up and said, 'It is necessary to circumcise them [Gentiles] and to order them to keep the law of Moses.'" (*Acts 15:5*)

However, a council was convened in Jerusalem to decide this matter.

173

- And after there had been much debate, Peter stood up and said to them, "Brothers, you know that in the early days God made a choice among you, that by my mouth the Gentiles should hear the word of the gospel and believe. And God, who knows the heart, bore witness to them, by giving them the Holy Spirit just as he did to us, and he made no distinction between us and them, having cleansed their hearts by faith. Now, therefore, why are you putting God to the test by placing a yoke on the neck of the disciples that neither our fathers nor we have been able to bear?"(*Acts 15:7-10*)

Peter argued that, now, Law-keeping was an unnecessary burden. James, the head of the council concurred:

- "Therefore my judgment is that we should not trouble those of the Gentiles who turn to God." (*Acts 15:19*)

Instead of requiring the Gentiles to follow the Law, James concluded that they should merely abstain from those Gentile practices that would alienate them from the Jews.

In light of this, could it possibly be, as some allege, that Jewish believers are required to follow certain commandments, like circumcision, while the Gentile believers are not? It doesn't appear so. Instead, the NT emphasis is about maintaining the unity of the Body of Christ for which God had died to create. Therefore, Paul urged the Church:

- ..."to maintain the unity of the Spirit in the bond of peace. There is one body and one Spirit—just as you were called to the one hope that belongs to your call— one Lord, one faith, one baptism, one God and Father of all, who is over all and through all and in all." (*Ephesians 4:3-6*)

This was accomplished:

- ..."by abolishing the law of commandments expressed in ordinances, that he might create in himself one new man in place of the two, so making peace, and might reconcile us both to God in one body through the cross, thereby killing the hostility." (*Ephesians 2:15-16*)

It is therefore unthinkable that certain believers would be *required* to be circumcised and others not – a theological basis for disunity. Sadly, we sometimes observe this disunity today.

In Paul's eyes, Peter "stood condemned" because his conduct was not in line with the truth – the unity of the Body:

- "For before certain men came from James, he [Peter] was eating with the Gentiles; but when they came he drew back and separated himself, fearing the circumcision party. And the rest of the Jews acted hypocritically along with him, so that even Barnabas was led astray by their hypocrisy." (*Galatians 2:12-13*)

According to Paul, Peter's behavior had violated the truth of the Gospel – the unity and brotherhood of all believers. If this is so, then the belief of some Jewish believers that they must still follow the law of Moses, while Gentiles need not, would certainly disrupt the unity of the Body of Christ.

Paul consistently taught that we are no longer under the Law and that being under the Law precluded being under Christ:

- "Likewise, my brothers, you also have died to the law through the body of Christ, so that you may belong to another, to him who has been raised from the dead, in order that we may bear fruit for God. For while we were living in the flesh, our sinful passions, aroused by the law, were at work in our members to bear fruit for death. But now we are released from the law, having

175

died to that which held us captive, so that we serve in the new way of the Spirit and not in the old way of the written code." (*Romans 7:4-6*)

According to Paul, being under the Covenant of the Law was to be in bondage:

- "For the law of the Spirit of life has set you free in Christ Jesus from the [Mosaic] law of sin and death." (*Romans 8:2*)

Instead, the bondage of the Covenant of the Law was necessary to prepare us for our liberty in Christ:

- "Now before faith came, we were held captive under the law, imprisoned until the coming faith would be revealed. So then, the law was our guardian until Christ came, in order that we might be justified by faith. But now that faith has come, we are no longer under a guardian." (*Galatians 3:23-25*)

This doesn't mean that the stipulations of the Law are no longer the Word of God or even that they are no longer normative for us all. There are stipulations we must continue to obey:

- "Do we then overthrow the law by this faith? By no means! On the contrary, we uphold the law." (*Romans 3:31*)

Laws, like those of The Ten Commandments, have been carried over into the New Covenant and should now be obeyed *Christologically*. For instance, we are still to keep the Sabbath, but now we have great freedom as to how to keep it:

- "One person esteems one day as better than another, while another esteems all days alike. Each one should be fully convinced in his own mind." (*Romans 14:5*)

Nevertheless, some commandments, like "Thou shall not kill," need no further NT re-interpretation. However, we are mandated to understand the Old through the lens of the New. After Paul taught that Christ had fulfilled the Law, he provided us with a principle to understand and apply their ongoing stipulations:

- "God made alive together with him, having forgiven us all our trespasses, by canceling the record of debt that stood against us with its legal demands. This he set aside, nailing it to the cross... Therefore let no one pass judgment on you in questions of food and drink, or with regard to a festival or a new moon or a Sabbath. These are a shadow of the things to come, but the substance belongs to Christ." (*Colossians 2:13-14, 16-17*)

The Law contained both shadow and substance, those teachings that remain Christologically normative for us today. Even the shadows or types of Christ remain instructive for us, but we need not rebuild the Temple and make animal sacrifices.

Those aspects of the Law that still provide moral guidance now fall under the "Law of Christ":

- "For though I am free from all, I have made myself a servant to all, that I might win more of them. To the Jews I became as a Jew, in order to win Jews. To those under the law I became as one under the law (though not being myself under the law) that I might win those under the law. To those outside the law I became as one outside the law (not being outside the law of

God but under the law of Christ) that I might win those outside the law." (*1 Corinthians 9:19-21*)

Paul contrasted being under the Law and being under Christ. It is either one master or the other. There cannot be two. (*Matthew 6:24*)

The *Book of Hebrews* explicitly indicates that we are no longer under the Law. It even goes further - that the Covenant of the Law has placed away, having been replaced by the New:

- "In speaking of a new covenant, he makes the first one obsolete. And what is becoming obsolete and growing old is ready to vanish away." (*Hebrews 8:13*)

This suggests that even the Jews, who don't believe that the Messiah has come, are also no longer under the Mosaic Covenant:

- "He does away with the first in order to establish the second. And by that will we have been sanctified through the offering of the body of Jesus Christ once for all." (*Hebrews 10:9-10*)

It was only through Christ that even the OT saints found a complete forgiveness for their sins (*Hebrews 9:14-15*). James also suggested that we are now under a new regime, the "*law of liberty*":

- "For whoever keeps the whole law but fails in one point has become accountable for all of it. For he who said, "Do not commit adultery," also said, "Do not murder." If you do not commit adultery but do murder, you have become a transgressor of the law. So speak and so act as those who are to be judged under the law of liberty." (*James 2:10-12*)

We are now under a new regime. However, some charge that the NT represents a perversion of the teachings of the Old rather than its fulfillment. Therefore, it is imperative that we also consult the OT evidence that the Old Covenant was only meant as a temporary measure.

We even see clues of this in the Mosaic legislation, where we find that the Covenant of the Law only pertained to the Land and the theocratic State of Israel:

- "You shall not do according to all that we are doing here today, everyone doing whatever is right in his own eyes, for you have not as yet come to the rest and to the inheritance that the Lord your God is giving you." (*Deuteronomy 12:8-9*)

Moses instructed Israel that the Law wasn't fully operative while they were wondering. Joshua reflects the same:

- At that time the Lord said to Joshua, "Make flint knives and circumcise the sons of Israel a second time." (*Joshua 5:2*)

Circumcision had been the sign of the Mosaic Covenant. However, it wasn't practiced during their 40 years of wandering. Evidently, the Covenant had only pertained to their time within the Promised Land. This also suggests that it is no longer relevant.

Jeremiah wrote that there would come a time when it would no longer be remembered or maintained:

- "And when you have multiplied and been fruitful in the land, in those days, declares the Lord, they shall no more say, 'The ark of the covenant of the Lord.' It shall not come to mind or be remembered or missed; it shall not be made again. At that time Jerusalem shall be called the throne of the Lord, and all nations shall gather to it, to the presence of the Lord in Jerusalem, and they shall no more stubbornly follow their own evil heart." (*Jeremiah 3:16-17*)

The Ark of the Covenant was the banner of the Mosaic Covenant. If the Ark would not come to mind, neither would the Law.

Besides, there are many indications that it would not be able to achieve God's final goal for His people. Instead, they would continue in their uncircumcised heart (*Deuteronomy 30:6*) until the arrival of the New:

- "But to this day the Lord has not given you a heart to understand or eyes to see or ears to hear." (*Deuteronomy 29:4*)

For God to accomplish His plans, some things would have to be changed. He had promised to marry Israel. However, the relationship remained very distant. Israel could not even endure the voice of God (*Exodus 20*) or come into His presence without being struck dead, but this would have to change:

- "And I will make for them a covenant on that day with the beasts of the field, the birds of the heavens, and the creeping things of the ground. And I will abolish the bow, the sword, and war from the land, and I will make you lie down in safety. And I will betroth you to me forever. I will betroth you to me in righteousness and in justice, in steadfast love and in mercy." (*Hosea 2:18-19*)

Such an idea was foreign to the Old Covenant. A New and radically different one would be required:

- "Behold, the days are coming, declares the Lord, when I will make a new covenant with the house of Israel and the house of Judah, not like the covenant that I made with their fathers on the day when I took them by the hand to bring them out of the land of Egypt, my covenant that they broke, though I was their husband, declares the Lord. For this is the covenant that I will make with the house of Israel after those days, declares the Lord: I will put my law within them, and I will write it on their hearts. And I will be their God, and they shall be my people. And no longer shall each one teach his neighbor and each his brother, saying, 'Know the Lord,' for they shall all know me, from the least of them to the greatest, declares the Lord. For I will forgive their iniquity, and I will remember their sin no more." (*Jeremiah 31:31-34*)

In order to salvage their claim that the Old will be eternal, the rabbis maintain that the New Covenant simply represents a minor modification of the Old. However, our Lord *explicitly* tells us that the New will "*not* [be] like the covenant that I made with their fathers on the day when I took them by the hand to bring them out of the land of Egypt."

The New Covenant had to be radically different in order to fulfill the promises of God, in view of the fact that the Law had placed Israel under an inevitable curse:

- "'Cursed be anyone who does not confirm the words of this law by doing them.' And all the people shall say, 'Amen.'" (*Deuteronomy 27:26*)

However, the OT extended the Messianic hope to Israel that the promised Savior would come and take upon Himself Israel's curse (*Isaiah 53; Psalm 40, 22, 69; Daniel 9:24-27*), indicating the insufficiency of the Old Covenant.

While the other covenants - the Noahic, Abrahamic, the Davidic, and the New Covenant - are termed "everlasting," not once is the Mosaic, the Covenant of the Law, described in this way (although certain of its stipulations are regarded as everlasting.) This is surprising because the OT says far more about the Mosaic than it does about all of the others combined.

The OT *never* claims that the Covenant of the Law is eternal. Instead, it shows many signs that it is incomplete, and that it will be superseded! Nor should any believers in Christ believe that they are still bound by it. Instead, we have died to the Law through the Body of Christ (*Romans 7:4*).

Nevertheless, the rabbis claim that the Mosaic Covenant is eternal by citing Isaiah:

- "The grass withers, the flower fades, but the word of our God will stand forever." (*Isaiah 40:8*)

But what does it mean that the "word...stands forever?" While God's Word does stand forever, this is *not* the case with *His activities*. His Word reflects many stages. He created the Garden of Eden and then closed its door. He created but now sustains. He rejected Israel but will again draw them to Himself. He fed Israel with mana but them required Israel to hunt up their own food. He gave the Mosaic Covenant but then revokes it in favor of the New. None of these changes mean that God's Word has changed. They merely reflect the fact that His plan has entered into a prophesied new stage.

This next chapter will elaborate more on this decisive shift into the New Covenant.

WORKS CITED

Dunning, Craig A., *Hebrew Roots Movement*
www.watchman.org/hr.pdf

Chapter 15

THE EVERLASTING COVENANT AND THE MOSAIC COVENANT

"In that He says, "A new covenant," He has made the first obsolete.
Now what is becoming obsolete and growing old is ready
to vanish away." (*Hebrews 8:13*)

The Bible provides a wealth of evidence of a New Covenant, which will supersede the Old. However, the rabbis claim that the Mosaic Covenant will last forever and that it provides everything that Israel needs, with only perhaps some minor adjustments (*Psalm 1; 119:32, 92, 104, 127, 144*), and the Word of God doesn't change (*Isaiah 40:8*). If they are correct, then the New Testament has it all wrong, and our faith is built upon a non-existent foundation. However, Jeremiah writes:

- "Behold, the days are coming, says the LORD, when I will make a new covenant with the house of Israel and with the house of Judah-- not according to the covenant that I made with their fathers in the day that I took them by the hand to lead them out of the land of Egypt, My covenant which they broke, though I was a husband to them, says the LORD. But this is the covenant that I will make with the house of Israel after those days, says the LORD: I will put My law in their minds, and write it on their hearts; and I will be their God, and they shall be My people. No more shall every man teach his neighbor, and every man his brother, saying, 'Know the LORD,'" for they all shall know Me, from the least of them to the greatest of them, says the LORD. For I will forgive their iniquity, and their sin I will remember no more." (*Jeremiah 31:31-34; Hebrews 8:8-9*).

This New Covenant will "*not* be according to the [Mosaic] covenant." Doesn't this settle the matter? Hasn't a "New

Covenant" superseded the Old? Not according to Jewish authorities:

- "By any objective reading of the text, one fails to see any reference to a substitution of a new covenant which will supersede the old. There is nothing in Jeremiah's statement to suggest that the new covenant will contain any changes in the Law (the Mosaic Covenant)." (Sigal, 70)

However, since Jeremiah writes that God will establish a "new covenant," wouldn't this explicitly rule out the continuation of the Mosaic Covenant, which Israel continued to break (*Jeremiah 31:31-32*)? Not according to Gerald Sigal:

- "Obviously, Jeremiah's 'new covenant' is not to be viewed as a replacement of the existing (Mosaic) covenant, but merely as a figure of speech for the reinvigoration and revitalization of the old (Mosaic) covenant." (Sigal, 73)

According to Sigal, the new covenant is the Mosaic covenant with a bit of a face-lift. However, Jeremiah claims that this "new covenant" will *not* resemble the Old (*Jeremiah 31:32*). Why not? Because it was a failure, at least from the perspective of Israel's obedience to it! Israel "broke it" as naturally as breathing. It had done its job and had to be scrapped and replaced by something new.

Furthermore, when we examine the features of the "new," we find that they represent more than a mere face-lift, but a major overhaul. There will be laws (and some of them will be brought over from the Old) but they will be inscribed upon the heart, and forgiveness will be permanent, whereas under the Mosaic scheme, sacrificial offerings had to be made on a *continual* basis for the sins of the people.

What type of evidence does Sigal offer in defense of his seemingly improbable interpretation? For one thing, he says that many prophetic writings indicate that Israel would ultimately keep God's Mosaic ordinances. In support of this, he cites *Ezekiel 11:19-20*:

- "Then I will give them one heart, and I will put a new spirit within them, and take the stony heart out of their flesh, and give them a heart of flesh, that they may walk in My statutes and keep My judgments and do them; and they shall be My people, and I will be their God."

Sigal wrongly assumes that this transplant would occur under the Mosaic administration. However, Ezekiel's prophecy bears a strong resemblance to Jeremiah's prophecy of the "new covenant," which also alludes to a change in heart. There is nothing here to suggest that the Mosaic Covenant is still functioning. Instead, the very fact that God will have to unilaterally take charge and convert Israel suggests that the Mosaic wasn't able to produce. Under this system, blessing depended upon obedience. However, in the eleven chapters prior, Ezekiel paints us a portrait of Israel's unmitigated unfaithfulness. It's therefore clear that this promise of blessing isn't the result of Israel's faithfulness to the Mosaic Covenant! Had it been the dominant factor, Israel would be cursed, not blessed!

Sigal then cites *Psalm 111:7-8* and *Isaiah 40:8*. Both maintain that God's Word doesn't change. However, a change in covenants doesn't imply that God's Word had changed or had been wrong. It just implies that a new time and situation might demand a new course of action. When Israel crossed the Jordan into the Promised Land, God's activity changed--the manna ceased falling—but God's Word hadn't changed! He never promised that manna would always fall from heaven.

Sigal's other defense is more to the point:

185

- "That the covenant of old is of eternal duration, never to be rescinded or to be superseded by a new covenant, is clearly stated in *Leviticus 26:44-45*." (Sigal, 71)

If Sigal is correct about this verse, it offers powerful support for his contention that the Mosaic covenant can never be superseded, and he might then be somewhat justified in his awkward interpretation to Jeremiah. However, this isn't the message of these verses:

- "Yet for all that, when they are in the land of their enemies, I will not cast them away, nor shall I abhor them, to utterly destroy them and break My covenant with them; for I am the LORD their God. But for their sake I will remember the <u>covenant of their ancestors</u>, whom I brought out of the land of Egypt in the sight of the nations, that I might be their God: I am the LORD." (*Leviticus 26:44-45*).

Is this "covenant of their ancestors" the Mosaic covenant? Instead, the "ancestors" must refer to those who came *before* Moses, to the Patriarchs—Abraham, Isaac, and Jacob. Moses is not an ancestor to the Israelites that he had led into the desert just one short year prior! Furthermore, the Hebrew word for "ancestors" ("rishone") meaning the "first" further solidifies this conclusion. It was the Patriarchs who had been the *first* Hebrews and the *first* to receive the Promise.

Had we no other context than the above two verses, this would be enough to dismiss Sigal's assertion. However, the preceding context allows us to pin down the meaning of "covenant of their ancestors," even more precisely:

- "Then I will remember <u>my covenant with Jacob, and my covenant with Isaac and my covenant with Abraham</u> I will remember; they will accept their guilt, because they despised My judgments and because their soul abhorred My statutes," (*Leviticus 26:42-43*).

This clearly is not a reference to the Mosaic covenant, but the covenant that God had made with the *Patriarchs*, one that was still in effect. It's because of God's unchanging, *unconditional* promises to the *Patriarchs* that Israel had hope, not because of the Mosaic Covenant which brought condemnation to Israel according to their deeds. This was the prime purpose of the highly conditional Mosaic Covenant—to show Israel the extent of her damning sins and their need of a Savior (*Galatians 3:22-24*). In this, the Mosaic is diametrically opposed to the other covenants. While blessing under the Mosaic depended upon Israel's obedience, the promises to the Patriarchs were guaranteed by God Himself.

How could Sigal have made such a mistake? Weren't there other verses to which he could have appealed to make his case that the Mosaic Covenant was everlasting? If so, he doesn't seem to be aware of them. Is there any evidence that the Mosaic is everlasting and therefore won't be replaced?

This question intrigued me. Do the Scriptures consistently bear witness against the permanence of the Mosaic Covenant, the centerpiece of the Hebrew Scriptures? They should, shouldn't they?

THE MOSAIC COVENANT WAS TEMPORARY

As already mentioned, Jeremiah prophesied that God would make a "new covenant" that would not be like the Old one. Would the Old remain side-by-side with the New? Evidently not!

- "Then it shall come to pass, when you are multiplied and increased in the land in those days,' says the LORD, 'that they will say no more, 'The *ark of the covenant* of

187

the LORD.' <u>It shall not come to mind, nor shall they remember it, nor shall they visit it, nor shall it be made anymore</u>'" (*Jeremiah 3:16*).

The "ark of the covenant" represented the Mosaic Covenant. It was the receptacle for the two tablets of the Ten Commandments, the centerpiece of the Mosaic institution. When Jeremiah said that the "ark of the covenant" will "not come to mind," he was also referring to the Mosaic Covenant. Why will it not come to mind? Because it will be replaced by another system which will "feed you with knowledge and understanding" (*Jeremiah 3:15*)! If it will not be remembered, then it will certainly not be in effect!

The Mosaic is not merely limited in its duration; it is also *limited* to its Promised Land setting. Moses cautioned Israel:

- "You shall not at all do as we are doing here today-- <u>every man doing whatever is right in his own eyes</u>-- for as yet you have not come to the rest and the inheritance which the LORD your God is giving you" (*Deuteronomy 12:8-9*).

As long as Israel was not as yet in the Promised Land, they were free from many of the legal stipulations. The fact that the Israelites born during their desert wanderings had not been circumcised provides strong evidence for the fact that many of Mosaic stipulations were not being enforced prior to entering Israel (*Joshua 5:5*). If this covenant pertained only to a particular time and place, then it is difficult to argue for its permanence.

The Mosaic Covenant is Never Referred to as "Everlasting"

This isn't because covenants, in general, are seldom referred as everlasting. Many covenants are so referenced, but *never* the Mosaic! The first time that the term "covenant" is used is in regards to the covenant with Noah.

- "The rainbow shall be in the cloud, and I will look on it to remember the *everlasting* covenant between God and every living creature of all flesh that is on the earth," (*Genesis 9:16; Isaiah 54:9-10*).

The next reference to "covenant" is the one made with Abraham, which was subsequently extended to Isaac and Jacob.

- "On the same day the LORD made a covenant with Abram, saying: 'To your descendants I have given this land, from the river of Egypt to the great river, the River Euphrates—'" (*Genesis 15:18*).

This too was an "everlasting" covenant (*Genesis 17:19, 13; Psalm 105:9-10, 42; 1 Chronicles 16:15-17*). This same covenant was subsequently extended to the other Patriarchs. (How could these covenants be called "everlasting" if the New Covenant is also described as "everlasting?" Simply because their promises were all absorbed by the New Covenant!)

So far, we're two for two. The Mosaic Covenant is the next at bat. This one formed the center of Israelite thought and practice and had center stage throughout the bulk of the Hebrew Scriptures. However, it is *never* referred to as "everlasting," "eternal," or by any other term to that effect. This *absence* is profound in light of the prominent place of this covenant and also that all the other divinely appointed covenants are everlasting!

The next covenant we encounter is a "perpetual covenant" given within the framework of the Mosaic, the Sabbath: "It is a *sign* between Me and the children of Israel *forever,* for in six days the LORD made the heavens and the earth, and on the seventh day He rested and was refreshed," (*Exodus 31:17*). However, the Sabbath shouldn't be understood to suggest that the Mosaic is also "perpetual." Had it been clearly established that the entire Mosaic regime is everlasting, then it would have been redundant to state that its various features were also everlasting. Instead, the Sabbath is distinguished as perpetual because it was obvious that the Mosaic wasn't!

The next mention of a "covenant" is also found within the context of the Mosaic Covenant. This was the promise to Phinehas of a "covenant of an everlasting priesthood" (*Numbers 25:13*). However, this covenant also stood in contrast with the Mosaic Covenant. Had the Mosaic also been "everlasting," it would have been redundant to offer Phinehas, the Levite, an everlasting priesthood since all the specifications of the Mosaic would have already been understood as everlasting, including the provision of an everlasting priesthood for the Levites. This covenant was also called "everlasting" because its promise was a done deal. The promise would ultimately be fulfilled in the priesthood of *all* believers (*Exodus 19:6; 1 Peter 2:5*).

The next mention of a divinely commissioned covenant is in regards to David. This too is an "everlasting covenant."

- "Although my house is not so with God, yet He has made with me an *everlasting* covenant, ordered in all things and secure. For this is all my salvation and all my desire; will He not make it increase?" (*2 Samuel 23:5; Isaiah 55:3*).

It seems as if the Mosaic covenant is deliberately contrasted with these others. Why is it that a covenant so important and central is the one *not* mentioned as "everlasting?" Fulfillment of the other covenants depended upon one thing—the faithfulness of God. The Mosaic depended upon the faithfulness of *humankind*. Scripture always places these two types of faithfulness into radical contrast. God is always faithful while humankind has habitually perverted themselves.

The Mosaic Covenant was Inadequate and would have to be Set Aside!

The New Testament maintains that although the Mosaic Covenant wasn't flawed, it was inadequate (*Romans 8:3; 7:5; Hebrews 7:18-19; 10:1*). A hammer might be perfectly crafted. However, it wasn't designed to drill a hole. Likewise, the Mosaic Covenant was perfect, but it wasn't equipped to cut through sin and backsliding. Is this understanding a pious Christian invention, or is this what we also encounter within the Hebrew Scriptures?

It should be obvious that the Mosaic Covenant was conditional. If Israel was obedient, she would receive blessing; if disobedient, she would be cursed (*Leviticus 26; Deuteronomy 28-29*). In contrast, the Noahic covenant *unconditionally promised* that God would never again destroy the world with a flood as he had done saving only Noah and his family. It would stand as such despite the extent of sin upon the earth. In contrast to this, the Mosaic "promises" *depended* upon the obedience of Israel to God's commands.

This meant that when sinful Israel required God's mercy, she could not appeal to the provisions of the Mosaic Covenant. These would only trigger condemnation. Israel had to appeal to former promises from the "covenant of your fathers:

- "When you are in distress, and all these things come upon you in the latter days, when you turn to the LORD your God and obey His voice (for the LORD your God is a merciful God), He will not forsake you nor destroy you, nor forget the covenant of your fathers which He swore to them" (*Deuteronomy 4:30-31*, also *Leviticus 26:42-45*).

191

The Mosaic Covenant was Grace-Deficient!

Hope sprang anew from "covenant of your fathers." Which covenant was this? Undeniably, this was the covenant of the Patriarchs, Abraham, Isaac, and Jacob (*Exodus 3; 13:5, 11; Deuteronomy 8:18; 29:13; 30:5, 20; 31:7*). Moses wasn't their "fathers." We find no Hebrew prophet crying out, "God will remember the covenant that He made with Moses and have mercy upon you!" However, just about all of the prophets explicitly proclaim the restoration of Israel, but this will not be based upon Israel's obedience to the Law. Instead, the Law had brought condemnation. Its requirement, that the curses had to be brought upon Israel (*Deuteronomy 27:26*), would have to be set aside in order for Israel to find mercy.

The Law was inadequate. It could never provide what Israel needed. Israel's problems were much deeper. They required more than rules upheld by positive and negative reinforcements. They required a change of heart, but this was the very thing they lacked. Moses had promised "stiff-necked" Israel that sometime in the *future* God would "circumcise your heart and the heart of your descendants to love the LORD your God with all your heart and with all your soul that you may live," (*Deuteronomy 30:6*). Israel would need a "circumcised" heart in order to love God and live, but that this hadn't happened yet! This was like telling Israel that she was doomed to failure!

Even more to the point, Moses told them, "Yet the LORD has not given you a heart to perceive and eyes to see and ears to hear, to this very day," (*Deuteronomy 29:4*). Something had to change! Israel lacked the heart for God despite all of her proclamations otherwise. She would turn her heart from the Covenant, and tragedy would overtake her. Moses was prophetically explicit about this in the Song he taught her: "Then he (Israel) forsook God who made him" (*Deuteronomy 32:15*).

192

Despite all the Mosaic warnings, this is exactly what Israel would do in the future. Moses was sure of it:

- "For I know that after my death you will become utterly corrupt, and turn aside from the way which I have commanded you; and evil will befall you in the latter days, because you will do evil in the sight of the LORD, to provoke Him to anger through the work of your hands." (*Deuteronomy 31:29*)

Joshua reiterated this message of gloom to Israel in the midst of Israel's protestations to the contrary.

- But Joshua said to the people, "You cannot serve the LORD, for He is a holy God. He is a jealous God; He will not forgive your transgressions nor your sins." (*Joshua 24:19*)

If hope couldn't spring forth from the Mosaic Covenant, there had to come something else. The Mosaic couldn't be everlasting. It would have been an everlasting flop. It had to be replaced, but Israel had to learn her lesson first, the hard way.

These types of statements are not to be found in other religious or political literature. What politician ever put forth a program and then stated, without any equivocation, that it was doomed to fail? What religious leader ever tried to promote a religion and then declared that it wouldn't work, and the followers wouldn't receive anything they wanted? Why do the Hebrew Scriptures contain such negative messages unless they were true and that the people were completely convinced that they were God's very words, even though they didn't like the messages?

Indications that the Mosaic Covenant had to be Replaced!

Israel had been promised that they would be a nation of priests (*Exodus 19:6; Isaiah 61:6*) and that God would dwell in their midst (*Leviticus 26:11-12; Joel 3:17, 21*). However, their *present* situation stood in direct contradiction to these promises. They couldn't bear God's presence (*Exodus 20:19*), and He couldn't bear theirs (*Exodus 33:2-3*). Although He would meet with Moses in the tent of meeting, this tent was placed far outside the camp and no one, apart from Moses and Joshua, could approach it (*Exodus 33:7*).

The Temple also communicated the same forbidding presence of the Lord. Only the priests could enter into the Holy Place, and only the High Priest could enter into the High Holy Place, but only once a year. When they did enter, it could only be after they had fulfilled every specification (*Leviticus 16:2*). God's presence was a terrifying reality. This was a far cry from what Israel had been promised. Israel would be so intimate with God, that it was described as a marriage (*Hosea 2:18-19; Isaiah 62:4*). For this portrait to be realized, the Law and its Temple curtain of separation would have to come down.

The institution of the Temple offerings also conveyed the inadequacy of the Mosaic Law and Covenant. The fact that they had to be continually offered meant that they never covered subsequent sins. This meant that whenever an Israelite entertained a covetous thought, he was again in sin and therefore deserved to be cursed. This placed them continuously under God's condemnation. Nor did these offerings remove the discomfort of the thought of this terrifying God. Indeed, discomfort was purposely a necessary part of Israel's relationship to her God. Israel was promised curses for any and every infraction (*Deuteronomy 27:15-26*).

Perhaps most significantly, the Mosaic Covenant never offered the promise of eternal life. If Law-keeping couldn't guarantee eternal life, what good was it? Paul had stated that Christians were the most pitiful people if there wasn't a heaven (*1 Corinthians 15:19*). It wasn't that there wasn't any indication of eternal life within the Mosaic revelation. Jesus had corrected the anti-resurrection beliefs of the Sadducees with *Exodus 3:6*: "I <u>am</u> the God of your father--the God of Abraham, the God of Isaac, and the God of Jacob." This proved that the three Patriarchs still existed. God doesn't say that He *was* their God, but that He *is* their God! Instead, the Law was disturbingly silent in regards to how to *obtain* this eternal life. Evidently, this was another way that God covertly hinted to Israel that this Mosaic Covenant was just temporary and would be superseded by a New Covenant that would guarantee eternal life.

In short, the Mosaic stipulations and experiences do not represent the ultimate portrait of Israel's future blessedness. They're miles behind! Something had to change.

The New Covenant will Supersede the Old!

The Mosaic Covenant is not pictured as part of the *ultimate* answer. The portrait that emerges from Hebrew Scriptures does not show Israel as finally developing more self-control and obedience to perform the Mosaic Law successfully in order to secure blessing and deliverance.

According to prophecy, God's eventual deliverance will not come because Israel wakes up, smells the coffee, and repents on her own. God will have to initiate Israel's return, and it will not occur because Israel will eventually deserve God's blessings. Rather, God will have mercy upon Israel.

- "For the LORD will judge His people and have compassion on His servants, when He sees that their <u>power is gone.</u>" (*Deuteronomy 32:36*)

Instead of doing something positive to warrant God's mercy, it is Israel's destitution that will move God. According to Moses,

195

Israel will violate the Mosaic Covenant and bring down upon themselves the promised curses. It is God who then will have "compassion." How will He do this? According to Jeremiah, it will be through a "new covenant" (*Jeremiah. 31:31-34*), but it will also be done in a radically different way. Moses knew that Israel would fail and that her problem was one of the heart, and if Israel had a heart problem, she would need a heart answer (*Deuteronomy 30:6*).

Without a changed heart, Israel inevitably went astray. They needed to be born again with a new heart. They needed a covenant that would go far further than the Mosaic.

Ezekiel states that even though Israel consistently disgraced God before the other nations, God would act lovingly on her behalf:

- "I will cleanse you from all your filthiness and from all your idols. I will give you a <u>new heart and put a new spirit within you</u>; I will <u>take the heart of stone out of your flesh and give you a heart of flesh. I will put My Spirit within you</u>..." (*Ezekiel 36:25-27; 11:19-20*).

The very thing Israel had lacked under the *Old*, they would receive under the *New*—a new heart and the indwelling Holy Spirit. Jeremiah associates this necessary change with a new and permanent covenant.

- "Then I will give them one heart and one way, that they may fear Me forever, for the good of them and their children after them. And I will make an *everlasting covenant* with them, that I will not turn away from doing them good; but I will put My fear in their hearts so that they will not depart from Me." (*Jeremiah 32:39-40*)

This is the *guarantee* of a hope which isn't found under the Mosaic Covenant. As a result of God's grace, "they will not depart from me." This is why the Mosaic couldn't be called "eternal." As long as blessing depended upon Israel, no guarantee could be made, but if it depended upon God, He could make an ironclad guarantee. God would succeed in securing Israel's love only through changing her.

In contrast to Israel's cycle of rebellion and devastation, the New Covenant would be characterized by unending peace.

- "Moreover I <u>will</u> make a covenant of peace with them, and it shall be an <u>everlasting covenant</u> with them; I will establish them and multiply them, and I will set My sanctuary in their midst forevermore. My tabernacle also shall be with them; indeed I will be their God, and they shall be My people." (*Ezekiel 37:26-27; 34:25-26; Isaiah 54:9-10*)

There's no reason to regard "sanctuary" and "tabernacle" as literal buildings (*Amos 9:11; 2 Samuel 7:11; Zechariah 6:12-13*). The intimacy between God and His people makes a building unnecessary and counterproductive. *He* will be the sanctuary! Walls will no longer separate. God will enter into the most intimate form of relationship with His people. Hosea points to a future, radical covenant that would ensure God's unfailing love:

- "In that day I will make a covenant for them with the beasts of the field...I will betroth you to Me *forever*; Yes, I will betroth you to Me in righteousness and justice, in lovingkindness and mercy." (*Hosea 2:18-19; Isaiah 62:4*)

This would be a "*forever*" covenant. It wasn't a covenant that had already been in place. Hosea says, "I *will* make a covenant!" He lays down no conditions that Israel must fulfill in order to enter into her blessedness as had been characteristic of the Mosaic Covenant. Instead, God will enter into a permanent relationship with Israel; He will *marry* His people.

197

As Hosea had been instructed to take his adulterous wife Gomer into seclusion, God would unilaterally do the same for Israel.

The idea of a marriage with God must have seemed somewhat blasphemous to Mosaic Israel. Her experience had been characterized by God's words to Moses-- "Tell Aaron your brother *not* to come at just any time into the Holy Place inside the veil, before the mercy seat which is on the ark, lest he die" (*Leviticus 16:2*)—a far cry from marriage!

Isaiah concurs that this "yet to be" covenant would be "*everlasting.*"

- "And (God) will make with them an everlasting covenant. Their descendants shall be known among the Gentiles, and their offspring among the people. All who see them shall acknowledge them, that they are the posterity whom the LORD has blessed." (*Isaiah 61:8-9*)

Under the Law, separation from the contaminating influence of other peoples was strictly enforced. Under the New, God's people would be among the nations!

Could the Mosaic have merely been emended to accommodate these radical changes? No! A covenant is a contract to which no one could add or subtract (*Deuteronomy 4:2*). Changes would require a new covenant and fresh blood to seal it! Therefore, the Mosaic had to be replaced and would no longer be remembered (*Jeremiah 3:14-16*).

While there are many verses that state that God will have mercy upon His people, there are *no* verses that affirm that God will have mercy by virtue of the covenant He made with Moses! This covenant had been instituted for a limited time and place (*Deuteronomy 12:8-9*). It wouldn't figure directly into the establishment of the New kingdom. Instead, God's mercy is predicated upon something radically different, but something to which the Mosaic bore witness. The prophetic passages look beyond a redemption based upon the offerings mediated by the Levitical priesthood, to a redeeming God's unmediated intervention.

A New Atonement

Deuteronomy 32 contains a song God directed Moses to teach to Israel. It represented both a disturbing warning and a prophetic overview of Israel's blessing, rebellion, and eventual deliverance. Surprisingly, the song ends on a positive note.

- "Rejoice, O Gentiles, with His people; for He will avenge the blood of His servants, and render vengeance to His adversaries; He will provide atonement for His land and His people." (*Deuteronomy 32:43*)

If the Mosaic system had been adequate, why didn't this feat of "atonement" fall upon the Levites, who had been divinely commissioned to provide atonement? Where are the Levites and the Mosaic system at the time of Israel's eventual deliverance? It is never this system that comes to the rescue but God Himself.

- "Help us, O God of our salvation, for the glory of Your name; and deliver us, and provide atonement for our sins, for Your name's sake!" (*Psalm 79:9*; also *65:3*)

A new High Priest, in line with the priesthood of the enigmatic Melchizedek (*Psalm 110:4*), will trump the Levitical priesthood, which required that all priests had to come from the tribe of Levi. This *"King* of Righteousness" only took the Scriptural stage once—three verses worth (*Genesis 14:18-20*)—but he made an enduring impact. One reason that he is enigmatic is

199

that he is both a king and a priest, something forbidden under Mosaic Law. This suggests a change in guard.

Zechariah prophesied about a distant individual who would also be a "priest on His throne." This Person will "build the temple of the Lord" (*Zechariah 6:13*). Christianity understands that Jesus "built" this very temple through His incarnation, taking on the form of a man and "tabernacling" among us." (*John 1:14; 2:19*)

Along with a radically different High Priest, a new priesthood is prophesied. Israel was promised that she would be a *nation* of priests (*Exodus 19:6; Isaiah 61:6*), something she had never experienced. This nation of priests, suggestive of the New Covenant, would have to replace the Levitical Mosaic order that restricted the priesthood to Levites.

At first glance, this seems to come into conflict with the New Testament promise that all believers would be priests (*1 Peter 2:5, 9; Revelations 1:6*). How could Israel assume the promised priesthood while this was a standing promise to the believers? This is easily understood by recognizing that Israel must *also* come to a faith in Christ in order to receive their promised priesthood along with all other believers.

This understanding also helps us reconcile the more difficult verses. Jeremiah said that to the degree that God's promises to David are unshakable, they are equally unshakable to the Levites (*Jeremiah 33:18, 20-21; Numbers 25:12-13*). On the *surface*, this is troubling for Christianity. If the Levitical priesthood remains, so too the Mosaic Covenant! However, the prophecies do not say that the Levitical priesthood will remain *unchanged*! They merely state that God will remain faithful to the Levitical priests. How will He remain faithful to them? They would become priests according to the same promise that would make all Israel priests. As we've seen, there are other ways to function as priests besides offering animal sacrifices. God instructed Israel to offer the "sacrifice (literally "calves") of our lips" as her offering of repentance (*Hosea 14:2*; also *Psalm 69:30-31; 50:13-14*), not actual calves.

God had to pay the price of "atonement." Levitical atonement was sorely inadequate. It was this "atonement" that would provide the basis of the "*everlasting covenant*."

- "And I will establish My covenant with you. Then you shall know that I am the LORD, that you may remember and be ashamed, and never open your mouth anymore because of your shame, when I provide you an atonement for all you have done." (*Ezekiel 16:59-63*)

This covenant will not be established on the basis of any Levitical ministrations, but on the basis of the unilateral grace of God as promised in the covenant God made with Abraham.

Israel's hope had always been Messianic, not Mosaic. It looked towards a Redeemer who would refine the Israel with His "fire," rather than the sprinkling of the blood of animals, which God never really desired (*Psalm 51:16-17*):

- "Behold, I send My messenger, and he will prepare the way before Me. And the Lord, whom you seek, will suddenly come to his temple, even the messenger of the covenant, in whom you delight. Behold, He is coming,' says the LORD of hosts. 'But who can endure the day of His coming? And who can stand when He appears? For He is like a refiner's fire and like launderer's soap." (*Malachi 3:1-2*)

"The Messenger of the covenant" is no less than God Himself, coming to make His atonement. He is "the Lord," and it's "His" temple. He is the "refiner's fire;" He will purify His people!

201

Blood of the New Atonement

A new covenant requires a fresh blood offering (*Exodus 24:8; Hebrews 9:18*). An *everlasting covenant* requires a special blood offering!

- "Thus says the LORD: 'In an acceptable time I have heard You, and in the day of salvation I have helped You; I will preserve You and give <u>You as a covenant</u> to the people, to restore the earth, to cause them to inherit the desolate heritages.'" (*Isaiah 49:8; 42:6*)

Presumably, God will "preserve" Him, because He will have to endure an ordeal through which He will need to be rescued from the dead. Zechariah adds that, "because of the blood of *your* covenant, I will set your prisoners free from the waterless pit" (*Zechariah 9:11*). To whom does the *"your"* refer? Obviously to the humble King Messiah who comes riding on a donkey and who will "speak peace to the nations" (*Zechariah 9:10*). What role do the Levites play here? None!

It's clear that Israel's hope wasn't in the Mosaic system but in a Savior who Himself would provide atonement. That's why He is often called the *"Redeemer"* (*Job 19:25; Psalm 19:14, 78:35; Isaiah 41:14, 43:14, 44:6, 24; 47:4...*). It is the Redeemer who will ultimately provide the payment to deliver His people from sin (*Psalm 49:15*). That's why His people are called the "ransomed" or the "redeemed" (*Isaiah 35:9-10; 51:11; 62:12*). Nor is redemption ever accomplished on the basis of Israel's righteousness, but upon the Lord's! (*Isaiah 61:10*)

How does the Mosaic Covenant fit into this gracious portrait? It doesn't! Although it is "holy and righteous" (*Romans 7:12; Psalm 119*), It's never portrayed as the source of hope but as the source of condemnation, which points to the Hope.

Result of the New Atonement

Under the Mosaic regime, "righteousness" was a matter of an individual's performance.

- "And the LORD commanded us to observe all these statutes, to fear the LORD our God, for our good always, that He might preserve us alive, as it is this day. Then it will be righteousness for us, if we are careful to observe all these commandments before the LORD our God, as He has commanded us." (*Deuteronomy 6:24-25; 24:15*)

Under the Messiah, this will all change. Righteousness will no longer be something that we attain to through our efforts. Instead, we will receive the Messiah's righteousness through the grace of God alone.

- "Behold, the days are coming," says the LORD, "That I will raise to David a Branch of righteousness; a King shall reign and prosper, and execute judgment and righteousness in the earth. In His days Judah will be saved, and Israel will dwell safely; now this is His name by which He will be called: THE LORD OUR RIGHTEOUSNESS." (*Jeremiah 23:5-6; 33:6; Isaiah 45:24-25; Daniel 9:24*)

This couldn't have occurred under the Mosaic Covenant, its antithesis (*Deuteronomy 6:25*)! These prophecies proclaim that it is no longer about us, but about a righteousness that will come to us as a gift rather than an earned salary.

The New Testament is the revelation of these truths—not that the Messiah will help us become righteous, but that He will become our imperishable righteousness (*1 Corinthians 1:30; 2 Corinthians 5:21*).

Why then the Mosaic Law if it was only temporary and would bring condemnation rather than salvation? Again, the New Testament provides the perfect answer, which knits together all the pieces:

- "Is the law then against the promises of God? Certainly not! For if there had been a law given which could have given life, truly righteousness would have been by the law. But the Scripture has confined all under sin, that the promise by faith in Jesus Christ might be given to those who believe. But before faith came, we were kept under guard by the law, kept for the faith which would afterward be revealed. Therefore the law was our tutor to bring us to Christ, that we might be justified by faith." (*Galatians 3:21-24*)

Throughout the writing of this chapter, I had to stop and worship, awed as I was by the beauty of God's design. I enjoy movies whose ending brings a harmonious resolution, knitting together all the loose ends. God's Word does the same thing. Not to say that there aren't any remaining rough edges! There should be by virtue of our limited understanding, but the overall contours are incredibly harmonious. These point to a grand design, one that I think requires a Grand Designer. If the Hebrew Scriptures were merely the product of various independent writers sharing a common faith, such a congruent design would scarcely have emerged.

Not only are the Hebrew Scriptures elegantly crafted, they also march in lock step with the New Testament. To behold this is awe-inspiring; it's like seeing the face of God.

WORKS CITED

Sigal, Gerald, *The Jew and the Christian Missionary*: *A Jewish Response to Missionary Christianity,* (New York: KTAV Publishing House, Inc., 1981)

Chapter 16

THE RABBIS HAVE PLACED THEIR FAITH IN KEEPING THE LAW OF MOSES AND NOT IN THE MESSIAH

Former rabbis had believed that the Messiah would bring in a new set of laws to replace the Mosaic laws. We find a number of indications of this in the Talmud, compiled around 550 AD. Jewish commentator Raphael Patai had written:

- The notion that the days of the messiah, the messiah's apocalyptic reign, will be served by a new law is a Jewish one. Paul is quite Jewish in seeking to extend his new, more accessible, religion to Gentiles in the interest of time as did some of his contemporaries among the rabbis. In his essay, "The Crisis of Tradition in Jewish Messianism," G. Scholem reviews the most important rabbinic statements that look forward to a utopian messianic age governed by a new, relaxed law:

  - Lev. Rabbah 9:7 - All sacrifices will be abolished except for the offer of thanksgiving.

  - Yalkut and Midrash Mishle (on *Proverbs 9:2*) - All festivals will be abolished except for Purim which will never be abolished (and the Day of Atonement will be like Purim)

  - Midrash Tehillim (in regard to *Psalm 146:7*) - The Lord allows the forbidden ... and will one day allow the eating of all animals now forbidden to be eaten ... In the time to come he will allow everything that he has forbidden.

  - Lev. Rabbah 13:3 - A new Torah [law or teaching] shall go forth from me.

206

- ➤ Yalkut (in regard to *Isaiah 26:2*) - the messiah himself will teach it (*The Jewish Messiahs*, Harris Lenowitz, page 270ff)

- ➤ Eccl. Rabbah 11:1 - R Hizqiya in the name of R. Simon bar Zibdi said: "The whole Tora which you learn in This World is vanity as against the Tora of the World to Come. For in This World a man learns Tora and forgets, but in the Future to Come (he will not forget) as it is written, I will put My Tora in their inward parts and in their heart will I write it (*Jeremiah 31:33*). (*The Messiah Texts, Raphael Patai*, pages 247-257) (www.hadavar.org/critical-issues/anti-missionary-arguments/additional-issues/the-law-of-moses-is-eternal/)

However, modern-day rabbis have gravitated to a different view – that the Mosaic Laws are eternally binding. *The Jewish Encyclopedia's* "New Testament" article states:

- • "The idea of the new covenant is based chiefly upon *Jeremiah 31:31–34*. That the prophet's words do not imply an abrogation of the Law is evidenced by his emphatic declaration of the immutability of the covenant with Israel (*Jeremiah 31:35–36*); he obviously looked for a renewal of the Law through a regeneration of the hearts of the people." (www.jewishencyclopedia.com/articles/4714-covenant#anchor8)

However, *Jeremiah 31:35-36* says *nothing* about the continuation of the Mosaic Covenant:

- • "Thus says the LORD, who gives the sun for light by day and the fixed order of the moon and the stars for light by night, who stirs up the sea so that its waves roar— the LORD of hosts is his name: 'If this fixed order departs from before me, declares the LORD, then shall the offspring of Israel cease from being a nation before me forever.'" (*Jeremiah 31:35-36*)

What remains unchanged are "the fixed order of the moon and the stars" and Israel as a nation. *Jeremiah 31:32* claims that the New Covenant will "not [be] like the covenant that I made with their fathers on the day when I took them by the hand to bring them out of the land of Egypt, my covenant that they broke, though I was their husband, declares the LORD.")

Elsewhere, *The Jewish Encyclopedia* reads:

- Judaism knows of no other than the old Sinaitic [Mosaic] covenant. Eternal as the covenant with heaven and earth is God's covenant with the seed of Jacob (*Jeremiah xxxiii. 25 et seq.*). (www.jewishencyclopedia.com/articles/4714-covenant)

However, Scripture reveals that the Mosaic Covenant would be unable to deliver what the Messiah and His New Covenant were finally able to provide. When we examine Messianic prophecy, we find that Israel's blessedness was not to be found in their adherence to the Mosaic Law but in their Messiah. The following are verses that the rabbis had also regarded as Messianic:

- "The Spirit of the Lord GOD is upon me, because the LORD has anointed me to bring good news to the poor; he has sent me to bind up the brokenhearted, to proclaim liberty to the captives, and the opening of the prison to those who are bound; to proclaim the year of the LORD's favor, and the day of vengeance of our God; to comfort all who mourn; to grant to those who mourn in Zion— to give them a beautiful headdress instead of ashes, the oil of gladness instead of mourning, the garment of praise instead of a faint spirit; that they may be called oaks of righteousness, the planting of the LORD, that he may be glorified…you shall be called the priests of the LORD; they shall speak of you as the ministers of our God; you shall eat the wealth of the nations, and in their glory you shall boast. Instead of your shame there shall be a double portion; instead of dishonor they shall rejoice in their lot; therefore in their land they shall possess a double portion; they shall have everlasting joy." (*Isaiah 61:1-7*)

In what state do we find Israel prior to the Messiah's return? One of shame and dishonor! It would be the Messiah, and not Mosaic Law keeping, that would "bind up the brokenhearted, to proclaim liberty to the captives, and the opening of the prison to those who are bound." Instead of exalting Israel, the Mosaic Law would evidently afflict Israel through their failure to keep it.

Elsewhere, Isaiah prophesies that the Messiah will bring justice, not the Mosaic Law:

- "Behold my servant, whom I uphold, my chosen, in whom my soul delights; I have put my Spirit upon him; he will bring forth justice to the nations… "I am the LORD; I have called you in righteousness; I will take you by the hand and keep you; I will give you as a covenant for the people, a light for the nations, to open the eyes that are blind, to bring out the prisoners from the dungeon, from the prison those who sit in darkness." (*Isaiah 42:1-7; 9:6-7; 11:1-10*)

The Messiah will also be the covenant and the light, which the Mosaic Covenant (MC) could not provide. He would open blind eyes and release those in bondage. Clearly, the MC would fail to do this.

- "The voice of your watchmen—they lift up their voice; together they sing for joy; for eye to eye they see the return of the LORD to Zion. Break forth together into singing, you waste places of Jerusalem, for the LORD has comforted his people; he has redeemed Jerusalem. The LORD has bared his holy arm before the eyes of all the nations, and all the ends of the earth shall see the salvation of our God." (*Isaiah 52:8-10*)

At the time of the Messiah's return, there will be "waste places of Jerusalem." Why would this be if Israel's adherence to the MC had been adequate? Evidently, it wouldn't be. Instead, Israel's hope would have to be in the Messiah and not in their ability to keep the MC.

Who is "his holy arm?" Isaiah tells us:

- "Who has believed what he has heard from us? And to whom has the arm of the LORD been revealed? For he grew up before him like a young plant, and like a root out of dry ground; he had no form or majesty that we should look at him, and no beauty that we should desire him. He was despised and rejected by men; a man of sorrows, and acquainted with grief; and as one from whom men hide their faces he was despised, and we esteemed him not. Surely he has borne our griefs and carried our sorrows; yet we esteemed him stricken, smitten by God, and afflicted." (*Isaiah 53:1-4*)

Why would the Messiah have to carry "our sorrows" if the MC had been adequate? Instead, the Messiah, the one who would bear Israel's sins, would ultimately be their hope.

The Messiah's return will mean comfort for the afflicted and a worldwide awakening:

- "The afflicted shall eat and be satisfied; those who seek him shall praise the LORD! May your hearts live forever! All the ends of the earth shall remember and turn to the LORD, and all the families of the nations shall worship before you. For kingship belongs to the LORD, and he rules over the nations." (*Psalm 22:26-28* [This Psalm might not have been considered Messianic by the rabbis]; also see *Psalm 2, 40, 69*)

Salvation wouldn't come through Israel's obedience to the MC. Instead, as so many prophecies indicate, it would come through the Messiah:

- "Rejoice greatly, O daughter of Zion! Shout aloud, O daughter of Jerusalem! Behold, your king is coming to you; righteous and having salvation is he, humble and mounted on a donkey, on a colt, the foal of a donkey...and he shall speak peace to the nations; his rule shall be from sea to sea, and from the River to the ends of the earth. As for you also, because of the blood of my covenant with you, I will set your prisoners free from the waterless pit...On that day the LORD their God will save them, as the flock of his people; for like the jewels of a crown they shall shine on his land." (*Zechariah 9:9-16*)

The MC would not bring salvation, but death, because of Israel's disobedience:

- "Why then has this people turned away in perpetual backsliding? They hold fast to deceit; they refuse to return. I have paid attention and listened, but they have not spoken rightly; no man relents of his evil, saying, 'What have I done?' Everyone turns to his own course." (*Jeremiah 8:5-6; 5:3; Isaiah 1:3-4; 9:3; 64:7; 65:2-3; 66:4; Hosea 4:6; 7:10*)

211

Instead of bringing glory to God, Israel under the MC would profane Him. This is why a New Covenant was necessary. Besides, the MC was governed by fear. Israel had been terrified to hear God's voice and dared not to come into His presence lest they be struck dead.

Why weren't the rabbis willing to see that the MC brought Israel under the curse of God, as so many verses indicate?

- "But if you will not obey the voice of the LORD your God or be careful to do all his commandments and his statutes that I command you today, then all these curses shall come upon you and overtake you…" (*Deuteronomy 28:15; 27:26*)

After this, God gave Moses a prophetic song to teach to His people that would illustrate their future rebellion under the Mosaic Covenant:

- "They [Israel] stirred him to jealousy with strange gods; with abominations they provoked him to anger. They sacrificed to demons that were no gods, to gods they had never known, to new gods that had come recently, whom your fathers had never dreaded. You were unmindful of the Rock that bore you, and you forgot the God who gave you birth." (*Deuteronomy 32:16-18*)

However, the song ended with a promise of God's mercy:

- "Rejoice, O Gentiles, with His people; For He will avenge the blood of His servants, And render vengeance to His adversaries; He will provide atonement for His land and His people." (*Deuteronomy 32:43 NKJV*)

There is no mention anywhere in this song of Israel successfully keeping the law and meriting God's mercy. Why

212

don't the rabbis see that an eternal MC offered them no hope and no blessedness? Why would they put their hope in their ability to keep the Law? Why do the rabbis reject the New Covenant and its promised blessedness through an intimate love-relationship with their Savior, something they could never enjoy under the MC?

- "And I will make for them a covenant…And I will betroth you to me forever. I will betroth you to me in righteousness and in justice, in steadfast love and in mercy. I will betroth you to me in faithfulness. And you shall know the LORD." (*Hosea 2:18-20*)

Sadly, my Jewish people continue to harden their heart against their Savior, and, by doing so, they have also hardened their heart against wisdom, plunging themselves headlong into the darkness. (*John 3:19-21*)

WORKS CITED

HaDavar Messianic Ministries, *The Law of Moses is Eternal,* (*The Messiah Texts, Raphael Patai*, pages 247-257) www.hadavar.org/critical-issues/anti-missionary-arguments/additional-issues/the-law-of-moses-is-eternal/

Jewish Encyclopedia, Executive Committee of the Editorial Board., Kaufmann Kohler, Louis Ginzberg, Richard Gottheil, Isaac Broydé, Emil G. Hirsch, J. Frederic McCurdy, "*Covenant*", www.jewishencyclopedia.com/articles/4714-covenant

Chapter 17

THE TEMPLE AND THE MOSAIC COVENANT

The rabbis often denounce the New Testament claiming that it misconstrues the Hebrew Scriptures to support its own doctrines. In *"The Jew and the Christian Missionary: A Jewish Response to Missionary Christianity,"* Gerald Sigal had written:

- "Misreading the essential meaning of the Torah, Christian theology developed along lines that are at variance with the message of Hebrew Scriptures." (Sigal, Introduction, xv)

For instance, in the NT, Jesus likened His own body to the Jerusalem Temple, in effect, proclaiming that His body had become the actual place to meet God and find His mercy, instead of the Temple. In a revealing account, the Jewish leadership demanded that Jesus justify His authority to drive the money-changers and animal-salesmen out from the Temple:

- Jesus answered them, "Destroy this temple, and in three days I will raise it up." The Jews then said, "It has taken forty-six years to build this temple, and will you raise it up in three days?" But he was speaking about the temple of his body. (*John 2:19-21; John 1:14*)

Jesus equated His body with the Temple. He had been hinting about this to a Samaritan woman who thought religion was just a matter of the geographical place of worship, pointing out that the Jews worshipped in the Jerusalem Temple and the Samaritans on Mount Gerizim. However, Jesus corrected her:

- "But the hour is coming, and is now here, when the true worshipers will worship the Father in spirit and truth, for

214

the Father is seeking such people to worship him. God is spirit, and those who worship him must worship in spirit and truth." (*John 4:23-24*)

According to Jesus, worship, ultimately, was not a matter of place but of truth. It is through belief in the truth that we meet God, not through a literal building but through a Person.

When the Pharisees criticized Jesus' disciples for eating standing grain on the Sabbath, Jesus retorted that priests who serve in the Temple also violate the Sabbath. If they could do it, so too could His disciples, because He was greater than both the Sabbath and the Temple:

- He said to them, "Have you not read what David did when he was hungry, and those who were with him: how he entered the house of God and ate the bread of the Presence, which it was not lawful for him to eat nor for those who were with him, but only for the priests? Or have you not read in the Law how on the Sabbath the priests in the temple profane the Sabbath and are guiltless? I tell you, something greater than the temple is here...For the Son of Man is lord of the Sabbath." (*Matthew 12:3-6, 8*)

How could Jesus imply, about Himself, that "something *greater* than the temple is here?" He understood that the Temple was merely a *symbol* or a *shadow* of the reality, and that He was ultimately the One to whom Israel must come to find mercy (*Colossians 2:16-17*).

The *Book of Revelation* also claims that the New Jerusalem would not contain a physical temple:

- "And I saw no temple in the city, for its temple is the Lord God the Almighty and the Lamb." (*Revelation 21:22; 13:6; 21:3*)

215

Has the NT perverted the teachings of the Mosaic revelation by spiritualizing the Temple? Moses had been given the plan for the Tabernacle (the moveable Temple) while on Mt. Sinai (*Exodus 25:40; 27:8; Numbers 8:4; Acts 7:44*). However, the NT interpreted this plan as symbolic (a shadow) of a deeper reality:

- "They [the Temple and its services] serve a copy and shadow of the heavenly things [of Christ]. For when Moses was about to erect the tent, he was instructed by God, saying, 'See that you make everything according to the pattern that was shown you on the mountain.'" (*Hebrews 8:5*)

Did God simply have a preference for certain physical forms and structures, or did He command these Temple forms, because they *symbolically* conveyed heavenly truths? The NT writers understood that the Temple and the prescribed forms of worship were symbolic of a *deeper reality*. Interestingly, the OT *also* suggests this. Even before there was a Tabernacle, God had been Israel's refuge and sanctuary:

- Lord, <u>you</u> have been our dwelling place in all generations. (*Psalm 90:1; 71:3; Isaiah 57:15*)

This suggests that the Temple was a shadow of a deeper reality, the actual presence of God, which God had wanted to convey symbolically. The NT claims that *God Himself* would be our sanctuary (Temple). This is *also* true of the OT revelation:

- "Therefore say, 'Thus says the Lord GOD: Though I removed them far off among the nations, and though I scattered them among the countries, yet <u>I have been a sanctuary</u> ["mikdash"] to them for a while in the countries where they have gone.'" (*Ezekiel 11:16; Isaiah 8:13:14*)

216

God would be a temple to Israel even in their exile. The physical Temple was therefore symbolic, suggesting that, instead, it *represented* a reality beyond itself. Besides, God promised that *He Himself* would "build" the ultimate Temple in conjunction with the New Covenant:

- "I will make a covenant of peace with them. It shall be an everlasting covenant with them. And I will set them in their land and multiply them, and will set my sanctuary ["mikdash"] in their midst forevermore. My dwelling place ["mishkan"] shall be with them, and I will be their God, and they shall be my people. Then the nations will know that I am the LORD who sanctifies Israel, when my sanctuary ["mikdash"] is in their midst forevermore." (*Ezekiel 37:26-28*)

Would this be a physical sanctuary? The fact that *God* would build it suggests otherwise. Besides, it seems that this "everlasting covenant" with Israel will replace the Mosaic Covenant and its Temple. In fact, nowhere in the Scriptures is the Mosaic ever described as everlasting.

Of what will "my sanctuary," which God will create, consist? First of all, it is not only associated with a new and eternal covenant, it is also a Messianic covenant, the work of the mysterious BRANCH:

- "And say to him, 'Thus says the LORD of hosts, "Behold, the man whose name is the Branch: for he shall branch out from his place, and he shall build the temple of the LORD. It is he who shall build the temple of the LORD and shall bear royal honor, and shall sit and rule on his throne. And there shall be a priest on his throne, and the counsel of peace shall be between them both."'" (*Zechariah 6:12-13*)

It is noteworthy that the physical Temple had already been rebuilt by the Israelite exiles returning from Babylon. Evidently, this temple constructed by God would be a very different kind of temple and even a different priesthood. This Priest, the Messianic BRANCH, was also regarded by the rabbis as the promised Davidic offspring, the Messiah who would create an everlasting kingdom (*Isaiah 9:6-7; Jeremiah 23:5-6*), would also be a King (*Psalm 110*). A single person fulfilling these two roles had been absolutely forbidden under the Mosaic Covenant (*Numbers 18:7*). The fact that the Messiah would fulfill *both* roles suggests a change in the Covenant, the Temple, its rituals, and even the end of animal sacrifices:

- "Before they call [for forgiveness as they sacrifice an animal] I will answer; while they are yet speaking I will hear. The wolf and the lamb shall graze together; the lion shall eat straw like the ox, and dust shall be the serpent's food. They shall not hurt or destroy in all my holy mountain," says the LORD. Thus says the LORD: "Heaven is my throne, and the earth is my footstool; what is the house that you would build for me, and what is the place of my rest? All these things my hand has made, and so all these things came to be, declares the LORD. But this is the one to whom I will look: he who is humble and contrite in spirit and trembles at my word. He who slaughters an ox is like one who kills a man; he who sacrifices a lamb, like one who breaks a dog's neck; he who presents a grain offering, like one who offers pig's blood; he who makes a memorial offering of frankincense, like one who blesses an idol. These have chosen their own ways, and their soul delights in their abominations." (*Isaiah 65:24 - 66:1-3; 11:6-9*)

Since there will be no more "destruction" in the Kingdom of the Messiah, the death of animals could no longer be required. Instead, the promised Messianic sacrifice will put an end to all sacrifices:

- Surely he [the promised Messiah] has borne our griefs and carried our sorrows; yet we esteemed him stricken, smitten by God, and afflicted. But he was pierced for our transgressions; he was crushed for our iniquities; upon him was the chastisement that brought us peace, and with his wounds we are healed. All we like sheep have gone astray; we have turned—every one—to his own way; and the LORD has laid on him the iniquity of us all. (*Isaiah 53:4-6*)

The Psalms also promise that one offering will put to end all subsequent offerings and the Temple system, which required them:

- Consequently, when Christ came into the world, he said, "Sacrifices and offerings you have not desired, but a body have you prepared for me; in burnt offerings and sin offerings you have taken no pleasure. Then I said, 'Behold, I have come to do your will, O God, as it is written of me in the scroll of the book.'" [*Psalm 40; LXX*] When he said above, "You have neither desired nor taken pleasure in sacrifices and offerings and burnt offerings and sin offerings" (these are offered according to the law), then he added, "Behold, I have come to do your will." He does away with the first [covenant] in order to establish the second. (*Hebrews 10:5-10*)

Evidently, the Temple animal sacrifices had been a shadow of the coming reality – the offering of the *Messiah Himself* for the sins of the world. How else can we explain the fact that God wasn't truly pleased with the animal sacrifices, although He had ordained and required them? They weren't pleasing to God because they and the Temple were *only* symbols. Besides, the Scriptures inform us that the true offerings of Israel were to be those of the mouth and the heart:

- "For you will not delight in sacrifice, or I would give it; you will not be pleased with a burnt offering. The sacrifices of God are a broken spirit; a broken and contrite heart, O God, you will not despise." (*Psalm 51:16-17; Hosea 6:6; 14:2; Malachi 1:10-11*)

God also desires the *figurative* sacrifice of the entire person (*Romans 12:2*):

- "For on my holy mountain, the mountain height of Israel, declares the Lord GOD, there all the house of Israel, all of them, shall serve me in the land. There I will accept them, and there I will require your contributions and the choicest of your gifts, with all your sacred offerings. As a pleasing aroma I will accept you, when I bring you out from the peoples and gather you out of the countries where you have been scattered." (*Ezekiel 20:40-41; Isaiah 66:20-21*)

We find that, in the Biblical prophecies, there are many indications that spiritual sacrifices will replace animal sacrifices. Hosea foresees that the sacrifice of words will be required instead of animal sacrifices:

- "Return, O Israel, to the LORD your God, for you have stumbled because of your iniquity. Take with you words and return to the LORD; say to him, 'Take away all iniquity; accept what is good, and we will pay with bulls the vows of our lips.'" (*Hosea 14:1-2*)

Bull offerings would be replaced by words. Malachi claims that, in the future, "in every place incense will be offered to my name, and a pure offering" (*Malachi 1:11*). No mention here of animal sacrifice! Also, Isaiah claims that the Gentile nations "shall bring all your [Israelite] brothers from all the nations as an offering to the LORD" (*Isaiah 66:20; 49:22*). Again, no mention of a physical temple or animal sacrifices!

The Temple and its prescribed worship were only meant to apply until the Messiah (*Hebrew 13:8*):

- "And when you have multiplied and been fruitful in the land, in those days," declares the LORD, "they shall no more say, 'The ark of the covenant of the LORD.' It shall not come to mind or be remembered or missed; it shall not be made again. At that time Jerusalem shall be called the throne of the LORD, and all nations shall gather to it, to the presence of the LORD in Jerusalem, and they shall no more stubbornly follow their own evil heart." (*Jeremiah 3:16-17*)

The Ark, which carried the centerpiece of the Mosaic Covenant, the Ten Commandments, would not be remembered or made again because this Covenant would be superseded by the New:

- "Behold, the days are coming, declares the LORD, when I will make a new covenant with the house of Israel and the house of Judah, not like the covenant that I made with their fathers on the day when I took them by the hand to bring them out of the land of Egypt, my covenant that they broke, though I was their husband, declares the LORD. For this is the covenant that I will make with the house of Israel after those days, declares the LORD: I will put my law within them, and I will write it on their hearts. And I will be their God, and they shall be my people." (*Jeremiah 31:31-33*)

The New would replace the Old with its Temple and its priests. The New would be predicated on the fact that God Himself would provide the payment or atonement for our sins:

- "I will establish my covenant with you, and you shall know that I am the LORD, that you may remember and be confounded, and never open your mouth again because of your shame, when I atone for you for all that you have done, declares the Lord GOD." (*Ezekiel 16:62-63; 36:25-26; Micah 7:19; Zechariah 3:4; Hosea 13:14; Deuteronomy 32:43; Psalm 130:8; 103:12*)

If it is God who does the atoning, then the Temple becomes superfluous. How do the rabbis answer this evidence of a new covenant, temple, Messianic offering, and priesthood? They respond that the New is a mere remodeling of the Mosaic Covenant. Rabbi Sigal had written:

- "By any objective reading of the text, one fails to see any reference to a substitution of a new covenant which will supersede the old." (Sigal, 70)

However, God *explicitly* declares that the New is "not like the [Mosaic] covenant that I made with their fathers on the day when I took them by the hand to bring them out of the land of Egypt." Nevertheless, Sigal claimed that:

- "...what Jeremiah meant by it was the renewing of the old covenant, which will thereby regain its full original vigor. Jeremiah is thus able to speak of a "new covenant," and still remain a true prophet among his people because there was absolutely no difference between the new and old." (Sigal, 72-73)

"Absolutely no difference?" Not according to Jeremiah! It will "not [be] like the covenant that I made with their fathers on the day when I took them by the hand to bring them out of the land of Egypt!" Once again, the rabbis have studiously side-stepped their promised Messiah (*Isaiah 8:13-14; 28:16; 53:1-3; Psalm 118:22*), as prophesied.

In contrast, the NT follows in the path laid out by the OT but with a lantern in hand to illuminate what had previously been obscured by the shadows. We find that the NT fits the OT like a glove fits the hand, demonstrating the internal consistency of the entire Bible, pointing to the fact that the Bible expresses a single, albeit cryptic, revelation by a single divine Author.

There are many other cryptic indications that the Mosaic Covenant would have to be replaced in order for the OT prophesies to be fulfilled. Under the Mosaic, no one except the high priest could come into the presence of God. However, this would have to change, because it had been prophesied that God would marry His people:

- "And I will make for them a covenant on that day with the beasts of the field, the birds of the heavens, and the creeping things of the ground. And I will abolish the bow, the sword, and war from the land, and I will make you lie down in safety. And I will betroth you to me forever. I will betroth you to me in righteousness and in justice, in steadfast love and in mercy. I will betroth you to me in faithfulness. And you shall know the LORD." (*Hosea 2:18-20*)

In order for God to marry His people, the New Covenant would have to replace the Old along with its Temple. In conclusion, there is a wealth of evidence that the NT writers didn't coerce the OT to agree with NT theology regarding the Temple. Instead, this theology was already embedded within the OT.

WORKS CITED

Sigal, Gerald, *The Jew and the Christian Missionary: A Jewish Response to Missionary Christianity,* (New York: KTAV Publishing House, Inc., 1981)

Chapter 18

DID THE CHURCH INVENT THE TRINITY
AND THE DEITY OF CHRIST?

The rabbis claim that the Deity of Jesus and the Trinity are merely New Testament fabrications. In *The Jew and the Christian Missionary*, Gerald Sigal wrote:

- "This belief, called the Trinity, is not only diametrically opposed to Jewish belief, but is the very antithesis of the teachings of the Torah, the Prophets, and the Writings concerning the oneness of God." (Sigal, 125)

I therefore want to offer these verses from the Hebrew Scriptures as a handy reference.

PLURAL PRONOUNS

- ***Genesis 1:26-27*** "And God said, Let <u>us</u> make man in **our** image, after <u>our</u> likeness: and let them have dominion over the fish of the sea, and over the fowl of the air, and over the cattle, and over all the earth, and over every creeping thing that creepeth upon the earth. So God created man in his *own* image, in the image of God created he him; male and female created he them."

The rabbis often claim that these plural pronouns refer to God and His angels. However, angels aren't introduced into the Bible until *Genesis 16*. Besides, angels are never described as having been created in the "image of God." Instead, it makes far better interpretive sense to understand the plural pronouns as including the "Spirit of God" who is already on stage (*Genesis 1:2*).

224

- *Genesis 3:22* "And the LORD God said, Behold, the man is become as one of <u>us</u>, to know good and evil: and now, lest he put forth his hand, and take also of the tree of life, and eat, and live forever":

- *Genesis 11:7* "Go to, let <u>us</u> go down, and there confound their language, that they may not understand one another's speech."

- *Isaiah 6:8* "Also I heard the voice of the Lord, saying, Whom shall I send, and who will go for <u>us</u>? Then said I, Here *am* I; send me."

DISTINCTION OF PERSONS IN THE GODHEAD
(also called "Plurality of Persons)

- *Genesis 19:24* "Then the LORD rained upon Sodom and upon Gomorrah brimstone and fire <u>from the LORD</u> out of heaven."

Wherever you find "LORD" written in Caps, it is a translation of the Hebrew "Yahweh," which *always* refers to God.

- *Psalm 110:1* "The <u>LORD said unto my Lord</u>, Sit thou at my right hand, until I make thine enemies thy footstool."

As Jesus had pointed out (*Matthew 22:42-45*), in this Psalm King David confessed that He had *two* Masters. How could that be if he was king, unless "my Lord" referred to the Messiah?

- *Isaiah 44:6* "Thus saith the LORD the King of Israel, <u>and his redeemer</u> the LORD <u>of hosts</u>; I am the first, and I am the last; and beside me there is no God."

- *Isaiah 48:16* "Come ye near unto me, hear ye this; <u>I</u> have not spoken in secret from the beginning; from the
225

time that it was, there am I: and now <u>the Lord GOD, and his Spirit</u>, hath sent <u>me</u>."

Here we see an illustration of the three Persons of the Trinity. However, it seems that God had carefully guarded this truth, perhaps because Israel might confuse Trinity with the polytheistic beliefs of their neighbors. Therefore, He added:

- ***Isaiah 48:12*** "Hearken unto me, O Jacob and Israel, my called; I am he; I am the first, I also am the last."

- ***Isaiah 63:9*** "In all their affliction he was afflicted, and the angel of his presence saved them: in his love and in his pity he redeemed them; and he bare them, and carried them all the days of old."

Who is this "angel of his presence?"

- ***Exodus 33:2*** "And I will send an angel before thee; and I will drive out the Canaanite, the Amorite, and the Hittite, and the Perizzite, the Hivite, and the Jebusite."

- ***Exodus 33:14*** "And he said, <u>My Presence</u> shall go with thee, and I will give thee rest."

This Angel (also translated as "Messenger") was the one who led Israel out of Egypt (*Numbers 20:16*), because God the Father couldn't be in the midst of Israel lest He destroy them (*Exodus 33:2-3*). However, *Exodus 12:51* claims that "*Yahweh*" had brought Israel out of Egypt. How do we resolve this paradox? The Angel must have also been "*Yahweh*," as the ancient Israelites understood. (We will read more about this in the next chapter.)

I capitalized the "P" in "My Presence," because many other verses make it clear that God is still with Israel even though God was not present.

- **Hosea 1:7** "But I will have mercy upon the house of Judah, and <u>will save them by the Lord their God</u>, and will not save them by bow, nor by sword, nor by battle, by horses, nor by horsemen."

- **Zechariah 2:10-11** "Sing and rejoice, O daughter of Zion: for, lo, I come, and I will dwell in the midst of thee, saith the Lord. And many nations shall be joined to the Lord in that day, and shall be my people: and I will dwell in the midst of thee, and thou shalt know that the <u>Lord of hosts hath sent me</u> unto thee."

- **Zechariah 12:10** "And I will pour upon the house of David, and upon the inhabitants of Jerusalem, the spirit of grace and of supplications: and they shall look upon <u>me</u> whom they have pierced, and they shall mourn for <u>him</u>, as one mourneth for his only son, and shall be in bitterness for him, as one that is in bitterness for his firstborn."

These verses each point to the fact that there is both oneness in the Godhead but also a distinction among the Persons, as the doctrine of the Trinity maintains.

DEITY OF THE SON (the Messiah)

- **Psalm 2:7** "I will declare the decree: the Lord hath said unto me, Thou art my Son; this day have I begotten thee."

- **Psalm 2:12** "Kiss the Son, lest he be angry, and ye perish from the way, when his wrath is kindled but a little. Blessed are all they that put their trust in him."

Only God is worthy of trust. No Prophet is ever described in this way. Therefore, the Son must also be God.

- **Isaiah 7:14** "Therefore the Lord himself shall give you a sign; Behold, a virgin shall conceive, and bear a son, and shall call his name Immanuel. [meaning "God with us." The Hebrew for "Immanuel" is found only two other times in Scripture, both in the next chapter (*Isaiah 8:8, 10*) For more on this, see chapter *Isaiah 20*].

- **Isaiah 9:6** "For unto us a child is born, unto us a son is given: and the government shall be upon his shoulder: and his name shall be called Wonderful, Counsellor, The mighty God, The everlasting Father, The Prince of Peace."

- **Jeremiah 23:5-6** "Behold, the days come, saith the LORD, that I will raise unto David a righteous Branch, and a King shall reign and prosper, and shall execute judgment and justice in the earth. In his days Judah shall be saved, and Israel shall dwell safely: and this is his name whereby he shall be called, THE LORD OUR RIGHTEOUSNESS."

The Messiah is explicitly referred to here as "Yahweh":

- **Jeremiah 33:15-16** "In those days, and at that time, will I cause the Branch of righteousness to grow up unto David; and he shall execute judgment and righteousness in the land. In those days shall Judah be saved, and Jerusalem shall dwell safely: and this is the name wherewith she shall be called, The LORD our righteousness."

- **Micah 5:2** "But thou, Bethlehem Ephratah, though thou be little among the thousands of Judah, yet out of thee shall he come forth unto me that is to be ruler in Israel; whose goings forth have been from of old, from everlasting."

- **Malachi 3:1-3** "Behold, I will send my messenger, and he shall prepare the way before me: and the Lord, whom ye seek, shall suddenly come to his temple, even the messenger of the covenant, whom ye delight in: behold, he shall come, saith the LORD of hosts. But who may abide the day of his coming? and who shall stand when he appeareth? for he is like a refiner's fire, and like fullers' sope: And he shall sit as a refiner and purifier of silver: and he shall purify the sons of Levi, and purge them as gold and silver, that they may offer unto the LORD an offering in righteousness."

THE DIVINE SPIRIT

While both Muslims and Jews believe in the existence of the Spirit, they either regard Him as a created being or an impersonal extension of God.

- **Zechariah 4:6** "Then he answered and spake unto me, saying, This is the word of the LORD unto Zerubbabel, saying, Not by might, nor by power, but by my spirit, saith the LORD of hosts."

These next verses indicate that the Spirit is a Being distinct from God the Father and having godlike characteristics:

- **Ezekiel 2:2-3** "Then the Spirit entered me when He spoke to me, and set me on my feet; and I heard Him who spoke to me. And He said to me: "Son of man, I am sending you to the children of Israel, to a rebellious nation that has rebelled against Me; they and their fathers have transgressed against Me to this very day."

- **Ezekiel 11:5** "Then the Spirit of the LORD fell upon me, and said to me, "Speak! 'Thus says the LORD: "Thus you have said, O house of Israel; for I know the things that come into your mind.""

These verses provide weighty OT evidence that the Messiah is God and a member of the Trinity. Of course, the NT teaches these truths far more explicitly. Nevertheless, the OT evidence remains integral to the Christian defense. This evidence also demonstrates that the doctrines of the Deity of Messiah and the Trinity weren't NT inventions or had been borrowed from other religions.

In the next chapter, I will be presenting evidence – the hidden portraits of Christ and His *Christophanies* in the Hebrew Scriptures – which I think is even weightier than these explicit passages.

WORKS CITED

Sigal, Gerald, *The Jew and the Christian Missionary: A Jewish Response to Missionary Christianity,* (New York: KTAV Publishing House, Inc., 1981)

Chapter 19

CHRISTOPHANIES IN THE TORAH

There is a wealth of evidence for the appearances of a Messianic God-Person in the *Five Books of Moses*, the Torah. We call these "Theophanies" or "Christophanies." We have good reason to the in terms of a Christophany whenever the "The Angel of the Lord" (in the singular) is mentioned in the Torah. Interestingly, in each one of these appearances, there is direct evidence that He is God. Take His first appearance:

- "The angel of the LORD found her by a spring of water in the wilderness, the spring on the way to Shur. And he said, "Hagar, servant of Sarai, where have you come from and where are you going?" She said, "I am fleeing from my mistress Sarai." The angel of the LORD said to her, "Return to your mistress and submit to her." The angel of the LORD also said to her, "I will surely multiply your offspring so that they cannot be numbered for multitude." And the angel of the LORD said to her, "Behold, you are pregnant and shall bear a son. You shall call his name Ishmael, because the LORD has listened to your affliction. He shall be a wild donkey of a man, his hand against everyone and everyone's hand against him, and he shall dwell over against all his kinsmen." So she called the name of the LORD [Yahweh] who spoke to her, "You are a God of seeing," for she said, "Truly here I have seen him who looks after me." (*Genesis 16:7-13; ESV*)

Here, the Angel is also identified by the narrative as the "LORD" ("Yahweh" in Hebrew, a term that is only used for God). Hagar then acknowledges that this Angel is "God."

This presents us with a paradox. How can this Angel also be God? Aren't there two people present – the Angel and

Yahweh? The paradox is heightened by the fact that the Hebrew word "malach," which is generally translated as "angel," is also translated in other contexts as "messenger." Whichever translation is chosen, "The Angel of God" or "messenger," both terms indicate that this individual is a distinct person from the God whom sent him. And yet, he is also called "God" or "Yahweh."

This, of course can be resolved from a Trinitarian perspective. The Son, Jesus, is both a distinct Person, the Angel, and yet God Himself.

In the next appearance of The Angel of the Lord, Yahweh is merely identified as a man:

- "And the <u>LORD</u> appeared to him by the oaks of Mamre, as he sat at the door of his tent in the heat of the day. He lifted up his eyes and looked, and behold, <u>three men</u> were standing in front of him. When he saw them, he ran from the tent door to meet them and bowed himself to the earth." (*Genesis 18:1-2*)

Although "The Angel of the Lord" is not mentioned in this account, we are again confronted with the same perplexity as before. Yahweh appears as a man along with two other "men," who are actually "angels" (*Genesis 19:1*). While the two go to investigate Sodom after enjoying a meal with Abraham, "Yahweh" remains behind, while Abraham intercedes with Him on behalf of his nephew Lot and his family:

- "So the [two] men turned from there and went toward Sodom, but Abraham still stood before the LORD [Yahweh]." (*Genesis 18:22*)

However, the rabbis claim that Yahweh cannot take on human form. Therefore, they claim that this "Yahweh" was only a *messenger* from Yahweh. Rabbi Gerald Sigal had written,

232

"God sends angels to act in His name, not in their own names" (Sigal,133).

However, the text will not allow such an interpretation. After Yahweh had assured Abraham that He would spare Sodom if ten righteous could be found within it, Scripture claims that Yahweh left Abraham:

- And the LORD ["Yahweh," not the "man"] went his way, when he had finished speaking to Abraham, and Abraham returned to his place. (*Genesis 18:33*)

From all indications, the text leads us to believe that *Yahweh* was actually present. Nevertheless, rabbinic authorities argue that this person could not possibly be Yahweh because Yahweh cannot be seen (*Exodus 33:20*). However, this doesn't discount the second Person of the Trinity, the Son. From an NT point of view, the impossibility of God being seen refers strictly to the *Father* (*John 1:18; 1 Timothy 6:16*).

Jacob later wrestled with a "man," whom he later understood was God:

- So Jacob called the name of the place Peniel, saying, "For I have seen God face to face, and yet my life has been delivered." (*Genesis 32:30*)

Jacob was convinced that he had wrestled with God. Later, Jacob identified God as the "Angel" with whom he had wrestled and equated the Angel with God:

- And he [Jacob] blessed Joseph and said, "The <u>God</u> before whom my fathers Abraham and Isaac walked, the <u>God</u> who has been my shepherd all my life long to this day, <u>the angel</u> who has redeemed me from all evil, <u>bless the boys</u>; and in them let my name be carried on, and the name of my fathers Abraham and Isaac; and let

233

them grow into a multitude in the midst of the earth."
(*Genesis 48:15-16*)

After Jacob invokes the name of God three times, he calls upon God to "bless the boys." However, "bless" is in the singular, which reflects the fact that although he had invoked God three times, he also recognized that they are all One!

(Why did Jacob refer to the Angel is the One who "has redeemed me from all evil?" He, God, had allowed Jacob to have his way with Him, even to humiliate and brutalize Him, as a foreshadowing of what would happen to Him on the Cross.)

Well, isn't this evidence of a Christophany? Not according to the rabbis. Gerald Sigal wrote:

- "The fact that Jacob sees "*elohim* face to face" only goes to prove that the divine being [a mere messenger from God] that Jacob wrestles with is not God. But, since the angel represents God, Jacob views the messenger as if it is God Himself. It is quite clear that this angel is not God manifested on earth as a human being. At no time does the Hebrew Bible teach this belief." (Sigal, 143)

Sigal once again appeals to *Exodus 33:20*, which claims that God cannot be seen. However, this evidently only pertains to God, the Father. Instead, the Torah repeatedly demonstrates that God can be seen in His human appearances.

Then the Angel appeared to Moses in the midst of the burning bush in the middle of the desert:

- "And the angel of the LORD appeared to him in a flame of fire out of the midst of a bush. He looked, and behold, the bush was burning, yet it was not consumed. And Moses said, 'I will turn aside to see this great sight, why the bush is not burned.' "When the LORD saw that he turned aside to see, God called to him out of the bush, "Moses, Moses!" And he said, 'Here I am.'" (*Exodus 3:2-4*)

First, the account claims that the Angel of the Lord had been in the midst of the bush; then it claims that it is actually "Yahweh" who is in the midst of the bush. Notice that this Angel is also called "LORD" (Yahweh) and "God!" To reinforce the claim that Yahweh is actually present, the account reads:

- "...<u>God</u> called to him out of the bush, "Moses, Moses!" And he said, 'Here I am.' Then he said, "Do not come near; take your sandals off your feet, for the place on which you are standing is <u>holy ground</u>" ...And Moses hid his face, for he was <u>afraid to look at God</u>." (*Exodus 3:4-6*)

Moses understood that this was "holy ground," because of Yahweh's presence and not the presence of a mere messenger. Besides, the fact that he was "afraid to look at God" meant that he knew that God was present in the bush.

Nevertheless, Sigal seems to believe that *both* the Angel and God were "present" in some sense:

- "...the textual evidence leans in favor of the view that this angel of the Lord functions here solely as a fiery manifestation which attracts Moses' attention, while it is the God of Israel who actually "appeared," that is, made Himself known and spoke to Moses...an angel of the Lord" can in no way be identified as part of the divine essence." (Sigal, 134-35)

Once again, contrary to the text, Sigal will not acknowledge that God actually appeared in the bush. Consequently, Moses was afraid to look upon Him and had been instructed that this was holy ground. Instead, Sigal has to awkwardly claim that both individuals were somehow present in the one bush. While Moses had been convinced that Yahweh was actually present, Sigal is convinced that he knows better.

Instead, all of these appearances provide us with evidence that God, Yahweh, is not as the present-day rabbi's claim. Instead, these appearances of a Messianic figure provide us with additional evidence for the Trinity in the Hebrew Scriptures.

Before the Battle of Jericho, the Angel, another Christophany, identifies Himself to Joshua as the "Commander of the Lord's army." Here too, we find out that this "Commander" is actually Yahweh:

- "And he said, 'No; but I am the commander of the army of the LORD. Now I have come.' And Joshua fell on his face to the earth and worshiped and said to him, 'What does my lord say to his servant?' And the commander of the LORD's army said to Joshua, 'Take off your sandals from your feet, for the place where you are standing is holy.' And Joshua did so." (*Joshua 5:14-15*)

A mere angel or messenger would never have received worship. Only the former archangel Satan demanded worship. Even though the Prophets of Israel were messengers of the Lord, they never asked anyone to take off their shoes in their presence. They understood that they were only human. Consequently, this Commander would have been usurping God's majesty to demand that Joshua take off his sandals had He not been God. Instead, this command signified that God was present as He stood before Joshua. The narrative also identifies Him as "Yahweh":

- And the LORD said to Joshua, "See, I have given Jericho into your hand, with its king and mighty men of valor." (*Joshua 6:2*)

The Angel had also manifested Himself to Samson's parents, Manoah and his previously barren wife to promise them as son. However, Manoah was beginning to suspect that this He was more than just a mere messenger:

- And Manoah said to the angel of the LORD, "What is your name [essence of being], so that, when your words come true, we may honor you?" And the angel of the LORD said to him, "Why do you ask my name, seeing it is wonderful?" (*Judges 13:17-18*)

The Angel responded that His name or essence was "wonderful," ("pawlee;" a term used in reference to the Messiah, *Isaiah 9:6*, but never to a mere messenger). The narrative also identifies Him as Yahweh:

- "So Manoah took the young goat with the grain offering, and offered it on the rock to the <u>LORD</u>, to the one who works <u>wonders</u>, and Manoah and his wife were watching. And when the flame went up toward heaven from the altar, the angel of the LORD went up in the flame of the altar. Now Manoah and his wife were watching, and they fell on their faces to the ground. The angel of the LORD appeared no more to Manoah and to his wife. Then Manoah knew that he was the angel of the LORD. And Manoah said to his wife, "We shall surely <u>die, for we have seen God.</u>"" (*Judges 13:19-22*). We find the same phenomenon in the account of Gideon – (*Judges 6:22-23*)

While Samson's parents were convinced that they had "seen God," Sigal is not. He correctly points out that God ("Elohim" in the Hebrew) is also used to refer to human judges (*Exodus*

22:8) (Sigal, 129). However, Sigal overlooks all of the other contextual evidence that this couple had actually seen "Yahweh" and had become convinced of this fact.

The Angel was also the One who brought Israel out of Egypt:

- "When we cried out to the Lord, He heard our voice and sent the Angel and brought us up out of Egypt." (*Numbers 20:16*)

However, other verses claim that it was *God* who brought Israel out of Egypt. Again, in order to make sense out of this recurring paradox, it is most easily resolved by concluding that the Angel Himself is God, but as another Person. We find many examples of distinction between the Angel and Yahweh and yet Oneness, exactly what the doctrine of the Trinity posits.

God is often identified as the "Redeemer of Israel." However, at closer examination, it seems that the "Angel of His Presence" had "saved" and "redeemed" Israel:

- "In all their affliction He was afflicted, and the Angel of His Presence saved them; in His love and in His pity He redeemed them; and He bore them and carried them all the days of old." (*Isaiah 63:9*)

Is this a contradiction? Not unless this Angel is God Himself, the second Member of the Trinity! Here is further evidence. God the Father claimed that He could never be seen:

- But He said, "You cannot see My face; for no man shall see Me, and live." (*Exodus 33:20; 1 Timothy 6:16*)

Nevertheless, God was seen:

- "So the Lord spoke to Moses face to face, as a man speaks to his friend. And he would return to the camp, but his servant Joshua the son of Nun, a young man, did not depart from the tabernacle." (*Exodus 33:11*)

- And he [God] said, "Hear my words: If there is a prophet among you, I the LORD make myself known to him in a vision; I speak with him in a dream. Not so with my servant Moses. He is faithful in all my house. With him I speak mouth to mouth, clearly, and not in riddles, and he beholds the <u>form of the LORD</u>. Why then were you [Miriam and Aaron] not afraid to speak against my servant Moses?" (*Numbers 12:6-8*)

This sounds like a contradiction, unless Moses had seen God the Angel, the second Person of the Trinity. Elsewhere, God says:

- "Behold, I send an Angel before you to keep you in the way and to bring you into the place which I have prepared. Beware of Him and obey His voice; do not provoke Him, for He will not pardon your transgressions; for My name *is* in Him… For My Angel will go before you… and I will cut them off." (*Exodus 23:20-23*)

If God's "name" is in Him, this is the same as saying that "My essence or nature is in Him." God the Father also makes a sharp distinction between Himself and His Angel:

- "And I will send My Angel before you, and I will drive out the Canaanite and the Amorite and the Hittite and the Perizzite and the Hivite and the Jebusite. Go up to a land flowing with milk and honey; for I will not go up in your midst, lest I consume you on the way, for you are a stiff-necked people." (*Exodus 33:2-3*)

239

God, the Father, could not be in the presence of Israel. Therefore, He sent His Angel, the second Person of the Trinity to be with Israel.

Elsewhere, the Angel is mentioned interchangeably with God, suggesting that the Angel is *also* God, Yahweh:

- "And the Angel of God, who went before the camp of Israel, moved and went behind them; and the pillar of cloud went from before them and stood behind them." (*Exodus 14:19*)

- "Now it came to pass, in the morning watch, that the Lord looked down upon the army of the Egyptians through the pillar of fire and cloud, and He troubled the army of the Egyptians." (*Exodus 14:24*)

- "And the Lord went before them by day in a pillar of cloud to lead the way, and by night in a pillar of fire to give them light, so as to go by day and night." (*Exodus 13:21*)

Again, the Angel seems to be God Himself but as another distinct Person. The rabbis and the various cults do not seem to want to engage the extensive Biblical evidence. It simply does not accord with their worldview. However, these verses provide for us a compelling glimpse of the Trinity in the Torah and also in the following books of the Tanach.

WORKS CITED

Sigal, Gerald, *The Jew and the Christian Missionary: A Jewish Response to Missionary Christianity,* (New York: KTAV Publishing House, Inc., 1981)

Chapter 20

DOES JESUS FULFILL THE PROPHECY OF A VIRGIN GIVING BIRTH?

> "Behold, the virgin shall be with child, and bear a Son, and they shall call His name Immanuel," which is translated, "God with us." (*Matthew 1:23*)

Arguably, Isaiah 7:14 is the most contested verse in the Old Testament. Although Matthew unequivocally states that this is fulfilled by the birth of the Messiah, the Old Testament indicates a fulfillment during the life of King Ahaz. These two perspectives can be reconciled using the concept of a "double fulfillment." But is this an understanding that Christianity has illegitimately imposed upon the Old Testament?

A young Jewish believer reluctantly confessed that he thought that the rabbis had a better understanding of Scripture, in at least one area. He was referring to *Isaiah 7:14*, perhaps the most contested Old Testament verse.

The birth of this sign child was given by God through Isaiah to King Ahaz of Judah, whose life was being threatened by two northern kings. Ahaz didn't want a sign, since he had devised his own godless plans, allying himself with the powerful king of Assyria, but God gave him the sign anyway:

- "Therefore the Lord himself will give you a sign. Behold, the virgin shall conceive and bear a son, and shall call his name Immanuel. He shall eat curds and honey when he knows how to refuse the evil and choose the good. For before the boy knows how to refuse the evil and choose the good, the land whose two kings you dread will be deserted." (*Isaiah 7:14-16*)

The *Book of Matthew* requires us to understand *Isaiah 7:14* as a prophecy fulfilled by the birth of the Messiah Jesus to the Virgin Mary. However, the rabbis raise four potent challenges against this interpretation:

1. There is no imperative to take "Immanuel" ("God with us" in the Hebrew) as a description of the "child" as the NT insists on understanding it – God *actually* with us in Jesus Christ. Instead, the Rabbis insist that "Immanu_el_" is merely a name like Dani_el_ or Nathani_el_ ("El" always means "God" in Hebrew) and not a description of the nature of the person.

2. The Rabbis correctly assert that the Hebrew word "almah," translated as "virgin" in *Isaiah 7:14* can possibly be translated as "young maiden." Furthermore, if Isaiah had wanted to unequivocally say "virgin," he could have used the unequivocal word, "betulah," in this context, not the perhaps equivocal "almah." "Betulah" *always* means "virgin."

3. The prophecy of *Isaiah 7:14* was given to King Ahaz (ca. 735 BC) as a divine sign of what God had promised him – that the two northern kings, Pekah (Israel) and Rezin (Syria), who were threatening his own nation of Judah, would soon be destroyed (*Isaiah 7:1-16*). The birth of Jesus, which took place over 700 years later, couldn't possibly be a sign for Ahaz.

4. Isaiah's prophecy seems to have already been fulfilled by the birth of his son. Isaiah had prophesied to Ahaz that the promised events of the demise of Damascus (Syria) and Samaria (the Northern kingdom of Israel) would precede the sign-child's maturation:

    • "Curds and honey He shall eat, that He may know to refuse the evil and choose the good. For *before* the Child shall know to refuse the evil and choose the good, the land that you dread will be forsaken by both her kings." (*Isaiah 7:15-16*).

This same prophecy seems to be reiterated shortly afterwards when Isaiah's wife gives birth to their own child, Maher-Shalal-Hash-Baz:

- "Then I [Isaiah] went to the prophetess, and she conceived and bore a son. Then the Lord said to me, 'Call his name Maher-Shalal-Hash-Baz; for before the child shall have knowledge to cry 'My father' and 'My mother,' the riches of Damascus and the spoil of Samaria will be taken away before the king of Assyria.'" (*Isaiah 8:3-4*)

Here again, we find the same two elements—the destruction of both Damascus and Samaria preceding the child's maturation. This seems to indicate that the prophecy had already been fulfilled 700 years before Christ. Therefore, according to the rabbis, by applying this prophecy to the birth of Christ, the Christian Church had illegitimately manipulated the Hebrew Scripture into saying what it never intended to say.

Let's start with the last challenge first. If the birth of Isaiah's son had already fulfilled *Isaiah 7:14*, then this is a clear case of a multiple fulfillment. This concept suggests that a single prophetic message is sometimes fulfilled at different times and in slightly different ways. It acknowledges that the final fulfillment is often preceded by types. This is clearly visible in the New Testament, which understands the entire sacrificial system, with its holidays and offerings, as pre-figurements of Christ. But do the Hebrew Scriptures also provide evidence of this type of foreshadowing, where prophecies and objects are often pre-figurements or types of some ultimate realities yet to be revealed? Yes! Although the Hebrew Scriptures are not often explicit about pointing out types, they nevertheless do allude to them. For example, the prophet Zechariah sees the broken, assailed high priest Joshua as a type of One to come.

- "Then he showed me Joshua the high priest standing before the Angel of the LORD, and Satan standing at his right hand to oppose him. And the LORD said to Satan, 'The LORD rebuke you, Satan!... Is this not a brand plucked from the fire?' Now Joshua was clothed with filthy garments, and was standing before the Angel. 4Then He answered and spoke to those who stood before Him, saying, 'Take away the filthy garments from him.' And to him He said, 'See, I have removed your iniquity from you, and I will clothe you with rich robes.' And I said, 'Let them put a clean turban on his head...Hear, O Joshua, the high priest, you and your companions who sit before you, for they are a wondrous *sign*; for behold, I am bringing forth My Servant the BRANCH...And I will remove the iniquity of that land in one day.'" (*Zechariah 3:1-9*)

This passage abounds in pre-figurements and types. Joshua and his companions are symbolic of what the Lord will ultimately do through the Messiah. The filthy garments are symbolic of the sins that God will remove "in one day!" This removal serves as a pre-figurement of a justification by grace through faith alone. Joshua was certainly sin-stained. God never corrected the damning accusations of Satan. They were probably true, but the righteous God did something Satan could never understand. He would remove sin through the undisclosed work of a mysterious individual, the BRANCH!

The identity of the "Branch" becomes clearer three Chapters later where Zechariah is given another assignment regarding Joshua in his symbolic role.

- "Take the silver and gold, make an elaborate crown, and set it on the head of Joshua the son of Jehozadak,

244

the high priest. Then speak to him, saying, 'Thus says the LORD of hosts, saying: 'Behold, the Man whose name is the BRANCH! From His place He shall branch out, and He shall build the temple of the LORD. Yes, He shall build the temple of the LORD. He shall bear the glory, and shall sit and rule on His throne; so He shall be a priest on His throne.'" (*Zechariah 6:11-13*)

This passage is also replete with types and symbols. A crown is placed upon the head of Joshua, ostensibly making this priest a king! However, Joshua never actually became a king nor was he supposed to. Israel already had a civil magistrate, Zerubbabel. If Joshua had become king, this would have brought him into direct conflict with Zerubbabel. However, we have no evidence that this ever happened. From all indications, they worked harmoniously together to build the Temple. Furthermore, a separation of powers had been strictly instituted in Israel. A priest couldn't become a king and a king couldn't become a priest. Only the Messiah was worthy of occupying both posts (*Psalm 110*). God was revealing through Joshua that He would ultimately bring the two offices together through the glorious BRANCH who would "sit and rule on His throne." Thus, Joshua was merely a type or pre-figurement of *Someone greater* who would ultimately fulfill the type.

Are we confronted with something similar in *Isaiah 7*? Could Isaiah's child be a sign of a more glorious Child? Isaiah says as much!

- "Here am I [Isaiah] and the children whom the LORD has given me! We are for *signs* and *wonders* in Israel from the LORD of hosts, who dwells in Mount Zion." (*Isaiah 8:18*)

Signs of what? Could Maher-Shalal-Hash-Baz have prefigured the Messiah as Joshua did? The narratives regarding Joshua clearly point to a Person beyond Joshua. Does the Isaiah

245

passage point beyond Isaiah's son? To answer this question, it is imperative that we regard the broader context (*Isaiah: 7-12*) where we find the same elements of the "Immanuel" prophecy – a child born with divine names and an everlasting Kingdom. These related passages illuminate the original prophecy.

The term "Immanuel" (the conjunction of two very common words: "Immanu", "with us," with "El", God) appears only three times in Hebrew Scripture. The first instance is found in *Isaiah 7:14*. The other two instances are both found in the *next Chapter*. This alone would suggest that the three instances are *related* in Isaiah's mind (and in God's)! Additionally, all three uses are unusual, provocative and thematically related.

"Immanuel" is encountered for the second time after a description of what Assyria will do to Judah after Assyria swallows up Syria (also called "Damascus" and "Aram") and Israel (also called "Ephraim") in 721 BC.

- "Now therefore, behold, the Lord brings up over them the waters of the River, strong and mighty--the king of Assyria and all his glory; he will go up over all his channels And go over all his banks. He will pass through Judah, he will overflow and pass over, he will reach up to the neck; and the stretching out of his wings will fill the breadth of *Your* land, *O Immanuel*." [or "God with us"] (*Isaiah 8:7-8*)

Assyria will conquer Judah "up to the neck" (*Isaiah* 8:8). This probably refers to Assyria's unsuccessful siege of Jerusalem in 701 BC, which culminated when the angel of the Lord "put to death 185,000 men in the Assyrian camp" (*Isaiah 37:36*). The prophecy ends with the cry, "O Immanuel," seemingly an outcry for help to the same individual of *Isaiah 7:14*. (Even if this appearance of "Immanuel" doesn't represent a cry for help, it does plainly demonstrate that "Immanuel" is a significant figure in the history of Israel.)   However, in this latter context,

246

Immanuel seems to be more than a mere human! It would be ridiculous to cry for help to a human in such a hopeless situation. Assyria's victory seemed assured without miraculous intervention. However, it was this very intervention that turned the tide.

The third instance of "Immanuel" is more striking. In *Isaiah 8:9-10*, a prophetic warning is issued against Assyria and the nations it had incorporated within its army:

- "Be shattered, O you peoples, and be broken in pieces! Give ear, all you from far countries. Gird yourselves, but be broken in pieces; gird yourselves, but be broken in pieces. Take counsel together, but it will come to nothing; speak the word, but it will not stand, for *God is with us."* [*"Immanuel"* in the Hebrew] (*Isaiah 8:9-10*)

Despite the overwhelming superiority of the Assyrian army, it will not succeed against the wobbling and panic-stricken Jerusalem ("the neck") for one simple reason--"for God is with us" (the third instance of "*Immanuel*")! What started out as a cry for help (*Isaiah 8:8*) has now become a declaration of triumph (*Isaiah 8:10*)! "Immanuel" is the cause of this triumph. Reading the account of the destruction of the Assyrian army (*Isaiah: 36-39*), it is clear that "Immanuel" can't pertain to Hezekiah, nor to any mere mortal. "Immanuel" (appropriately translated here as "God is with us") holds the destiny of nations within His hands. (It's interesting to observe that English translations all render the Hebrew as "God is with us" rather than simply "Immanuel" which consistency among the two prior instances would ordinarily demand.)

To suggest that these three "Immanuels" represent three different people is more than sound interpretation will bear, especially since they are all found in adjacent Chapters. The more natural interpretation demands that the same titles or names pertain to the *same* person. Furthermore, this individual appears to be both human (a "child") and Divine! This conclusion will be born out as we track this "child" Immanuel in two subsequent and related contexts (*Isaiah 9:6-7; 11:1-12*).

Let's now look at another concept found in *Isaiah 7:14* which is also repeated within the context of Chapters *Isaiah 7-12* and serves to unify them. This is the concept of the birth of a child:

- "For unto us a Child is born, unto us a Son is given; and the government will be upon His shoulder. And His name will be called Wonderful, Counselor, Mighty God, Everlasting Father, Prince of Peace. Of the increase of His government and peace here will be no end, upon the throne of David and over His kingdom, to order it and establish it with judgment and justice from that time forward, even forever..." (*Isaiah 9:6-7*)

This prophecy is not only related to *Isaiah 7:14* by virtue of a birth of a special child, but also by the divine names. In *Isaiah 7:14*, we encountered a single divine name ("Immanuel") or is it a description of the child? In *Isaiah 9:6* we encounter *four* divine titles. I don't say "names" because at this point, it should be clear that these can't be mere names – not all four! – but rather *descriptive titles* of the Child. These four titles contain eight words—too cumbersome for actual names. It would be like naming a child "Anthony Robert Spencer Alan Thomas Arthur Andrew Timothy."

The first title, "Wonderful Counselor" ("Pele Yoetz" in Hebrew), is clearly divine. "Pele" might better have been translated "awesome" because this term only refers to God or to the wonders He miraculously brings into existence (for example, *Exodus 15:11; Daniel 12:6*).

"Mighty God" ("El Gibor") is clearly a divine designation because "El" as a free-standing word always refers to God. In addition to this, note that "Immanu El" of *Isaiah 7:14* also carries the free-standing "El" (along with *Isaiah 8:8 and 8:10*), establishing another parallel with *Isaiah 7:14*. This also serves to rule against "Immanu El" as merely a name (as Nathani<u>el</u>), as the Rabbis propose, instead of a description.

"Everlasting Father" is also a divine description. Who can be everlasting apart from God Himself? Even "Prince of Peace" seems to be a divine reference, for it is God Himself who will bring peace. Some Jewish interpreters want to understand these divine names as mere reminders that it is God who is performing His works through this child. However, all Jewish commentators argue that this prophecy cannot pertain to Jesus. For example, Gerald Sigal has written:

- The fact remains that Jesus did not literally or figuratively fulfill any of Isaiah's words. A "wonderful counselor" does not advise his followers that if they have faith they can be agents of destruction (*Matthew 21:19-21; Mark 11:14, 20-23*). (Sigal, 32)

The rest of Sigal's commentary is also so absurd that it is not worth reciting. However, it is this very Child who is called these descriptive titles. Nowhere does the text suggest that He is given these divine titles in remembrance of God!

It strains credulity to say that the "child" of Isaiah 9:6 is different from the "child" of *Isaiah 7:14*. As the "Immanu El" of *Isaiah 7:14* (*Isaiah 8:8, 10*) will reign supreme, so too will the "El Gibor" of *Isaiah 9:6*. Are we looking at two different Child Deities or at One? The Child of *Isaiah 9:6* will set up a kingdom with "no end," in harmony with the Immanuel we had encountered in two previous Chapters. This argues against two divine children or kingdoms.

This context is not complete without Chapter 11, where we find a third allusion to the Child:

- "There shall come forth a *Rod from the stem of Jesse*, and a *Branch shall grow out of his roots*. The Spirit of the LORD shall rest upon Him, the Spirit of wisdom and understanding, the Spirit of counsel and might, the Spirit of knowledge and of the fear of the LORD. His delight is in the fear of the LORD, and He shall not judge by the sight of His eyes, nor decide by the hearing of His ears; but with righteousness He shall judge the poor, and decide with equity for the meek of the earth; He shall strike the earth with the rod of His mouth, and with the breath of His lips He shall slay the wicked. Righteousness shall be the belt of His loins, and faithfulness the belt of His waist. The wolf also shall dwell with the lamb… They shall not hurt nor destroy in all My holy mountain, for the earth shall be full of the knowledge of the LORD as the waters cover the sea." (*Isaiah 11:1-9*)

Here we find an enlargement of the Messianic portrait established earlier. We find the Child, at long last, reigning in His own kingdom. However, in Chapter 11 this child is referred to with slightly different terms. Here He is a "Rod" and a "Branch," born from the "stump of Jesse" (*Isaiah 11.1*), the father of King David. Therefore, we are looking at the same lineage! Unmistakably, this is the same Child who "will reign upon the throne of David and over his kingdom" (*Isaiah 9:7*).

Other parallels are also clear. Both kingdoms "will have no end" (*Isaiah 9:7*), an idea which is expressed in Isaiah *11:9*. Both kingdoms will entail the establishment of "justice and righteousness" (*Isaiah 9:6*; compare with *Isaiah 11:3-5*) and endless "peace" (*Isaiah 9:7; 11:6-9*).

The Chapters build upon one another. In addition to the above elaborations upon the initial prophetic germ, the four divine titles (*Isaiah 9:6*; and the fifth of *Isaiah 7:14*) seem to receive an expanded treatment in Chapter 11: "Wonderful Counselor" in

Isaiah 11:2-5; "Prince of Peace" in Isaiah 11:6-9. (Perhaps "El Gibor" and "Everlasting Father" are reflected within the entire prophecy of Chapter 11 and the prayer of Chapter 12.) These parallels each serve to demonstrate that these prophecies are closely related. If this is the case, then one prophecy is illuminated and enhanced by the others, and we must understand "Immanu El" and "child" (*Isaiah 7:14*) in a way that accords with the other above-mentioned prophecies.

The seed of a prophecy that Isaiah proclaimed in *Isaiah 7:14* and amplified in *Isaiah 8:6-10* and *Isaiah 9:6-7*, he trumpets out in Chapter 11. This child is indeed the cause of all of the world's rejoicing, and it is only natural that this great revelation should culminate in a song of praise (Chapter 12).

This song has several interesting characteristics. There are three references to "salvation" ("Yeshua" in Hebrew, which is believed to be Jesus' Hebrew name):

- "Behold, God is <u>my salvation</u> ["My Yeshua"]; I will trust, and will not be afraid; for the LORD GOD is my strength and my song, and he has become <u>my salvation</u>." With joy you will draw water from the wells of <u>salvation</u>…Shout, and sing for joy, O inhabitant of Zion, for great in your midst is the Holy One of Israel." (*Isaiah 12:2-3, 6*)

Chapter 12 of Isaiah is part of a single related prophecy (Chapter 7-12). It concludes with "for great in your midst is the Holy One of Israel." (*Isaiah 12:6*). This seems to be a play on "God with us" ("Immanu El"). The words are different but the theme is the same. All of this suggests that Chapters 7 through 12 must be regarded together, as one inseparable prophetic utterance.

If *Isaiah 7:14* is part of a greater prophecy (Chapters 7-12), then this verse must be understood within the context of this entire prophecy. Any word or phrase needs the context of the sentence, paragraph, and narrative to be truly understood. Understanding "Immanu El" as merely a human child who was born during the reign of King Ahaz fails to see *Isaiah 7:14* in its broader context. This is an interpretive failure that an unbiased eye would not make.

When the rabbis translated the Hebrew Bible into Greek many years before Christ for the Jewish world of the Diaspora, they had to deal with *Isaiah 7:14*. If "almah" was equivocal and could be translated by either "virgin" or "young maiden," the Rabbis had an important choice to make. (It should be noted that in each of the seven appearances of "almah" in Scripture, there is no compelling reason to *not* translate it as "virgin.") If they translated it as "young maiden," it meant that they understood the prophecy as having been fulfilled in its *totality* at the time of Ahaz. If they translated "almah" as "virgin," then they understood that this referred to a *miraculous* birth that had not yet taken place, a fulfillment which was still awaiting its day. They translated "almah" as "Parthenos," in the Greek, a term that means "virgin!" In light of this, Matthew was simply walking in the expectation of the rabbis when he applied this prophecy to the birth of the Messiah, Yeshua.

Let's return to the third objection of the Rabbis--that the birth of Jesus (Yeshua) couldn't possibly be a sign for Ahaz, to whom the prophecy was addressed. However, a closer look at the text shows that the prophecy *wasn't* intended for Ahaz *alone*. The *entire* "house of David" was in view.

- Then he said, "Hear now, O <u>house of David</u>! Is it a small thing for you to weary men, but will you weary my God also? Therefore the Lord Himself will give <u>you</u> (plural) a sign: Behold, the virgin shall conceive and bear a Son, and shall call His name Immanuel." (*Isaiah 7:13-14*)

Isaiah recognized that the audience for his prophecy went

252

beyond Ahaz. His message transcended its temporal boundaries, and he knew it! The prophecies constituted a sign of something far greater (*Isaiah* 8:18).

There is another reason why neither Hezekiah nor Isaiah's son could have fulfilled *Isaiah 7:14* in its entirety. A natural birth is hardly a "sign" (*Isaiah 7:14*). Young maidens are giving birth all of the time. There is nothing unusual about this, nothing that would have the persuasive weight to confirm a seemingly improbable prophecy. Only an unusual birth, a virgin birth, would constitute a legitimate sign, although an embarrassing one for the virgin herself.

Clearly, this prophecy reaches beyond the person and time of Ahaz. In many ways it points to a divine Person standing at the headwaters of both history and the future, to a Person who holds the destiny of Israel in His hand. In the strongest terms, it cries out that this is the One for whom Israel has been waiting, the One who would fulfill all the promises of God seated upon "David's throne" (*Isaiah 9:7*). It would be this Child who would set up an everlasting kingdom (*Isaiah 9:7, 11:9*) in which there would be no end to peace and the knowledge of the Lord. Although there was a type or a shadow of fulfillment in Ahaz's time, the ultimate fulfillment of *Isaiah 7:14* awaited the Messiah.

My Jewish friend believed that Jesus is the prophesied Messiah, but he was also very conflicted in his understanding of the prophecies. This deprived him of peace. The antidote to the conflict that rages in so many of us is a *resolution* of the conflict, the perceiving of God's hidden treasures in the midst of the confusion. This requires persistent work, but even more than work, the grace of God, which He pours out liberally upon those weary souls who seek His wisdom (*James 1:5, Psalm 51:6; 25:14*).

WORKS CITED

Sigal, Gerald, *The Jew and the Christian Missionary: A Jewish Response to Missionary Christianity,* (New York: KTAV Publishing House, Inc., 1981)

Chapter 21

IS ISAIAH 53 ABOUT ISRAEL OR THE MESSIAH?

www.mannsword.blogspot.com/2019/03/is-isaiah-53-about-israel-or-messiah.html

It is beyond dispute that the ancient rabbis regarded *Isaiah 53* as Messianic. In *The Life and Times of Jesus the Messiah*, the Jewish Christian scholar, Alfred Edersheim, provided two references, where these rabbis regarded *Isaiah 53* as Messianic – one from the Midrash on Samuel, and the other from a Targum (Edersheim, 727).

However, there are many other rabbinic references regarding *Isaiah 53* as Messianic. Rabbi Moshe Alshekh, a famous 16th century rabbinic scholar asserted:

- "[Our] Rabbis with one voice, accept and affirm the opinion that the prophet [*Isaiah 53*] is speaking of king Messiah."   (Frydland, 53)

Frydland also quotes the Talmud tractate *Sanhedrin*:

- The Rabanan [rabbis] say that Messiah's name is The Suffering Scholar…for it is written, "Surely He hath borne our grief and carried our sorrows, yet we did esteem him stricken, smitten of God and afflicted." [*Isaiah 53*] (Frydland, 54)

- "Generally then, the Talmud, the Targum, the Midrashim, the Zohar and Pesikta Rabbati recognized a suffering Messiah in fulfillment of *Isaiah 53* and other similar descriptions in the Tenach." (Frydland, 54)

However today, many rabbis, starting with Rashi, have rallied around the assertion that the "Suffering Servant" of *Isaiah 53* is the nation of Israel and *not the Messiah*.

- "The chief representative of the non-Messianic, collective interpretation was the 11th century French-Jewish scholar, Rabbi Shlomo Itzhaki (1040-1105), best known by his initials as Rashi.... In time the non-Messianic interpretation of *Isaiah 53* practically became an official dogma among most Jewish people." (Brown, 16-17)

Furthermore, instead of the Messiah dying for the sins of the people, Rashi claimed that Israel died for the Gentiles. However, is this assertion at all tenable? I have presented the verses from *Isaiah 53* in order and inserted what the rabbinic interpretation suggests to demonstrate how their interpretation violates Scripture and common sense:

Isaiah 53:1-3 **"Who has believed our report? And to whom has the arm of the Lord been revealed? For He [Israel] shall grow up before Him as a tender plant, and as a root out of dry ground. He has no form or comeliness; and when we [Gentiles] see Him [Israel], there is no beauty that we [Gentiles] should desire Him [Israel]. He [Israel] is despised and rejected by [Gentile] men, a Man of sorrows and acquainted with grief. And we [Gentiles] hid, as it were, our faces from Him [Israel]; He [Israel] was despised, and we [Gentiles] did not esteem Him."** (All of these *Isaiah 53* verses come from the NKJV.)

The present rabbinic understanding is highly improbable. The narrator is no longer Isaiah but *Gentile spokesmen* ["we," *Isaiah 53:3*] who has incredibly slipped in and dislodged the author, Isaiah. However, there is no precedent for such a thing in all of the Scriptures. This alone should disqualify the rabbinic interpretation.

In a vain attempt to eliminate Jesus from consideration, the modern rabbis have stumbled upon an absurd interpretation, in which Israel dies for *"we" Gentiles*. Is there any Biblical evidence that Israel would die a redemptive death for the Gentiles? No! All of the evidence points to the Messiah as the Redeemer and not sinful Israel! Israel is always characterized as the object of mercy, not its source.

In *The Jew and the Christian Missionary*, Rabbi Gerald Sigal also argues that this chapter could not possibly refer to Jesus:

- "Jesus, as portrayed in the Gospels, does not at all fit that of the Suffering Servant of the Lord as portrayed in Isaiah." (Sigal, 39)

Why not? Sigal argues that the Jesus of the Gospels was popular. However the Suffering Servant of *Isaiah 53* was not. In support of this charge, he cites:

- "Then Jesus returned in the power of the Spirit to Galilee, and news of Him went out through all the surrounding region. And He taught in their synagogues, being glorified by all." (Sigal, p.39 - quoting *Luke 4:14-15*; similarly, *Luke 8:4; Matthew 27:57*)

However, Jesus' "popularity" was only *temporary and skin-deep*. Ultimately, the world turned against Him. Jesus informed His biological brethren:

- "The world cannot hate you, but it hates Me because I testify of it that its works are evil." (*John 7:7; 15:18-20*)

The crowd only followed Him as long as they could benefit from His miracles and free meals:

- "From that time many of His disciples went back and walked with Him no more." (*John 6:66*)

257

- "Pilate said to [the crowd of assembled Jews], 'What then shall I do with Jesus who is called Christ?' They all said to him, "Let Him be crucified!" (*Matthew 27:22*)

Isaiah 53:4-6 **"Surely He [Israel] has borne our [Gentile] griefs and carried our sorrows; Yet we [Gentiles] esteemed Him [Israel] stricken, smitten by God, and afflicted. But He [Israel] was wounded for our [Gentile] transgressions, He was bruised for our [Gentile] iniquities; the chastisement for our peace was upon Him [Israel], and by His [Israel's] stripes we [Gentiles] are healed. All we [Gentiles] like sheep have gone astray; We [Gentiles] have turned, every one, to his own way; and the Lord has laid on Him [Israel] the iniquity of us [Gentiles] all."**

According to the rabbinic interpretation, the salvation of God's chosen people is not an issue, as if Israel didn't need it, just the salvation of the Gentiles. Remarkably, Sigal, following other rabbis, claimed that the narrators are Gentiles:

- "The Gentile spokesmen depict the Servant (the Nation of Israel) as bearing the "diseases" and carrying the "pains" which they themselves should have suffered." (Sigal, 42)

However, just a quick read through the Prophets of Israel will show that Israel wasn't in any position to carry the sins of others. They could not even bear their own sins. The Prophets make it plain that it was Israel who has "gone astray" and "turned, every one, to his own way." The Gentiles could not have been described as "gone astray." They were never in a position to have "gone astray" from God.

Traditionally, Israel-as-Redeemer hadn't been the Jewish position. Moses Maimonides, (1135-1204), perhaps the most famous rabbi of all time, in a letter to Jacob Alfajumi, commenting on *Isaiah 52:15 and 53:2*:

- "What is to be the manner of Messiah's advent...He came up as a sucker before him, and as a root out of dry earth [*53:2*], . . . in the words of Isaiah, when describing the manner in which the kings will hearken to him, at him the kings will shut their mouth; for that which had not been told them they have seen, and that which they had not heard they have perceived. (Quoted in The Fifty-Third Chapter of Isaiah According to the Jewish Interpreters" (translations by S.R. Driver and A.D. Neubauer, 374-375.)

According to Maimonides, the Redeemer is the Messiah. We even find this thinking reflected in the Day of Atonement Musaf (additional) prayer:

- "Our righteous anointed [Messiah] is departed from us: horror hath seized us, and we have none to justify us. He hath borne the yoke of our iniquities, and our transgression [*Isaiah 53:5*]. He beareth our sins on his shoulder, that he may find pardon for our iniquities. We shall be healed by his wound, at the time that the Eternal will create him as a new creature."

Isaiah 53:7 He [Israel] was oppressed and He was afflicted, yet He [Israel] opened not His mouth; He was led as a lamb to the slaughter, and as a sheep before its shearers is silent, so He opened not His mouth.

Although we cannot find any Biblical references to affirm that Israel had been silent in the face of oppression, we do find that this is true of Jesus. Nevertheless, Sigal claims that:

- "Jesus presented a strong defense both before the Sanhedrin and Pilate!" (Sigal, 50)

In support of this absurd claim, Sigal cites *John 18:20-21*:

- Jesus answered him, "I spoke openly to the world. I always taught in synagogues and in the temple, where the Jews always meet, and in secret I have said nothing. Why do you ask Me? Ask those who have heard Me what I said to them. Indeed they know what I said."

This was no defense. Jesus acted provocatively in order to be found "guilty," as the next two verses indicate:

- And when He had said these things, one of the officers who stood by struck Jesus with the palm of his hand, saying, "Do You answer the high priest like that?" Jesus answered him, "If I have spoken evil, bear witness of the evil; but if well, why do you strike Me?" (*John 18:22-23*)

According to the standards of that day, Jesus had answered confrontationally and was therefore struck. This was the opposite of a defense. Before the Sanhedrin, He remained silent, opening His mouth only to aid the prosecution:

- But He kept silent and answered nothing. Again the high priest asked Him, saying to Him, "Are You the Christ, the Son of the Blessed?" Jesus said, "I am. And you will see the Son of Man sitting at the right hand of the Power, and coming with the clouds of heaven." Then the high priest tore his clothes and said, "What further need do we have of witnesses?" (*Mark 14:61-63*)

Before Pilate, Jesus admitted He had a kingdom. However, this would place Him in competition with Pilate's boss, Caesar, who had zero tolerance for any kingdoms besides his own:

- "What have You done?" [Pilate asked.] Jesus answered, "My kingdom is not of this world. If My kingdom were of this world, My servants would fight, so that I should not be delivered to the Jews; but now My kingdom is not from here." Pilate therefore said to Him, "Are You a king then?" Jesus answered, "You say rightly that I am a king. For this cause I was born, and for this cause I have come into the world." (*John 18:35-37*)

At this point, to exonerate a "rival" king was to betray Caesar – risky business! Jesus then further infuriated both Pilate and King Herod with His silence:

- "And while He was being accused by the chief priests and elders, He answered nothing. Then Pilate said to Him, 'Do You not hear how many things they testify against You?' "But He answered him not one word [in defense], so that the governor marveled greatly." (*Matthew 27:12-14*)

- Then he questioned Him with many words, but He answered him nothing. And the chief priests and scribes stood and vehemently accused Him. (*Luke 23:9-10*)

Contrary to Sigal's claim, we find *no* semblance of any defense here. Instead, Jesus helped the prosecution to condemn Him.

Isaiah 53:8-9 **"He [Israel] was taken from prison and from judgment ["By oppression and judgment he was taken away," ESV, NIV], and who will declare His generation [his future offspring]? For He [Israel] was cut off from the land of the living; for the transgressions of My [Gentile] people He [Israel] was stricken. And they made His [Israel's] grave with the wicked--but with the rich at His [Israel's]**

death, because He [Israel] had done no violence. Nor was any deceit in His [Israel's] mouth."

Jesus was deprived of justice ("judgment") and was killed. Therefore, no one could talk about His progeny ("generation"). However, this hadn't been the case with Israel. Israel was not "cut off from the land of the living." Israel remained to produce progeny. It is also clearly untrue that Israel "had done no violence. Nor was any deceit in His [Israel's] mouth." At times, the Prophets charged that Israel had morally descended below the Gentiles.

How was Israel's grave with both the wicked and the rich? Sigal claims that, somehow, this was *figuratively* true. However, the Gospels declare that this was literally the case with Jesus, dying with sinners and buried in a rich man's tomb. These are claims that could have been very easily disproved had they not been true!

However, Sigal claims that this description could not fit Jesus because Jesus had done much "violence," contrary to Isaiah's description of the Suffering Servant. In support of this charge, Sigal cites Jesus' "violence" to the money-changers (*Matthew 21:12*), His casting demons out into swine (*Mark 5:13*), and His teaching about bringing a sword to divide families (*Matthew 10:34-35*).

However, this is a desperate attempt to disqualify Jesus. In none of these three instances did Jesus perform or advocate *sinful* violence. Clearly, there was no attempt to bring charges against Him for expelling the money-changers. If Jesus had broken the law, the Sanhedrin would have promptly brought charges against him.

Sigal then claims that "no deceit in his mouth" (*Isaiah 53:9*) could not apply to Jesus! This is because Jesus had been misleading when He promised to raise the Temple up in three days (*John 2:19-21*), which He didn't do, simply because He was talking figuratively about His body as the Temple.

Sigal also indicts Jesus because He hid the truth, talking in parables (*Matthew 13:10-11*). According to him, this practice was deceitful. However, according to this thinking, poets are also deceitful.

Isaiah 53:10-11 "Yet it pleased the Lord to bruise Him [Israel]; He has put Him to grief. When You make His [Israel's] soul an offering for sin, He [Israel] shall see His seed ("offspring"), He [Israel] shall prolong His days, and the pleasure of the Lord shall prosper in His hand. He shall see the labor of His soul, and be satisfied. By His knowledge [of Israel] My righteous Servant [Israel] shall justify many, for He shall bear their [Gentile] iniquities."

In place of the Messiah, the rabbis have made Israel into the savior of the world. However, there is no reason to suppose that Israel's death could represent "an offering for sin." Sin offerings had to be without any blemish. Meanwhile, Israel was covered with moral blemishes. Consequently, Israel could not qualify to "bear their [Gentile] iniquities."

We should also ask how it could possibly be that the knowledge about Israel "shall justify many?" There is absolutely no Biblical precedent for such an idea. However, it is true that faith (knowledge) in the Messiah will "justify many!" (*Psalm 2:12*).

Also, throughout, the masculine singular pronoun "he" is used to designate the suffering servant. Such a pronoun is very rarely used in regards to Israel. More usually, Israel is referred to as "you," she/her." and "they/them." However, there is absolutely no problem at all in using "he" in reference to the Messiah.

Sigal claims that "offspring" or "seed" (*53:10*) could not pertain to believers in Christ, as Christians allege, because, according to him, this term is always used to designate one's own children and not figurative or spiritual children.

However, even though this is the usual usage for "offspring," there are exceptions. Sometimes, it can be used figuratively:

- "But come here, you sons of the sorceress, you offspring of the adulterer and the harlot! Whom do you ridicule? Against whom do you make a wide mouth and stick out the tongue? Are you not children of transgression, offspring of falsehood?" (*Isaiah 57:3-4*)

It is also interesting to note that this Servant, who dies as a burnt offering for the people, will eventually "see the labor of His soul, and be satisfied." This implies that He will again live subsequent to His death. Therefore, this prophecy also represents a cryptic reference to the resurrection.

In fact, all of the verses envisioning the death of the Messiah also seem to contain a cryptic reference to His subsequent resurrection! I'll just offer one more example:

- "Therefore my heart is glad and my tongue rejoices; my body also will rest secure, because you will not abandon me to the grave, nor will you let your Holy One see decay." (*Psalm 16:9-10*)

Interestingly, this verse cryptically portrays the Messiah's death and subsequent life. As David, He too will be in the grave (death). However, He will not remain and decay there (resurrection) as David's body had!

If this isn't enough, let's take a look at the preceding verses, which have also been regarded as Messianic:

Isaiah 52:13-15 **"Behold, My Servant shall deal prudently; He [Israel] shall be exalted and extolled and be very high. Just as many were astonished at you, so His visage was marred more than any man, and His form more than the sons of men; So shall He [Israel] sprinkle many nations. Kings shall shut their mouths [in humility] at Him; for what had not been told them they shall see, and what they had not heard they shall consider."**

"He shall be exalted and extolled and be very high." This is true for the Messiah but not for Israel. Instead, Israel will mourn when they look upon the Messiah whom they have "pierced" (*Zechariah 12:10*). Yet, they will also be forgiven.

"His visage was marred more than any man" describes what had happened to the Messiah. He had been so terribly beaten that when Pilate re-introduced Him before the people, he needed to inform them that this marred man was Jesus: "Behold the Man!" (*John 19:5*)

The passage also claims that, "So shall He sprinkle many nations," something that Israel's blood could not accomplish. This Hebrew term refers only to ceremonial/sanctifying sprinkling of blood or water.

"Kings shall shut their mouths" in fear before Him. This is something that would be true for the Messiah (*Isaiah 49:7, 23*) but not for Israel.

This entire discourse will raise the question, "Why then isn't God more explicit about these critical matters?" While I think that there are many reasons for this, I'll just address one. There is knowledge that we are not ready to handle. The Apostle Paul writes:

- "No, we speak of God's secret wisdom, a wisdom that has been hidden and that God destined for our glory before time began. None of the rulers of this age understood it, for if they had, they would not have crucified the Lord of glory. However, as it is written: 'No eye has seen, no ear has heard, no mind has conceived what God has prepared for those who love him.'" (*1 Corinthians 2:7-9 NIV*)

It is not just God's enemies who are kept in the dark. It is we too, and I trust for good reason! Meanwhile, He has granted "those who have eyes to see" a body of knowledge, which are we mandated to defend (*Jude 3*) against the Gospel's many detractors. May our Lord enable us!

WORKS CITED

Brown, Michael, *Answering Jewish Objections to Jesus*, Vol. Three (Grand Rapids: Baker Books, 2007)

Edersheim, Alfred*, The Life and Times of Jesus the Messiah*, (McClean, VA: Macdonald Publishing, no publication date given)

Frydland, Rachmiel, *What the Rabbis Know about the Messiah*, Messianic Publishing Company, 4th Edition, 2011) www.amazon.com/What-Rabbis-Know-About-Messiah/dp/0917842073

Mamonidies, Jewish Interpreters, (translations by S.R. Driver and A.D. Neubauer), KTAV publishing House, New York, 1969.) www.jewishroots.net/library/prophecy/isaiah/isaiah-53/what-rabbis-said-2.html

Mann, Daniel, *"Is Isaiah 53 About Israel or the Messiah?"* www.mannsword.blogspot.com/2019/03/is-isaiah-53-about-israel-or-messiah.html

Sigal, Gerald, *The Jew and the Christian Missionary: A Jewish Response to Missionary Christianity,* (New York: KTAV Publishing House, Inc., 1981),

Chapter 22

WAS THE RESURRECTION PROOF THAT JESUS IS THE PROMISED MESSIAH?

In *"Why the Jews Rejected Jesus,"* Orthodox Jewish writer, David Klinghoffer, attempted to argue that the Jews of Jesus' day didn't have any adequate reasons to believe that Jesus was their Messiah. Why not? For one thing, they would have discounted the Resurrection as proof:

- "If no verse in the prophets unambiguously presented resurrection as a criterion for recognizing the Messiah—and none does—then such a hypothetical wonder [Jesus' resurrection] would prove nothing." (Klinghoffer, 88)

Although Klinghoffer is correct that the Old Testament doesn't provide any *explicit* statements that the Messiah will be resurrected, there is a wealth of implicit evidence—*every* Old Testament portrait of the Messiah's death is accompanied by a cryptic glimpse of His "resurrection," or at least a portrait of His life after death! If this is the case, it defies all odds and suggests that the collected books of the Hebrew Scriptures reflect a design or pattern that could only originate from above.

I'll just provide the eight clearest examples of this highly unlikely association between the Messiah's death and His return to life. Peter quoted *Psalm 16* in his first evangelistic speech (*Acts 2:25-32*) in reference to Jesus' resurrection:

- "For You will not leave my [David's] soul in Sheol, nor will You allow Your Holy One to see corruption [the decay of His body in the grave]." (*Psalm 16:10*)

268

Here, in one quick snapshot, we see the Messiah's death, but also a promise of His future life! Perhaps more dramatically, Isaiah pictures the Messiah living once again following His ordeal:

- "And they made His grave with the wicked--but with the rich at His death, because He had done no violence, nor was any deceit in His mouth. Yet it pleased the LORD to bruise Him; He has put Him to grief. When You make His soul an offering for sin, He shall see His seed, He shall prolong His days, and the pleasure of the LORD shall prosper in His hand. He shall see the labor of His soul, and be satisfied. By His knowledge My righteous Servant shall justify many, for He shall bear their iniquities." (*Isaiah 53:9-11.* Because it might be difficult to see the evidence that the Messiah will live again, I will underline the evidence.)

Although Jesus died, becoming an "offering for sin," He nevertheless "prolonged His days."

The Psalms provide us with a number of remarkable, albeit opaque, portraits of the crucifixion and the subsequent life of the Messiah. Although modern rabbis reject these portraits as Messianic. The Talmud, compiled around 550 AD, contains ancient rabbinic confirmation that these Psalms as Messianic:

- "For dogs have surrounded Me; the congregation of the wicked has enclosed Me. They pierced My hands and My feet; I can count all My bones. They look and stare at Me. They divide My garments among them, and for My clothing they cast lots...I will declare Your name to My brethren; In the midst of the assembly I will praise You. You who fear the LORD, praise Him! All you descendants of Jacob, glorify Him, and fear Him, all you offspring of Israel! For He has not despised nor abhorred the affliction of the afflicted; nor has He hidden His face from Him; but when He cried to Him, <u>He heard</u>." (*Psalm 22:16-18, 22-24*)

- "Reproach has broken my heart, and I am full of heaviness; I looked for someone to take pity, but there was none; and for comforters, but I found none. They also gave me gall for my food, and for my thirst they gave me vinegar to drink…For they persecute the ones You [God] have struck, and talk of the grief of those You have wounded…<u>I will praise</u> the name of God with a song, and will magnify Him with thanksgiving. This also shall please the LORD better than an ox or bull, which has horns and hooves. The humble shall see this and be glad; And you who seek God, your hearts shall live." (*Psalm 69:20-21, 26, 30-32*)

- "Sacrifice and offering You did not desire; my ears You have opened. ("A body Thou hast prepared for Me." - LXX; *Hebrews 10:5*) Burnt offering and sin offering You did not require. Then I said, "Behold, I come; in the scroll of the book it is written of me. I delight to do Your will, O my God, and Your law is within my heart." 9I have proclaimed the good news of righteousness in the great assembly; indeed, I do not restrain my lips, O LORD, You Yourself know. I have not hidden Your righteousness within my heart; <u>I have declared</u> Your faithfulness and Your salvation; <u>I have not concealed</u> Your lovingkindness and Your truth from the great assembly." (*Psalm 40:6-10*)

In each of these above three Psalms, there is both an indication that this Messianic figure will die but yet will later exist.

- "And <u>I</u> will pour on the house of David and on the inhabitants of Jerusalem the Spirit of grace and supplication; then <u>they will look on Me whom they</u>

pierced. Yes, they will <u>mourn for Him</u> as one mourns for his only son, and grieve for Him as one grieves for a firstborn"…And one will say to him, "What are these wounds between your arms?" Then he will answer, "Those with which I was wounded in the house of my friends…Awake, O sword, against My Shepherd, against the Man who is My companion," Says the LORD of hosts. "Strike the Shepherd, and the sheep will be scattered." (*Zechariah 12:10;13:6-7*)

Notice that in the above passage from Zechariah, the one who is pierced and later mourned is also the One who is now speaking, God who will pour out His Spirit upon Israel.

In the next two passages that had broadly been regarded as Messianic by the ancient rabbis, Messiah is pictured as the victim, who will also live again:

- "Seventy weeks are determined for your people and for your holy city, to finish the transgression, to make an end of sins, to make reconciliation ("atonement" KJV) for iniquity, to bring in everlasting righteousness, to seal up vision and prophecy, and to anoint the Most Holy. Know therefore and understand, that from the going forth of the command to restore and build Jerusalem until <u>Messiah the Prince [comes]</u>, there shall be seven weeks and sixty-two weeks [week 69]; the street shall be built again, and the wall, even in troublesome times. And after the sixty-two weeks <u>Messiah shall be cut off</u> [week 62], but not for Himself; and the people of the prince who is to come shall destroy the city and the sanctuary. The end of it shall be with a flood, and till the end of the war desolations are determined." (*Daniel 9:24-26*)

The Messiah will be cut off, but afterwards, He will return in week 69! Psalm 2 presents a similar picture:

- "The kings of the earth set themselves, and the rulers take counsel together, against the LORD and against His Anointed, saying, "Let us break Their bonds in pieces and cast away Their cords from us."..."Yet I have set My King on My holy hill of Zion. I will declare the decree: The LORD has said to Me, 'You are My Son, today I have begotten You' [*Acts 13:33; Hebrews 1:5; 5:5*]...Kiss the Son, lest He be angry, and you perish in the way, when His wrath is kindled but a little. Blessed are all those who put their trust in Him." (*Psalm 2:2-3, 6-7, 12*)

Despite this attempt of the nations to put an end to Jesus (*Acts 4:23-28*), God raised Him. As a result, the nations, over which He rules, will have to "put their trust in Him."

Admittedly, these passages are highly cryptic but purposely so. There are many things that God claimed that He had hidden (*Deuteronomy 29:29*). However, we might think it unbelievable that God would hide the centerpiece of His redemptive plan so carefully, but this is just what He did! He hide the "mercy seat," the covering of the Ark of the Ten Commandments, in the Holy of Holies under the outstretched wings of the Seraphim. Even when the High Priest would enter, only once a year, on the Day of Atonement, he would have to further obscure this "mercy seat" with billows of smoke from his censor lest he see this object and be struck dead (*Leviticus 16:11-13*). This was the only object that carried with it the threat of death if seen, symbolizing the fact that the Source of His mercy could not yet be disclosed to Israel.

Why did our Lord hide His stunning truth so diligently? Perhaps Paul provided the best explanation:

- "But we speak the wisdom of God in a mystery, the hidden wisdom which God ordained before the ages for our glory, which none of the rulers of this age knew; for had they known, **they would not have crucified the Lord of glory.**" (*1 Corinthians 2:7-8*).

Even though these passages are obscure, if these are cryptic portraits of both the Messiah's death and resurrection, they are pointing to a profound underlying design. In *each* of these eight passages where the Messiah's death is portrayed, there is even a more cryptic indication that He will live again – eight out of eight times. What are the chances of this? Even if we *only* are willing to assign the odds at one-chance-in-two that each time we see Messiah's death, we also see His subsequent life, the probability of this occurring is only one time out of 256 times. This is something worth contemplating.

WORKS CITED

Klinghoffer, David, *Why the Jews Rejected Jesus*, (New York: Doubleday, First Edition, 2005)

Chapter 23

WOULD ISRAEL REJECT THEIR PROMISED MESSIAH?

In *Why the Jews Rejected Jesus*, Orthodox Jewish writer David Klinghoffer claimed that the Jews had rejected Jesus because of a lack of evidence. In contrast to Klinghoffer, Jesus explained that their rejection of Him was not a matter of a lack of evidence but a disdain for their God and for His Prophets:

- "But I know that you do not have the love of God within you...For if you believed Moses, you would believe me; for he wrote of me. But if you do not believe his writings, how will you believe my words?" (*John 5:42, 45-47*)

Later, Jesus further charged the Jewish leadership:

- "...you witness against yourselves that you are sons of those who murdered the prophets. Fill up, then, the measure of your fathers. You serpents, you brood of vipers, how are you to escape being sentenced to hell? Therefore I send you prophets and wise men and scribes, some of whom you will kill and crucify, and some you will flog in your synagogues and persecute from town to town...O Jerusalem, Jerusalem, the city that kills the prophets and stones those who are sent to it! How often would I have gathered your children together as a hen gathers her brood under her wings, and you were not willing!" (*Matthew 23:31-34, 37*)

Jesus understood that these hardened leaders needed a blow-torch to soften their calcified hearts. In love, He intended His words to melt and to humble. It is in this hope that I repeat His damning words along with the words of their own Prophets, many of whom had been reluctant to speak God's

Words of censure. For example, God warned the Prophet Ezekiel that he had to speak the fiery words of his God or face the consequences:

- "So you, son of man: I have made you a watchman for the house of Israel; therefore you shall hear a word from My mouth and warn them for Me. When I say to the wicked, 'O wicked man, you shall surely die!' and you do not speak to warn the wicked from his way, that wicked man shall die in his iniquity; but his blood I will require at your hand. Nevertheless if you warn the wicked to turn from his way, and he does not turn from his way, he shall die in his iniquity; but you have delivered your soul." (*Ezekiel 33:7-11*)

Therefore, we must speak, but we also must pray that our Jewish people would reconsider their rejection of their Messiah. There are several reasons for this reconsideration. For one thing, according to the Prophets of Israel, Israel has almost always turned their back on their God. Take the Prophet Isaiah, for example:

- "Even an ox knows its owner, and a donkey recognizes its master's care— but Israel doesn't know its master. My people don't recognize my care for them. Oh, what a sinful nation they are— loaded down with a burden of guilt. They are evil people, corrupt children who have rejected the LORD. They have despised the Holy One of Israel and turned their backs on him." (*Isaiah 1:3-4*)

This denunciation is uniformly found among the Prophets. How should these indictments affect us? We should at least ask, "Are we still so blind and rebellious? Are we still incurring God's displeasure? Is it possible that our promised Savior, the Messiah, has already come and we have missed Him?" We claim that "When the Messiah comes, there will be world

275

peace. Jesus didn't bring world peace. Therefore, he cannot be the Messiah."

However, this is to ignore the many prophecies that indicate that the Messiah will first come in humility, as many of our Rabbis have noted:

- "Rejoice, O people of Zion! Shout in triumph, O people of Jerusalem! Look, your king is coming to you. He is righteous and victorious, yet he is <u>humble</u>, riding on a donkey— riding on a donkey's colt." (*Zechariah 9:9*)

By anyone's reckoning the prophecy of Daniel has been accomplished by the coming and humbling unto death of the Messiah:

- "A period of seventy sets of seven has been decreed for your people and your holy city to finish their rebellion, to put an end to their sin, to atone for their guilt, to bring in everlasting righteousness, to confirm the prophetic vision, and to anoint the Most Holy Place. Now listen and understand! Seven sets of seven plus sixty-two sets of seven will pass from the time the command is given to rebuild Jerusalem until a ruler— the Anointed One—comes. Jerusalem will be rebuilt with streets and strong defenses, despite the perilous times. After this period of sixty-two sets of seven, the <u>Anointed One will be killed</u>, appearing to have accomplished nothing, and a ruler will arise whose armies will destroy the city and the Temple. The end will come with a flood, and war and its miseries are decreed from that time to the very end." (*Daniel 9:24-26*)

It had been Israel's pattern to reject their God. The writer of the *Book of the Chronicles* explained the demise of Judah:

- "All the officers of the priests and the people likewise were exceedingly unfaithful, following all the abominations of the nations. And they polluted the house of the LORD that he had made holy in Jerusalem. The LORD, the God of their fathers, sent persistently to them by his messengers [prophets], because he had compassion on his people and on his dwelling place. But they kept mocking the messengers of God, despising his words and scoffing at his prophets, until the wrath of the LORD rose against his people, until there was no remedy. Therefore he brought up against them the king of the Chaldeans [Babylonians], who killed their young men with the sword in the house of their sanctuary and had no compassion on young man or virgin, old man or aged. He gave them all into his hand." (2 *Chronicles 36:14-17; Ezra 5:12*)

During the Babylonian exile, the Prophet Daniel had likewise prayed:

- "…we have sinned and done wrong and acted wickedly and rebelled, turning aside from your commandments and rules. We have not listened to your servants the prophets, who spoke in your name to our kings, our princes, and our fathers, and to all the people of the land." (*Daniel 9:5-6*)

The northern kingdom of Israel had been taken by the Assyrians into captivity more than a hundred years earlier for the same reasons:

- "And this occurred because the people of Israel had sinned against the LORD their God, who had brought them up out of the land of Egypt from under the hand of Pharaoh king of Egypt, and had feared other gods…And the people of Israel did secretly against the

LORD their God things that were not right. They built for themselves high places in all their towns, from watchtower to fortified city...Yet the LORD warned Israel and Judah by every prophet and every seer, saying, "Turn from your evil ways and keep my commandments and my statutes, in accordance with all the Law that I commanded your fathers, and that I sent to you by my servants the prophets." But they would not listen, but were stubborn, as their fathers had been, who did not believe in the LORD their God. They despised his statutes and his covenant that he made with their fathers and the warnings that he gave them. They went after false idols and became false, and they followed the nations that were around them, concerning whom the LORD had commanded them that they should not do like them...And they burned their sons and their daughters as offerings and used divination and omens and sold themselves to do evil in the sight of the LORD, provoking him to anger. Therefore the LORD was very angry with Israel and removed them out of his sight. None was left but the tribe of Judah only." (*2 Kings 17:7, 9, 13-15, 17-18*)

In view of this pattern, it is not surprising that we would also reject our Messiah, as had often been prophesied:

- "He was despised and rejected by men, a man of sorrows, and familiar with suffering. Like one from whom men hide their faces he was despised, and <u>we esteemed him not</u>. Surely he took up our infirmities and carried our sorrows, yet <u>we considered him stricken by God, smitten by him</u>, and afflicted. But he was pierced for our transgressions, he was crushed for our iniquities; the punishment that brought us peace was upon him, and by his wounds we are healed. We all, like sheep, have gone astray, each of us has turned to

278

his own way; and the LORD has laid on him the iniquity of us all." (*Isaiah 53:3-6*)

- "The stone [the Messiah] the <u>builders rejected</u> has become the capstone; the LORD has done this, and it is marvelous in our eyes. This is the day the LORD has made; let us rejoice and be glad in it." (*Psalm 118:22-24*)

- "...and he [the Messiah] will be a sanctuary; but for both houses of Israel he will be a stone that causes men to stumble and a rock that makes them fall. And for the people of Jerusalem <u>he will be a trap and a snare</u> [through their rejection of Him]." (*Isaiah 8:14*)

- "It is too small a thing for you [Messiah] to be my servant to restore the tribes of Jacob and bring back those of Israel I have kept. I will also make you a light for the Gentiles, that you may bring my salvation to the ends of the earth." This is what the LORD says--the Redeemer and Holy One of Israel--to him who was <u>despised and abhorred by the nation</u> [of Israel], to the servant of rulers: "Kings will see you and rise up, princes will see and bow down, because of the LORD, who is faithful, the Holy One of Israel, who has chosen you." (*Isaiah 49:6-7*)

- "And I will pour out on the house of David and the inhabitants of Jerusalem a spirit of grace and pleas for mercy, so that, when they look on me [the Messiah], on him whom they have pierced, they shall mourn for him, as one mourns for an only child, and weep bitterly over him, as one weeps over a firstborn." (*Zechariah 12:10*)

Israel will weep and repent that they had rejected their Messiah. However, they will also come to faith as their long-suffering God had promised. This point needs to be clearly stated ~ lest anti-Semites manipulate the abundant examples of Israel's unfaithfulness for the purpose of hate and the denigration of Israel. God's rejection of Israel is only *temporary*:

This will be followed by forgiveness and the restoration of Israel. As the New Testament affirms, "God's gifts and calling are without revocation" (*Romans 11:29*). According to Paul, all Israel will be saved:

- "I want you to understand this mystery, dear brothers and sisters, so that you will not feel proud about yourselves. Some of the people of Israel have hard hearts, but this will last only until the full number of Gentiles comes to Christ. And so all Israel will be saved. As the Scriptures say:

    - 'The one who rescues will come from Jerusalem, and he will turn Israel away from ungodliness. And this is my covenant with them, that I will take away their sins.'" (*Romans 11:25-27 quoting Isaiah 59:20-21*)

There are also many other prophecies that promise that God will not permanently abandon His people Israel:

- Then the LORD said, "Call him Lo-Ammi, for you are not my people, and I am not your God." Yet the Israelites will be like the sand on the seashore, which cannot be measured or counted. In the place where it was said to them, 'You are not my people,' they will be called 'sons of the living God.' The people of Judah and the people of Israel will be reunited..." (*Hosea 1:9-11*)

- But Zion said, "The LORD has forsaken me, the Lord has forgotten me." "Can a mother forget the baby at her breast and have no compassion on the child she has borne? Though she may forget, I will not forget you! See, I have engraved you on the palms of my hands; your walls are ever before me. Your sons hasten back, and those who laid you waste depart from you." (*Isaiah 49:14-17*)

However, God will not deliver His people Israel until they have been humbled away from their self-trust and arrogance and see that their only hope is in their Savior:

- "For the LORD will vindicate his people and have compassion on his servants, when he sees that their power is gone…" (*Deuteronomy 32:36*)

The proud will not receive a Savior as long as they believe that they have no need of One. Sadly, Israel is not presently trusting in their Savior but in their military might to always save them – a hope that has always been exposed as empty.

However, in the next chapter, I want to challenge the anti-Semitic narrative more extensively.

NO WORKS CITED

Chapter 24

ANTI-SEMITISM, ISLAM, AND THE HOPE OF ISRAEL

Recent polls have reported that, because of anti-Semitic violence, 25% of the Jews of the UK are thinking of leaving. In France, the percentage is 75%.

The horrid reality of anti-Semitism is even growing in the USA at an alarming rate. Attorney Jay Sekulow reported:

- "It's being called a "new anti-Semitism." Radical professors are punishing Jewish students for making pro-Israel statements. Christian students who support Israel are being intimidated. Radical Hamas supporters are issuing fake eviction notices to Jewish students. And it's happening on college campuses all across America. The threats of violence, intimidation, and discrimination against Jewish students and anyone who supports Israel..."

His observations are supported by FBI *2012 Hate Crime Statistics*:

- Approximately two-thirds of religious hate crimes are anti-Jewish. The FBI reported that of the 1,340 religious hate crimes, 62 percent were victims of an offender's anti-Jewish bias. The number two targeted group victimized on a religious bias were Muslims, as only 12 percent were victims of an anti-Islamic bias.

After the Holocaust, my Jewish people vowed, "Never again!" However, many of the most influential Jewish organizations remain silent in the face of growing anti-Semitism. One NYC Jewish history organization, while never ceasing to look back at the Holocaust, refuses to introduce any programming about the present threats to the Jewish people. They are not oblivious to this present threat. You cannot enter into their building without passing through security and a metal detector. However, they seem to be in denial regarding the extent and growth of this threat.

On several occasions, I have asked the staff why their programming remains silent on this critical issue of Islamic anti-Semitism. They have blandly responded that this simply isn't their focus. It also doesn't seem to be the focus of the media, universities, or the U.S. government. All remain relatively silent.

The Prophets of Israel saw it coming. Jeremiah cried:

- "Since my people are crushed, I am crushed; I mourn, and horror grips me. Is there no balm in Gilead? Is there no physician there? Why then is there no healing for the wound of my people?" (*Jeremiah 8:21-22*)

But there was little Jeremiah could do. The problem was a stage four cancer, and his countrymen were loath to examine it, let alone to correct it:

- "Oh, that my head were a spring of water and my eyes a fountain of tears! I would weep day and night for the slain of my people. Oh, that I had in the desert a lodging place for travelers, so that I might leave my people and go away from them; for they are all adulterers, a crowd of unfaithful people. "They make ready their tongue like a bow, to shoot lies; it is not by truth that they triumph in the land. They go from one sin to another; they do not acknowledge me," declares the LORD. "Beware of your friends; do not trust your brothers. For every brother is a deceiver, and every friend a slanderer. Friend deceives friend, and no one speaks the truth. They have taught their tongues to lie; they weary themselves with sinning. You live in the midst of deception; in their deceit they refuse to acknowledge me," declares the LORD." (*Jeremiah 9:1-6*)

I do not wish to blame the victim. However, this is just what the Prophets of Israel did at the bequest of their Master. Even Moses warned his people through a prophetic song that God had given him to teach to Israel:

- "He [God] shielded [Israel] him and cared for him; he guarded him as the apple of his eye, like an eagle that stirs up its nest and hovers over its young, that spreads its wings to catch them and carries them on its pinions. The LORD alone led him; no foreign god was with him. He made him ride on the heights of the land and fed him with the fruit of the fields. He nourished him with honey from the rock, and with oil from the flinty crag, with curds and milk from herd and flock and with fattened lambs and goats, with choice rams of Bashan and the finest kernels of wheat. You drank the foaming blood of the grape... He abandoned the God who made him and rejected the Rock his Savior. They made him jealous with their foreign gods and angered him with their detestable idols. They sacrificed to demons, which are not God-- gods they had not known, gods that recently appeared, gods your fathers did not fear. You deserted the Rock, who fathered you; you forgot the God who gave you birth. The LORD saw this and rejected them because he was angered by his sons and daughters. "I will hide my face from them," he said, "and see what their end will be; for they are a perverse generation, children who are unfaithful." (*Deuteronomy 32:10-20*)

Instead of returning and placing their trust in the God who had fathered and shepherded them for millennium, Israel has placed its trust in *themselves*, the very thing that Moses had warned them against:

- "You may say to yourself, '<u>My</u> power and the strength of <u>my</u> hands have produced this wealth for me.' But remember the LORD your God, for it is <u>he</u> who gives you the ability to produce wealth, and so confirms his covenant, which he swore to your forefathers, as it is today. If you ever forget the LORD your God and follow other gods and worship and bow down to them, I testify against you today that you will surely be destroyed. Like the nations the LORD destroyed before you, so you will be destroyed for not obeying the LORD your God." (*Deuteronomy 8:17-20*)

Throughout their history, my people Israel have suffered these promised woes. Even the Orthodox Jews have turned away. Instead of acknowledging God, they fill themselves with a sense of racial superiority.

In *Why the Jews Rejected Jesus*, Orthodox Jewish writer David Klinghoffer concludes that Jewish rejection of Jesus is founded in "the mystic uniqueness of the Jewish essence or nature. There was something distinct about the Jewish soul…The Jewish soul feels the worlds, in a remarkably visceral way, as unredeemed."

He bases this opinion upon Judah Loeb's famous interpretation of the Talmudic tractate, *Avodah Zarah*, which stated that God had offered the Torah to all the other nations first, "to see if they possessed a predisposition to the Torah, and did not find it in them," in contrast to the holy disposition God found in the Jews (Klinghoffer, 215-217).

This understanding, of course, is *not* at all reflective of the Hebrew Bible but instead, of much of the Talmud and is an affront to God.

I cry for my foolish people. Jeremiah's lament has become mine. What to do? Continue in prayer to point them back to their sins and the promised hope of repentance before their rejected Messiah.

What is my consolation? It is found only in our Savior Jesus. Through Paul, He promised:

- "I do not want you to be ignorant of this mystery, brothers, so that you may not be conceited: Israel has experienced a hardening in part until the full number of the Gentiles has come in. And so all Israel will be saved, as it is written: "The deliverer will come from Zion; he will turn godlessness away from Jacob. And this is my covenant with them when I take away their sins." As far as the gospel is concerned, they are enemies on your account; but as far as election is concerned, they are loved on account of the patriarchs, for God's gifts and his call are <u>irrevocable</u>." (*Romans 11:25-29*)

To Him be the glory!

***

ANTI-SEMITISM, ISLAM, AND NATIONAL SOCIALIST PROPAGANDA

Muslims are not only yelling "kill the Jews" as the Nazis had done, but they are also reviving Nazi propaganda. One Muslim woman posted this YouTube video on my Facebook. It amazes me that anyone could take this video seriously, but tragically many do.
(www.youtube.com/watch?v=uQwuaXo5T-4)

It also saddens me that instead of exposing and resisting the horror of Jewish-hatred at the core of Islam, the Western media has been bullied into silence, as they had been under Hitler. Here is my response to the Muslim woman:

What God thinks of the Jews is far more important than what others think. Yes, you are correct. They have rebelled against their God, but this hasn't prevented Him from loving them, nor will it change the glorious future that He has so often promised them:

- *Isaiah 49:13-15: "Shout for joy, O heavens; rejoice, O earth; burst into song, O mountains! For the Lord comforts his people and will have compassion on his afflicted ones." But Zion said, "The Lord has forsaken me, the Lord has forgotten me." "Can a mother forget the baby at her breast and have no compassion on the child she has borne? Though she may forget, I will not forget you!"*

- *Ezekiel 36:24-31: "For I will take you out of the nations; I will gather you from all the countries and bring you back into your own land. I will sprinkle clean water on you, and you will be clean; I will cleanse you from all your impurities and from all your idols. I will give you a new heart and put a new spirit in you; I will remove from you your heart of stone and give you a heart of flesh. And I will put my Spirit in you and move you to follow my decrees and be careful to keep my laws. You will live in the land I gave your forefathers; you will be my people, and I will be your God. I will save you from all your uncleanness. I will call for the grain and make it plentiful and will not bring famine upon you. I will increase the fruit of the trees and the crops of the field, so that you will no longer suffer disgrace among the nations because of famine. Then you will remember your evil ways and wicked deeds, and you will loathe yourselves for your sins and detestable practices."*

- *Isaiah 44:21-22: "Remember these things, O Jacob, for you are my servant, O Israel. I have made you, you are my servant; O Israel, I will not forget you. I have swept away your offenses like a cloud, your sins like the morning mist. Return to me, for I have redeemed you."*

- *Jeremiah 33:6-8: "I will bring health and healing to it; I will heal my people and will let them enjoy abundant peace and security. I will bring Judah and Israel back from captivity and will rebuild them as they were before. I will cleanse them from all the sin they have committed against me and will forgive all their sins of rebellion against me."*

- *Hosea 3:5: "Afterward the Israelites will return and seek the Lord their God and David their king. They will come trembling to the Lord and to his blessings in the last days."*

- *Zech. 12:10: "And I will pour out on the house of David and the inhabitants of Jerusalem a spirit of grace and supplication."*

- *Deut. 32:43: Rejoice, O nations, with his people, for he will avenge the blood of his servants; he will take vengeance on his enemies and make atonement for his land and people.*

- *Hosea 14:4-5: "I will heal their waywardness and love them freely, for my anger has turned away from them. I will be like the dew to Israel; he will blossom like a lily. Like a cedar of Lebanon he will send down his roots;*

- *Amos 9:14-15: "I will bring back my exiled people Israel; they will rebuild the ruined cities and live in them. They will plant vineyards and drink their wine; they will make gardens and eat their fruit. I will plant Israel in their own land, never again to be uprooted from the land I have given them," says the Lord your God.*

- *Micah 4:1-2: In the last days the mountain of the Lord's temple will be established as chief among the mountains; it will be raised above the hills, and peoples will stream to it. Many nations will come and say, "Come, let us go up to the mountain of the Lord, to the house of the God of Jacob. He will teach us his ways, so that we may walk in his paths." The law will go out from Zion, the word of the Lord from Jerusalem.*

- *Micah 7:18-20: "You do not stay angry forever but delight to show mercy. You will again have compassion on us; you will tread our sins underfoot and hurl all our iniquities into the depths of the sea. You will be true to Jacob, and show mercy to Abraham, as you pledged on oath to our fathers in days long ago."*

- *Zephaniah 3:15-20: "The Lord has taken away your punishment, he has turned back your enemy. The Lord, the King of Israel, is with you; never again will you fear any harm. At that time I will deal with all who oppressed you...At that time I will gather you; at that time I will bring you home. I will give you honor and praise among all the peoples of the earth when I restore your fortunes before your very eyes," says the Lord."*

The very fact that God came as a Jew reaffirms the fact that of His love for His chosen people. This is also the message of the New Testament:

- *Romans 11:26-29: "And so all Israel will be saved, as it is written: "The deliverer will come from Zion; he will turn godlessness away from Jacob. And this is my covenant with them when I take away their sins. "As far as the gospel is concerned, they are enemies on your account; but as far as election is concerned, they are loved on account of the patriarchs, for God's gifts and his call are irrevocable."*

I am therefore concerned for you and also for your Muslim brethren, who hate the Jewish people. You mustn't blind yourself to God's purpose regarding those who continue in their hatred to Israel:

- *Isaiah 41:11: "All who rage against you will surely be ashamed and disgraced; those who oppose you will be as nothing and perish."*

- *Isaiah 51:21-23: This is what your Sovereign Lord says, your God, who defends his people: "See, I have taken out of your hand the cup that made you stagger; from that cup, the goblet of my wrath, you will never drink again. I will put it into the hands of your tormentors, who said to you, 'Fall prostrate that we may walk over you.' And you made your back like the ground, like a street to be walked over."*

- *Joel 3:19-21: "But Egypt will be desolate, Edom a desert waste, because of violence done to the people of Judah, in whose land they shed innocent blood. Judah will be inhabited forever and Jerusalem through all generations. Their bloodguilt, which I have not pardoned, I will pardon."*

You can either continue in hatred or confess it to Allah, the One who wrote the Bible, according to your Koran. I pray that you will repent and seek peace which is pleasing to our God. He promises that if you seek, you will find:

- *Matthew 7:7-8: "Ask and it will be given to you; seek and you will find; knock and the door will be opened to you. For everyone who asks receives; he who seeks finds; and to him who knocks, the door will be opened."*

Wisdom would beckon us to get on the right side of God and His plans. Hating His chosen but errant people is certainly not to be on God's side.

WORKS CITED

FBI *2012 Hate Crime Statistics*:
www.jewishvirtuallibrary.org/fbi-hate-crime-statistics-2012

Klinghoffer, David, *Why the Jews Rejected Jesus*, (New York: Doubleday, First Edition, 2005)

Sekulow, Jay – American Center for Law and Justice – may not be exact article for quote
www.aclj.org/israel/major-university-allowing-anti-semitic-anti-israel-organization-to-hold-conference-on-campus

YouTube video posted on Daniel Mann's Facebook
www.youtube.com/watch?v=uQwuaXo5T-4

Chapter 25

THE TALMUD'S SUPPORT OF THE NEW TESTAMENT

According to Jewish sources, the Babylonian Talmud is the center of mainstream Judaism. It represents the commentary on the Hebrew Scriptures, a compilation of the writings of many sages and rabbis over a period of hundreds of years, perhaps even pre-dating Jesus. However, it is much more than a commentary. Often, the rabbis had inserted their own thoughts where they felt that the Scriptures had left many things unsaid.

It is a massive work. By one count, it contains 6,200 pages, and is comprised to two parts:

- The Talmud consists of what are known as the Gemara [complied around 550 AD] and the Mishnah [compiled around 200 AD].
  (www.gotquestions.org/Talmud.html)

There are actually two Talmuds: the Palestinian and the Babylonian Talmud, which is far more comprehensive and the one most people mean when they say "the Talmud."

The Babylonian Talmud, also called the "Oral Law," is claimed by many Orthodox Jews to have been given to Moses on Mt. Sinai. It has become even more authoritative in practice than the Hebrew Bible, which we know as the "Old Testament":

- Judaism has an 'Oral Torah' which is a tradition explaining what these scriptures mean and how to interpret them and apply the laws. Orthodox Jews believe God taught this Oral Torah to Moses, and to others, down to the present day. This tradition was maintained only in oral form until about the 2nd century

A.D., when the oral law was compiled and written down in a document called the Mishnah." (Ibid.)

The Talmud has even arrogated for itself a position superior to that of Scripture:

- "Those who devote themselves to reading the Bible exercise a certain virtue, but not very much; those who study the Mischnah exercise virtue for which they will receive a reward; those, however, who take upon themselves to study the Gemarah exercise the highest virtue." (Babha Metsia, fol. 33a)

- "The Sacred Scriptures is like water, the Mischnah wine, and the Gemarah aromatic wine. (Sopherim XV, 7, fol. 13b)

- "He who transgresses the words of the scribes sins more gravely than the transgressors of the words of the law." (Sanhedrin X, 3, f.88b)

JUSTIFYING THE CLAIM

The rabbis cannot appeal to any historical evidence. Instead, they cite the Mishnah tractate, Pirke Avot 1, perhaps written 1500 years after Moses:

- Moses passed it [the "Oral Law"] on to Joshua. Joshua gave it to the Elders. The Elders gave it to the Prophets, and the Prophets gave it to the Men of the Great Assembly [including Ezra and Nehemiah].

Orthodox Jews believe that the Hebrew Scriptures cannot be understood and applied without the commentary from the Talmud. Therefore, they reason, the Talmud itself must also have been given to Moses on Mt. Sinai. Why? Since the Torah is incomplete by itself, there must have been other instructions given:

- The Oral Torah [Talmud] is needed in order to maintain the context of the Written Torah. It therefore contains much more information than the Written Torah. The Written Torah needs the Oral Torah to make certain that the correct meaning is conveyed and understood. (www.beingjewish.com/mesorah/whynotwritten.html)

However, there are many problems connected with this claim:

1. The contents of the Talmud are clearly uninspired. Here's one example: "When a man talks too much to his wife, he causes evil to himself, disregards the words of Torah and in the end will inherit Gehenna." (Pirke Avot)

2. The Talmud often contradicts the Hebrew Scriptures. In fact, one Talmudic Rabbi often contradicts another.

3. Rather than declaring, "Thus says the Lord," the Talmud is comprised of rabbinic discussions, one rabbi disagreeing with another.

4. The Hebrew Scriptures give absolutely no support for the simultaneous existence of an Oral Law.

Scripture even contradicts such a claim. For instance:

- "Moses came and told the people ALL the words of the LORD and all the rules. And all the people answered with one voice and said, 'All the words that the LORD has spoken we will do.' And MOSES WROTE DOWN ALL THE WORDS of the LORD." (*Exodus 24:3-4*, emphasis added; all Bible quotations come from the ESV.)

All of the words of the Lord had been written down by Moses. These were the very words that Israel had sworn to keep, and no others! This leaves no room for the existence of an authoritative Oral Law.

Furthermore, God had covenanted with Israel to follow a *written* Law, not an Oral Law:

- "If you are not careful to do all the words of this law that are written in this book, that you may fear this glorious and awesome name, the LORD your God, then the LORD will bring on you and your offspring extraordinary afflictions..." (Deuteron*omy 28:58-59*)

Moreover, we fail to encounter the existence of a second law—an Oral Law—anywhere in Scripture:

- "And afterward he read all the words of the law, the blessing and the curse, according to all that is written in the Book of the Law. There was not a word of all that Moses commanded that Joshua did not read before all the assembly of Israel, and the women, and the little ones, and the sojourners who lived among them." (*Joshua 8:34-35*)

If Moses had passed on the Oral Law to Joshua, as the Talmud claims, then it should have been recited. However, Joshua had read **everything** that Moses had commanded him. This leaves no room for the existence of any unwritten law.

Later, Joshua charged the Israelites:

- "Be very strong; be careful to obey all that is written in the Book of the Law of Moses, without turning aside to the right or to the left." (*Joshua 23:6*)

Had Joshua been in possession of an Oral Law, why would he not have commanded Israel to obey it along with the written law? Certainly, the rabbis would not claim that Joshua had failed in his duty. This question becomes even more troubling in light of the fact that the Jews regard the Oral Law as more authoritative than the written.

Throughout the entirety of the Hebrew Scriptures, there is not the slightest hint of the presence of an Oral Law. Not once did a Prophet of Israel indict the people for having neglected the Oral Law! This kind of condemnation is nowhere to be found.

Besides this, the Torah was often read at Covenant renewals and revivals (*Exodus 24:7; 2 Kings 23:1-3; Nehemiah 8:1-18*). However, there is absolutely *no* indication that the Oral Law was ever recited. It seems to have been entirely absent.

All of this contradicts the claim of the rabbis that the Talmud was given to Moses on Mt. Sinai and is therefore authoritative. As a matter of fact, the Jewish exaltation of the Talmud to the level of Scripture represents the serious offense of adding to the Law (*Deuteronomy 4:2; 12:32*)!

THE TALMUD AND CHRISTIANITY

Does this suggest that the Talmud is worthless in terms of supporting Christian truth claims? Not at all! Even though the Talmud is not God-given and is even blasphemous in many regards, it is still a valuable historical document.

Why is this important? For one thing Talmud sometimes contradicts present-day rabbinic assertions! For example, the New Testament (*John 19:37; Revelations 1:7*) regards Zechariah 12:10 as Messianic:

- "And I will pour out on the house of David and the inhabitants of Jerusalem a spirit of grace and pleas for mercy, so that, when they look on me, on him [Messiah] whom they [Israel] have pierced, they shall mourn for him, as one mourns for an only child, and weep bitterly over him, as one weeps over a firstborn."

Against the Christian Messianic interpretation, Rabbi Gerald Sigal has written that the one pierced is actually the nation of Israel:

- "God cannot literally be pierced. The idea of piercing God expresses the fact that Israel stands in a very special relationship to God among all the nations of the earth. God identifies with His people to the degree that He takes part figuratively in the nation's destiny. To attack (pierce) Israel is to attack God." (Sigal, 79-80)

Yet, the context of *Zechariah 12:10* argues against Sigal. As a result of this "piercing," Israel mourns for her sin (*Zechariah 13:1*). This would not at all have been likely if Israel had been the victim of the piercing.

Besides, the Talmud doesn't affirm Segal's interpretation. Instead, it acknowledges that Zechariah might be prophesying about the death of Messiah:

- And the land shall mourn, every family apart; the family of the house of David apart, and their wives apart [*Zechariah 12:12*]... What is the cause of the mourning mentioned in the last cited verse? — R. Dosa and the Rabbis differ on the point. One explained, The cause is the slaying of Messiah the son of Joseph, and the other explained, The cause is the slaying of the Evil Inclination. It is well according to him who explains that the cause is the slaying of Messiah the son of Joseph, since that well agrees with the Scriptural verse, And they shall look upon me because they have thrust him through, and they shall mourn for him as one mourneth for his only son. (Sukkah 52A)

This Talmudic commentary contradicts the modern rabbis. This same commentary also acknowledges the possibility of two separate Messiahs—the first would come humbly and die; the second would set up an everlasting kingdom.

Why is this important? Because the modern Rabbis reject the Christian narrative of two Messianic comings, claiming instead that when the Messiah initially comes, there will be peace and an everlasting kingdom. But when Jesus came, there was neither.

We see evidence that modern rabbis conveniently ignore much Talmudic thought. The late Hebraic scholar turned Christian, Rachmiel Frydland, pointed out that the Talmud perceives two distinct portraits of the Messiah within Scripture: "A second explanation of the seemingly contradictory portrayals of Messiah as one both humiliated and exalted appears elsewhere in the Talmud":

- Sanhedrin 98A: [Rabbi] Alexandri said that [Rabbi] Joshua bar Levi combined the two paradoxical passages; the one that says, 'Behold, one like the Son of Man came with the clouds of heaven (*Daniel 7:13*; showing Messiah's glory) and the other verse that say, 'poor and riding upon a donkey' (*Zechariah 9:9*; showing Messiah's humility).'" (*What the Rabbis Know about the Messiah* (Cincinnati, Ohio: Messianic Publishing Company, 1993) (Frydland, 5)

GOSPEL AGREEMENT

In other places, the Talmud dramatically endorses the Gospel narrative, albeit indirectly. In a book devoted to explaining why the Jewish rejection of Jesus was entirely reasonable,

298

Orthodox Jewish scholar, David Klinghoffer, admitted:

- The Talmud states that from forty years before the Temple's destruction and onward, there were supernatural omens of the disaster to come--that is, starting from the inception of the Christian religion following the death of Jesus. The eternal fire of the Temple altar would not stay lit. The monumental bronze Temple gates opened by themselves. Josephus confirms the Talmud's account of the inner Sanctuary's east gate and its mysterious openings. He adds other portents from these years: a bright light shining around the altar and the Sanctuary at three in the morning, a cow brought for sacrifice giving birth to a lamb, apparitions of chariots and armies flying through the sky above the whole land of Israel. (Klinghoffer, 117)

Renowned Jewish scholar, Jacob Neusner, quotes these same omens from the *Jerusalem Talmud*:

- "Forty years before the destruction of the Temple, the western light went out, the crimson thread remained crimson, and the lot for the Lord always came up in the left hand. They would close the gates of the Temple by night and get up in the morning and find them wide open." (*The Yerushalmi* - Neusner,156-157)

Amazingly, after the Crucifixion (Cir. 30 AD) and for the next 40 years until the destruction of the Temple in 70 AD, Israel had been saturated by a series of miraculous omens pointing ominously to its future destruction.

Why would Jewish sources trying to debunk Christianity make such incredible admissions, admissions that validate Jesus? Klinghoffer tried to interpret the miraculous events as omens directed against the Jewish believers in Christ: "Was God not warning the people of the disastrous course some [the Jewish

Christians]   had   set   out   upon?"

However, the Christians had fled to safety across the Jordan to Pella! According to Klinghoffer, it was the Christians who should have been penalized for their heresy. And yet, it was the Jews who didn't believe in Christ who were left to pay the price.

What is even more unbelievable about Klinghoffer's explanation is the timing of the omens. They began at approximately the time of the Crucifixion (30 AD) and lasted for forty years until the destruction of the Temple.

If Klinghoffer is correct that the omens were intended to demonstrate God's displeasure with *Jesus*, they should have ended at the Crucifixion, at which point, God should have been appeased. Instead, since the omens *began* with the Crucifixion, it seems likely that they would have served as a call to repentance for those who had rejected Jesus, not for those who had followed Him.

And when did the omens end? After the destruction of the Temple and the death of millions of unrepentant Jews! Why did the omens cease at this time? Presumably, because the time for repentance had already passed! Now it was too late.

Klinghoffer asserts that the warnings were directed towards the Jewish Christians who had gone astray. However, if this had been the case, calamity should have fallen on them. Instead, it fell upon the nation of Israel. Why? Because Israel had refused to repent of their sins and seek God's mercy,   as Jesus had warned:

- "O Jerusalem, Jerusalem, the city that kills the prophets and stones those who are sent to it! How often would I have gathered your children together as a hen gathers her brood under her wings, and you were not willing!

See, your house is left to you desolate." (*Matthew 23:37-38*)

ANOTHER INTERESTING EXAMPLE FROM THE TALMUD

In his response to the question, "Why didn't the red ribbon on the head of the Scapegoat [on Yom Kippur] turn white in 30 CE [AD]?" Jewish anti-Christian apologist, Rabbi Tovia Singer reluctantly admits:

- "In Tractate Yoma 39b, the Talmud… discusses numerous remarkable phenomena that occurred in the Temple during the Yom Kippur service… There was a strip of scarlet-dyed wool tied to the head of the scapegoat which would turn white in the presence of the large crowd gathered at the Temple on the Day of Atonement. The Jewish people perceived this miraculous transformation as a heavenly sign that their sins were forgiven. The Talmud relates, however, that 40 years before the destruction of the second Temple [approximately 30 AD at the time of the Crucifixion] the scarlet colored strip of wool did not turn white." (www.outreachjudaism.org/about-us/)

This is a damning admission. Following the Crucifixion, the scarlet wool would no longer miraculously become white! It seems that God had put Israel on notice that He would no longer accept animal sacrifices now that the ultimate offering of Jesus had been accomplished.

How does Singer explain this cessation at the very time of the Cross? He claims that various miracles were gradually disappearing because Israel's "dedication to the golden rule slacked off." However, the timing of this cessation could not have been worse for the Jews who had rejected their Messianic Hope.

Singer also insists that God had been angry with Jesus for deceiving Israel. However, if that was true, we would have expected Him to grant signs of His approval of the Crucifixion. Instead, there was this major sign of His disapproval—that He no longer honored the scapegoat to take away Israel's sins. God's timing could not have been worse for Singer's argument!

ACCORDING TO THE TALMUD, JESUS WAS A WORKER OF MIRACLES

Miracles had validated Jesus' claims, and His detractors would have to offer an alternative explanation or deny the miracles altogether. The safest thing for them to do was to simply deny that He had performed miracles. However, it is likely that Jesus' miracles were so thoroughly accepted that the Talmud had little other choice but to ascribe them to Satan's black magic. This is exactly what we find in many of the Talmudic writings:

- Shabbath 104B: "Jesus was a magician and a fool. Mary was an adulteress".

- Sanhedrin 107B of the Babylonian Talmud: "Jesus ("Yeshu" in the Talmud)... stood up a brick to symbolize an idol and bowed down to it. Jesus performed magic and incited the people of Israel and led them astray."

- Sanhedrin 43A: "On Passover Eve they hanged Jesus ("Yeshu" in the Talmud) of Nazareth. He practiced sorcery, incited and led Israel astray...Was Jesus of Nazareth deserving of a search for an argument in his favor? He was an enticer and the Torah says, 'You shall not spare, nor shall you conceal him!"

However, do the Talmud's charges of "magic" or "sorcery" mean that it acknowledges that Jesus actually performed miracles?

It would seem so. In the New Testament, the Jewish leadership customarily accused Jesus of performing *supernatural* works, but by the hand of Satan (*Matthew 9:34; 12:24; Mark 3:22; Luke 11:15*). Why not by slight-of-the-hand? Jesus had, plainly to all, been performing miracles. Therefore, the Pharisees *never* attempted to allege that Jesus' miracles were merely a matter of deception. Israelites delivered from their infirmities and from Satanic possession could not have been a matter of deception. We have no Jewish rebuttals claiming that those seemingly healed really weren't.

Consistent with these original allegations and the Talmud's testimony, *The Jewish Encyclopedia* (1901-1906) acknowledged:

- According to Celsus (in Origen, "Contra Celsum," i. 28) and to the Talmud (Shab. 104b), Jesus learned magic in Egypt and performed his miracles by means of it; the latter work, in addition, states that he cut the magic formulas into his skin. It does not mention, however, the nature of his magic performances (Tosef., Shab. xi. 4; Yer. Shab. 18d); but as it states that the disciples of Jesus healed the sick "in the name of Jesus Pandera" (Yer. Shab. 14d; Ab. Zarah 27b; Eccl. R. i. 8) it may be assumed that its author held the miracles of Jesus also to have been miraculous cures. Different in nature is the witchcraft attributed to Jesus in the "Toledot." When Jesus was expelled from the circle of scholars, he is said to have returned secretly from Galilee to Jerusalem, where he inserted a parchment containing the "declared name of God" ("Shem ha-Meforash"), which was guarded in the Temple, into his skin, carried it away, and then, taking it out of his skin, he performed

303

his miracles by its means. (The Jewish Encyclopedia, s.v. "Jesus," Vol. VII, pages 171 and 172. Facsimile pages available as The Jewish Religion. (www.jewishencyclopedia.com/view.jsp?artid=254&letter=J&search=jesus#1017)

Based upon their understanding of the Talmud, *The Jewish Encyclopedia* equates miracles with witchcraft (the power of Satan) as the Pharisees had. It therefore makes far more sense to interpret the Talmud's charges of "magic" as referring to miraculous events.

Although the Talmud contains other useful apologetic material, which validates New Testament claims, due its sheer size and various interpretive difficulties, it might be better to leave Talmudic research to Talmudic Christian apologists to illuminate this material.

WORKS CITED

Frydland, Rachmiel, *What the Rabbis Know about the Messiah,* (Cincinnati, Ohio: Messianic Publishing Company, 1993)

Klinghoffer, *Why the Jews Rejected Jesus*, (New York: Three Leaves Press, Doubleday, 2006)

Jacobs, Joseph / Kohler, Kaufmann / Gottheil, Richard / Krauss, Samuel, "*Jesus of Nazareth*" www.jewishencyclopedia.com/view.jsp?artid=254&letter=J&search=jesus#1017
Neusner, Jacob, *The Yerushalmi*, (New York, New York: Jason Aronson, Inc., 1994)

Oral Talmud, Mishnah tractate, Pirke Avot 1 www.beingjewish.com/mesorah/whynotwritten.html

Sigal, Gerald, (*The Jew and the Christian Missionary*, New York, New York: KTAV Publishing House, Inc., 1981)

Singer, Tovia www.outreachjudaism.org/about-us/

The Talmud www.gotquestions.org/Talmud.html www.jewishvirtuallibrary.org/babylonian-talmud-full-text

Chapter 26

GOSPEL CRITICS AND GOSPEL AUTHENTICITY

Have you observed that the New Testament critics criticize the Four Gospels when they are too similar – they claim that they borrowed from each other and therefore do not represent four independent accounts – but then they also criticize them because they are dissimilar (The *Gospel of John* vs. the *Synoptics*).

Jesus made a similar observation about the critics of His day. They criticized both John's seriousness and Jesus' merriment:

- "For John the Baptist came neither eating bread nor drinking wine, and you say, 'He has a demon.' The Son of Man came eating and drinking, and you say, 'Here is a glutton and a drunkard, a friend of tax collectors and sinners." (*Luke 7:33-34*)

According to Jesus, these critics weren't motivated by a desire to understand but rather by a hatred of the Light (*John 3:19-20*).

We often find this same critical spirit underlying many disputes. Regarding Jesus' belief about His own identity – Some critics allege that if Jesus believed He was the Messiah, He would have stated this fact *more plainly*. Meanwhile, other critics charge that the Gospels are *overly plain*, contrived by the early Greek-speaking church to bring Jesus' words into conformity with their own messianic beliefs. Consequently, the Gospels fundamentally represent the words and concepts of the early Church. As a result, their contrived "Jesus" of the Gospels plainly proclaimed Himself to be both Messiah and God.

However, Orthodox Jewish scholar, David Klinghoffer, represents a more balanced position. In *Why the Jews Rejected Jesus*, he tries to justify the Jewish rejection of Jesus:

- "If he [Jesus] ever preached his messiahship openly, why did none of the Gospels record this? It stands to reason that he did not...[But] to reject Jesus, in his lifetime or after, was to condemn oneself as an unbeliever [according to the New Testament]. This hardly seems fair. You were supposed to acknowledge Jesus in a role he refused to publicly to claim?" (Klinghoffer, 61)

Klinghoffer raises a fair point. Many of Jesus' teachings weren't very explicit. Therefore, you can't indict a man for gambling if there's no law against it! Nor can you indict the Jews for rejecting Jesus! By Klinghoffer's analysis, it would seem that the early Church *hadn't invented a Jesus* who had clearly proclaimed his Deity and messiah-ship.

Yet Klinghoffer does admit that, privately, Jesus did acknowledge His messiah-ship. Here are the three examples Klinghoffer cited:

1. After Peter acknowledged that Jesus is "the Christ, the Son of the living God," Jesus affirmed, "Blessed are you, Simon son of Jonah, for this was not revealed to you by man, but by my Father in heaven." (*Matthew 16:17*)

2. After Caiaphas asked Jesus, "Are you then the Son of God?" Jesus answered, "You are right in saying I am." (*Luke 22:70; Matthew 26:64; Mark 14:62*)

3. After the Samaritan woman at the well mentioned the Messiah, Jesus responded, "I who speak to you am

307

he." (*John 4:26*. To these acknowledgments—as opposed to directly preaching that He was the Messiah—can be added numerous other passages— *John 5:16-28; John 8:28; John 10:24-38; Mark 13:26; 14:64*)

Ironically, these passages and other equally cryptic passages demonstrate the *authenticity* of the Gospels:

1. The early church wouldn't have concocted these subtle references of Jesus acknowledging His messiah-ship, as the skeptics allege regarding the Gospel accounts. Instead, the church would have fabricated verses where Jesus would have preached His divine identity loud and clear.

2. All four Gospels preserve equally cryptic expressions regarding Jesus' self-disclosures, even while they record very different incidents and sermons. Why hadn't the enthusiasm of the Apostles commandeer their pen to craft more direct and compelling disclosures? Their concern for accurate reporting evidently trumped their enthusiasm and theological concerns!

3. In addition to this, the Gospels preserve the same cryptic, parabolic quality in Jesus' teachings about other essential doctrines. He never taught clearly or exhaustively on the New Covenant – words that the early church would most assuredly have placed in His mouth. Only in the end did He explicitly refer to a New Covenant (*Matthew 26:28; Mark 14:24; Luke 22:20*). Although the Gospel of John doesn't explicitly mention Jesus bringing the "New Covenant," this concept may be conveyed in the idea that Jesus is the new Temple, suggesting that He is replacing the Old – (*John 1:14; 2:19*)

Klinghoffer believes that Jesus' indirect self-disclosures reflect His uncertainty about His calling and identity. However, in keeping with Jesus' strategy, He often commanded those He had healed to keep the lid on the light. Also, He was hesitant about giving His opponents the quotable ammunition they wanted to bring charges and crucify Him before His time. By explicitly saying, "I am the Messiah," or "I am God," Jesus would have served Himself upon an eager Pharisaic platter.

Klinghoffer is wrong for another reason. His veiled manner of speech could not have been a cloak for uncertainty. He purposely talked in perplexing parables so that only His chosen ones would understand (*Matthew 13:10-15*). And they could only understand once Jesus explained the parables to them. The early Church would never have invented such perplexing speech to support their theology.

It is interesting to note that even the foremost Bible critic and agnostic, Bart D. Ehrman, has acknowledged the reliability of the Gospel accounts:

- The oldest and best sources we have for knowing about the life of Jesus...are the four Gospels of the NT...This is not simply the view of Christian historians who have a high opinion of the NT and in its historical worth; it is the view of all serious historians of antiquity...it is the conclusion that has been reached by every one of the hundreds (thousands, even) of scholars." (Ehrman, 102)

And what about Klinghoffer's claim that Jesus' countrymen couldn't be held accountable for something that He never clearly preached? Jesus explains it best:

- "If I had not done among them what no one else did, they would not be guilty of sin. But now they have seen these miracles, and yet they have hated both me and my Father." (*John 15:24*)

WORKS CITED

Ehrman, Bart D., (*Truth and Fiction in the DaVinci Code: A Historian Reveals What We Really Know about Jesus, Mary Magdalene, and Constantine 1st Edition,* (New York: Oxford University Press; 1 edition, 2006)

Klinghoffer, David*, Why the Jews Rejected Jesus*, (New York: Doubleday, First Edition, 2005)

Chapter 27

WHAT DOES LOVE REQUIRE OF US?

We Messianic Jews – I just call myself a "Jewish Christian" – claim that we have unique contributions to make to the Church and even to the Synagogue. However, these contributions have to be in accord with God's Word. If we fail to expose sin and to show the way back through faith and repentance, we fail to be prophetic as the Hebrew Prophets had been.

God has been faithful. He has blessed His chosen people abundantly. To fulfill His promises to our Patriarchs, He has made the Jewish people fantastically successful, as He had promised (*Deuteronomy 8:16-19*). He has also exhibited His faithfulness by bringing Israel back to their Promised Land on three separate occasions, something that no other people group has experienced even once. Yet, despite His many blessings, we have turned away from our God:

- Thus says the LORD: "What wrong did your fathers find in me that they went far from me, and went after worthlessness, and became worthless? They did not say, 'Where is the LORD who brought us up from the land of Egypt, who led us in the wilderness, in a land of deserts and pits, in a land of drought and deep darkness, in a land that none passes through, where no man dwells?' And I brought you into a plentiful land to enjoy its fruits and its good things. But when you came in, you defiled my land and made my heritage an abomination. The priests did not say, 'Where is the LORD?' Those who handle the law did not know me; the shepherds transgressed against me; the prophets prophesied by Baal and went after things that do not profit." (*Jeremiah 2:5-8*)

We have rejected the Lord and His Word. Jesus also had accused the Jewish leadership of turning their backs on the Words and teachings of their Redeemer:

- But Jesus answered them, "You are wrong, because you know neither the Scriptures nor the power of God." (*Matthew 22:29; John 5:39-47*)

Yet even Orthodox Jews have replaced the Bible, the Word of God, with the Talmud, the words of mere men. Israel had habitually sought out false religions and false prophets to tell them what they wanted to hear:

- Thus says the LORD of hosts: "Do not listen to the words of the prophets who prophesy to you, filling you with vain hopes. They speak visions of their own minds, not from the mouth of the LORD. They say continually to those who despise the word of the LORD, 'It shall be well with you'; and to everyone who stubbornly follows his own heart, they say, 'No disaster shall come upon you.'" (*Jeremiah 23:16-17*)

While our Jewish people no longer turn to Moloch and the Ashtoreth, other "gods" have taken their place. The *Zohar* reads:

- "And he created every living thing, that is, the Israelites, because they are the children of the Most High God, and their holy souls come out from Him. But where do the souls of the idolatrous gentiles come from? Rabbi Eliezer says: from the left side, which makes their souls unclean. They are therefore all unclean and they pollute all who come in contact with them." (*Zohar*, I, 46b, 47a)

Such self- and national-aggrandizement is the very thing that the Bible had consistently forbade (*Deuteronomy 9:4-9*). However, it is very appealing to make a god out of oneself or one's people.

Our people have also made a god out of mammon (money) as Jesus had warned against:

- "No one can serve two masters, for either he will hate the one and love the other, or he will be devoted to the one and despise the other. You cannot serve God and money." (*Matthew 6:24*)

Secular Jews have adopted the psychologist as their guru and rabbi. The psychologist is another form of false prophet who offers comfort without repentance. He is skilled at convincing our people that they are good and have to learn how to forgive themselves without any mention of the forgiveness of God. Meanwhile, God has a very different estimation:

- "I did not send the prophets, yet they ran; I did not speak to them, yet they prophesied. But if they had stood in my council, then they would have proclaimed my words to my people, and they would have turned them from their evil way, and from the evil of their deeds." (*Jeremiah 23:21-22*)

Along with the false prophet, the psychologist runs a profit-making business. Therefore, they need to tell their clientele what they want to hear. They know that turning their clientele away from their sins will not produce returning clients. Instead, a true prophet must preach confession and repentance, the source of healing.

If we Jewish believers in Jesus fail to heed this calling, we fail to walk in the steps of the Hebrew Prophets who preached a message of healing through exposing sin.

- "I have heard what the prophets have said who prophesy lies in my name, saying, 'I have dreamed, I have dreamed!' How long shall there be lies in the heart of the prophets who prophesy lies, and who prophesy the deceit of their own heart, who think to make my people forget my name by their dreams that they tell one another, even as their fathers forgot my name for Baal? Let the prophet who has a dream tell the dream, but let him who has my word speak my word faithfully. What has straw in common with wheat? declares the LORD. Is not my word like fire, declares the LORD, and like a hammer that breaks the rock in pieces?" (*Jeremiah 23:25-29*)

What does it mean to speak God's Word faithfully? It is to expose the source of the breach and to point to the way of return. It must cut its way through layers of pride and self-satisfaction to bring the infection to the healing light. Love is not always about providing comfort. Love must first humble before it can comfort. Jesus was a model of this kind of love (*Matthew 23*). Those who are in rebellion against God and seek out false comforters must first be humbled before they can be healed.

Great Jerusalem had been utterly destroyed by King Nebuchadnezzar of Babylon. God, through the Prophet Jeremiah, had been warning closed ears and hardened hearts for years about their impending doom:

- "What can I say for you, to what compare you, O daughter of Jerusalem? What can I liken to you, that I may comfort you, O virgin daughter of Zion? For your ruin is vast as the sea; who can heal you? Your prophets have seen for you false and deceptive visions; they have not exposed your iniquity to restore your fortunes, but have seen for you oracles that are false and misleading." (*Lamentations 2:13-14*)

314

The false prophets had comforted Israel in the midst of their rebellion. Instead, restoration and healing requires the exposure of the iniquities of our people. This might be experienced as a severe love, but it is love nevertheless. It is also truth, the way we are required to worship our God (*John 4:23-24*).

Please understand that I am not holding myself above my Jewish brethren. Anything good that I might have comes as a gift from the Savior. Therefore, I cannot take pride in these things, just gratitude.

I applaud the many who love Israel and the chosen people of God, and for good reason. Despite Israel's rebellion against their Savior, Jesus came as a Jew and all of His Apostles were Jews to reinforce the longstanding promise and commitment of God to His errant people. It was the Jewish people who had been entrusted with the Scriptures:

- "Then what advantage has the Jew? Or what is the value of circumcision? Much in every way. To begin with, the Jews were entrusted with the oracles of God. What if some were unfaithful? Does their faithlessness nullify the faithfulness of God?" (*Romans 3:1-3*)

Not at all!
There is absolutely no justification to disdain the Jewish people.

According to Paul:

- "For if their rejection means the reconciliation of the world, what will their acceptance mean but life from the dead? If the dough offered as first fruits is holy, so is the whole lump, and if the root is holy, so are the branches. But if some of the branches were broken off, and you, although a wild olive shoot, were grafted in among the others and now share in the nourishing root of the olive tree, do not be arrogant toward the branches. If you are, remember it is not you who support the root, but the root that supports you." (*Romans 11:15-18*)

Rather ~ it is our duty to pray for them
and to love them.